TROPHY STRIPERS & HYBRIDS

INNOVATIVE TACTICS
AND TECHNIQUES FOR
CATCHING FRESHWATER
STRIPERS & HYBRIDS

By
Steve Baker
& Neil Ward

All rights reserved. This book or parts thereof must not be reproduced in any form without permission from the author.

Copyright 1990 by
Neil Ward & Steve Baker

First Printing 1990

Published
by
Atlantic Publishing Company
Tabor City, N.C. 28463

Library of Congress Card Number 89-82206

ISBN Number 0-937866-22-9

Printed in the United States of America
by
Atlantic Publishing Company
Tabor City, North Carolina 28463

Artwork
by
Michael Roane

DEDICATIONS

To my parents, C. E. and Jean Baker, and my wife, Pam, for their encouragement and love.

Steve Baker

To my parents, Grant and Rosalie Ward, who always supported my love of the outdoors, and to my wife, Meryl.

Neil Ward

ACKNOWLEDGEMENTS

The authors wish to thank all the people who helped with the production of this book. While there is not room to name all the people who helped and encouraged the authors, we would like to especially thank: Dave Bishop, David Fritts, Charlie Guffey and Arthur "Bear" Kelso for the major contributions of knowledge that they made to this book; Horace Carter for his editorial skills that produced this book; Michael Roane for his artwork and his patience in listening to how we wanted it drawn; Pam Baker for compiling the recipes and helping with the photography work; Meryl R. Ward, J. R. Golden and John Golden for their editing and proofreading and Judy Neal for her diligent typing.

INTRODUCTION

Before this book was written, I had caught a few stripers, and some of my friends had caught a few stripers, but I wanted to know how to consistently catch the fish, instead of just catching them during a few peak periods every year. Because of that desire, I started talking to a few dedicated striper fishermen, and I soon became amazed at the advanced knowledge they had acquired and the techniques they had developed. At the time, I knew bass and trout fishermen had become very sophisticated, but I soon found out that they had nothing on an experienced striper chaser.

It was this discovery that caused me to recognize the need for a striper fishing book that would make this wealth of knowledge available to other novices like myself. In researching the material for the book, I met nationally famous striper guide Steve Baker of Maynardville, Tennessee. Baker has been a striper guide for over seventeen years, and the number of stripers over thirty pounds that he and his guide parties have caught is in excess of eight hundred fish.

His best striper to date weighed forty-eight pounds, fourteen ounces. Five times he has come within a pound of breaking the Tennessee state record.

Steve Baker's house overlooks a well known striper haven, Norris Lake, which is situated approximately forty miles from Knoxville, Tennessee. Baker and his wife, Pam, run Trophy Striper, Inc., the most successful striper fishing guide service in the country. Fishermen from as far away as Alaska have traveled to the banks of Norris Lake to spend a day in the boat with Baker.

He has appeared on a number of national television shows about fishing and has also been featured in a number of outdoor magazines. Baker personally publishes an educational magazine about striper fishing entitled *Trophy Striped Bass* which is distributed nationwide.

Every year he works a number of boat shows and other promotions from Indianapolis to Atlanta. He has traveled to Oklahoma and Texas as well as the Carolinas to share his knowledge about striper and hybrid fishing. Baker has developed a reputation among striper fishermen as the "Roland Martin" of striper fishing.

Baker first became hooked on striper fishing back in 1971. He and a friend traveled from Chattanooga, his home at the time, to East Tennessee's Cherokee Lake for a weekend. They caught sixteen stripers weighing up to eighteen pounds, and Baker has never been interested in catching any other fish since.

Striper fishing is an obsession with Baker, and his whole life, including his livelihood, now revolves around striper fishing. Besides guiding and publishing a magazine, he manufactures a number of items to help fishermen catch more stripers, including a specially designed bait tank for keeping baitfish alive and a striper-size topwater lure.

In addition to Steve Baker's wealth of striper and hybrid fishing knowledge gleaned from fishing two hundred to two hundred fifty days a year, this book also contains the fishing secrets of a number of other expert striper fishermen, especially Charlie Guffey of Somerset, Kentucky, and Arthur "Bear" Kelso of Loudon, Tennessee. Both fishermen have freely shared their knowledge to help other striper addicts.

Stripers are now stocked in thirty-six states from Raystown Lake in Pennsylvania to Lake Havasu in Arizona, and the number of freshwater impoundments where they are prospering continues to grow. Steve Baker refers to stripers as "America's freshwater big-game fish," and as more and more fishermen learn how to tangle with this transplanted giant from the sea, the "big-game fish" is going to win a lot of fans.

The information revealed in this book is going to advance your striper fishing skills by light years. If it is a trophy striper or hybrid that you desire, then read this book and clear off a place on your den wall before your next fishing trip.

For more information about Striped Bass magazine, which is dedicated to the preservation and promotion of freshwater striper and hybrid fishing, write: *Striped Bass,* 128 Dogwood Trail, Maynardville, Tennessee 37807.

Neil Ward

TABLE OF CONTENTS

Chapter 1: "Understanding Stripers and Hybrids"

Explains how the saltwater striped bass became a freshwater species that is now stocked in thirty-six states. It also details how the hybrid, which is a cross between a female striped bass and a male white bass, was developed in 1965 and is now flourishing in many lakes around the country, especially in Florida, Texas and other states where warm, shallow water is unsuitable for stripers. Fisheries biologist David Bishop from Morristown, Tennessee, provided a lot of information, including scientific reports, for this chapter. Bishop, along with biologist Bob Stevens, who is now employed by the federal government in Washington, D.C., was responsible for creating the hybrid in 1965.

The chapter also discusses the characteristics and traits of stripers and hybrids, explaining how water temperature, oxygen and light affect the fish.

Chapter 2: "Topwater Fishing" 19

This chapter discusses the different types of topwater lures used to fool stripers with detailed instructions on how to fish them.

Chapter 3: "Catching and Caring for Live Bait" 33

Explains how to catch shad and other baitfish using a cast net, dip net and wire basket. Tells the reader how and where to catch baitfish during different seasons of the year. Details how to keep fragile baitfish alive during the summer months using specially designed bait tanks and a variety of chemicals.

Chapter 4: "Live Bait Fishing" 55

Explains how to catch stripers and hybrids using live bait on free lines and down rods. Describes where to find deep-water stripers.

Chapter 5: "Tailrace Fishing" 77

Discusses how to catch stripers and hybrids from below dams where swift currents control the fishing.

Chapter 6: "Seasonal Patterns" 99

Discusses where and how to catch stripers during the four seasons. Explains the migration patterns of stripers, and how the weather and water affect the striper's location.

Chapter 7: "Crankbait Fishing" 111

Even though a lot of fishermen use live bait when fishing for stripers, the saltwater transplants readily attack artificial lures. This chapter tells how and where to catch stripers on deep-diving crankbaits with valuable tips from professional fisherman David Fritts, who lives near Winston-Salem, North Carolina.

Chapter 8: "Jigs and Spoons" 119

Similar to Chapter 7. Discusses how and where to use jigs and spoons to catch stripers and hybrids.

Chapter 9: "Night Fishing" 131

Describes the new equipment developed in the past few years to help make night fishing more productive, including the fluorescent black light which causes monofilament line to glow in the dark so that you can watch your line at all times. Also discusses the advantages of night fishing for stripers, and where and how to do it.

Chapter 10: "River Fishing" 143

Details how to catch stripers from rivers as opposed to manmade impoundments. Contrasts the differences in habits of a river striper versus a lake striper. Explains how current, the most important factor in river fishing, positions the fish so that you can easily locate the most likely striper hangouts.

Chapter 11: "Warm-water Discharges" 165

Explains how and when to fish the warm water emptied into many lakes and rivers around the country from steam plants to catch more stripers and hybrids. The former world-record striper which weighed sixty pounds, eight ounces was caught on February 13, 1988, from a steam plant discharge near Knoxville, Tennessee.

Chapter 12: "Fishing with Downriggers" 173

A complete discussion on downriggers for striper fishing. Downriggers have been used for years on the Great Lakes to catch salmon and trout that frequently suspend in thirty to sixty feet of water, but it has only been during the past five years that a few innovative anglers have started using downriggers to catch stripers from deepwater haunts. Nationally famous striper guide Charlie Guffey, who lives on Kentucky's Lake Cumberland, shares the secrets of his downrigging system for stripers. Guffey was one of the first anglers to ever use downriggers for striper fishing.

Chapter 13: "Culinary Skills" 189

Since stripers have only been introduced to freshwater for fifteen to twenty years in most parts of the country, many anglers, who grew up catching and eating black bass, crappies, trout and bluegills, often wonder if a striper makes good eating. This chapter explains how to clean and prepare a striper for excellent table fare. Contains many recipes, including smoked striper dip and barbecued striper.

Chapter 14: "Striper Savvy" 199

Some of the questions most frequently asked Steve Baker during his seventeen years as a striper guide are answered in this chapter.

Chapter 15: "More Striper Savvy"..................223
   Additional questions and answers covering a wide variety of striper and hybrid fishing information.

Chapter 16: "Weekend Angling".........................245
   Steve Baker's advice to weekend anglers regarding how to catch more stripers on today's hard-fished waters.

Chapter 17: "Special Techniques for Trophy Stripers"
....251
   A number of little-known methods for catching trophy-size stripers, including fishing with balloons, using tiny minnows to catch giant stripers, fishing springs for cold-water stripers, how to catch stripers during low water conditions, and more.

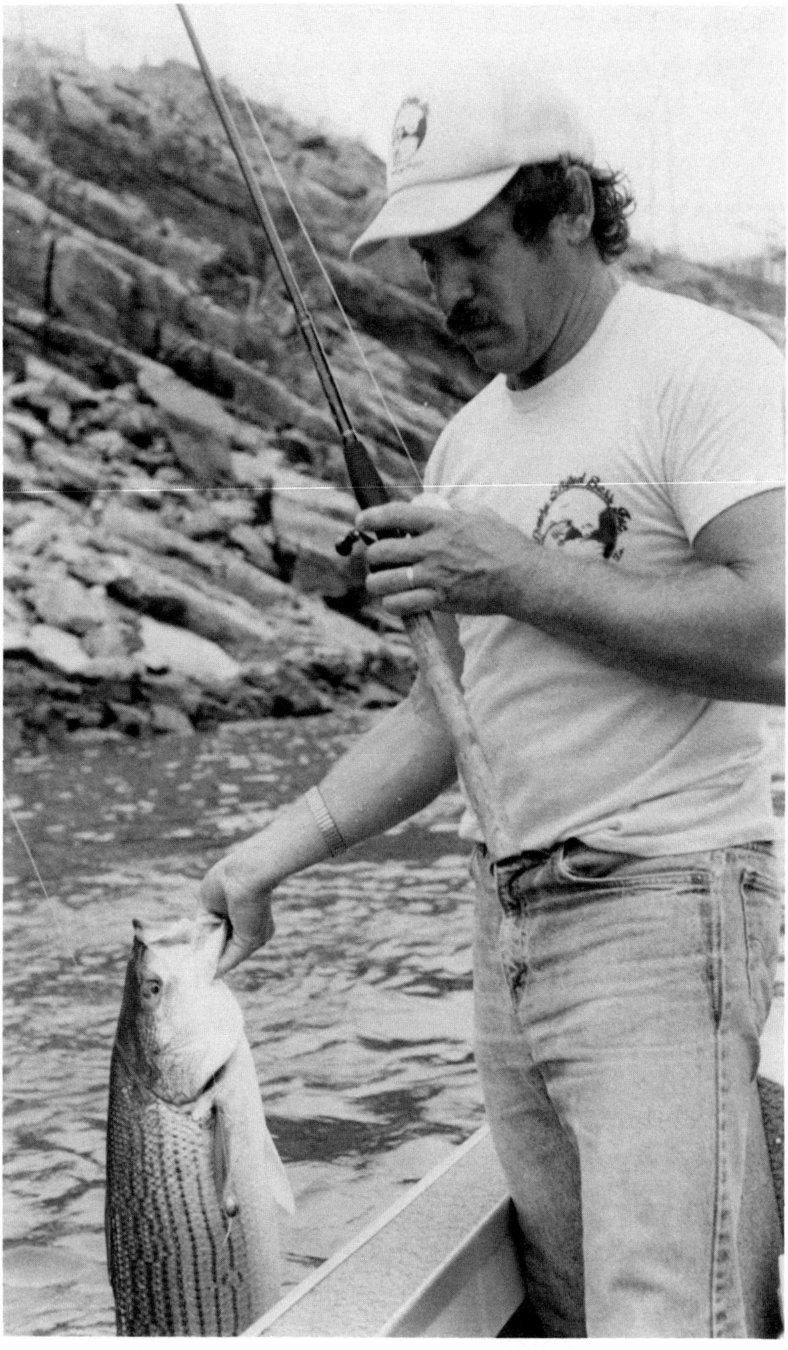

Chapter 1
UNDERSTANDING STRIPERS AND HYBRIDS

The striped bass, which is also called a striper, rockfish, rock or linesides was originally found only in saltwater. It was, and is, a highly prized gamefish that ranges from the New England Coast to Florida as well as in the Pacific Ocean off the coast of California. Saltwater anglers have found the striped bass to be a hard-fighting fish that can be caught on a variety of artificial lures as well as live bait. Fishermen catch the saltwater striped bass casting from the shore as well as fishing from a boat.

The striped bass in the ocean are andronomous, which means the species lives in saltwater but spawns in freshwater. It was this characteristic that led to the first landlocked striped bass.

Along the coasts of North and South Carolina there are a number of rivers that empty into the Atlantic Ocean. Striped bass run up the rivers in the spring from their home in the ocean to spawn. Once the spawning ritual is over, striped bass return to the ocean.

At Charleston, South Carolina, the Cooper River empties into Charleston Harbor. Striped bass from the Atlantic travel up the Cooper River every spring to spawn.

In the late 1930's, plans were approved to dam the Cooper River and flood over 170,000 acres of South Carolina lowland to form Lake Marion and Lake Moultrie which together are known as the Santee Cooper Complex. The purpose of the project was to provide hydroelectricity for the area.

Loggers were contracted to remove the timber from the

lakes before closing the dam on the Cooper River. Lake Moultrie was cleared and parts of Lake Marion were logged off before World War II broke out. With the United States' involvement in the war, the authorities decided that the power that could be generated by impounding Santee Cooper was needed right away. So, in 1941, the dam gates were closed without the majority of the upper lake being cleared as originally planned.

When the gates were closed, fisheries biologists knew that striped bass which had migrated up the Cooper River to spawn were trapped in the freshwater lakes. It was assumed that the bass could not survive in a totally freshwater environment and that they would die.

With World War II going on there was not a lot of fishing that took place at the newly impounded Santee Cooper. After the War, however, fishermen began to sample the fishing in the new lakes. But since the area around the lakes was sparsely populated, Santee Cooper did not receive much fishing attention other than cane pole fishermen who usually fished near the banks.

In the early 1950's, anglers began to hook huge fish that easily popped their lines and raced away. Most of the freshwater fishermen had no idea what they had hooked. As time went on, fishermen, using heavier line and better tackle than most bream and crappie anglers were using, started landing striped bass from Lakes Moultrie and Marion. Fisheries biologists were surprised to find that the saltwater species had not only survived but thrived in Santee Cooper. A combination of practically no fishing pressure, areas of the lakes that were almost totally inaccessible to boats due to stands of heavy timber, and an abundance of baitfish had combined to create a population of stripers in the thirty- to fifty-pound class.

As word of the giant striped bass in Santee Cooper spread, fishermen from all over the country traveled to Santee Cooper to try their hands at landing the refugees from saltwater. Interest in Santee Cooper soared in the early 1960's after race car driver Tiny Lund landed a world-record freshwater striper from Lake Moultrie on January

29, 1963. The fish was eighteen years old and weighed fifty-five pounds.

As evidence of how the striped bass were thriving in Santee Cooper came to the attention of fisheries biologists in other states, plans were made to see if stripers could survive in other freshwater reservoirs. During the 1960's and 1970's, billions of striper fry were shipped to lakes around the country and even some foreign countries from the hatchery at Moncks Corner, situated near the lower end of Lake Moultrie. In many states, the initial stockings of striper were unsuccessful because the lakes stocked with fry were not suitable for stripers' survival. As biologists learned more about the habits of a striped bass in freshwater, lakes with the environment needed to sustain stripers in a landlocked setting were stocked, and freshwater stripers have been flourishing around the country ever since.

Dave Bishop, a fisheries biologist and an assistant regional manager for the Tennessee Wildlife Resources Agency, first became interested in striped bass while serving a tour of duty in the Navy. After he returned to civilian life and started working for the TWRA, Bishop was pleased to hear about how the striper could thrive in freshwater. He thought about the number of large impoundments in Tennessee and how stripers might adapt to his state's inland waters.

In 1960, Dave Bishop started going to Weldon, North Carolina. Weldon is the site of the oldest striped bass hatchery in the world. Striped bass from Albemarle Sound annually run up the Roanoke River at Weldon to spawn in the spring. Striped bass are netted from the river and taken to the hatchery where the females are stripped of their eggs and then fertilized by sperm stripped from a male striper.

Bishop went to Weldon to capture stripers from the Roanoke River in order to obtain fry to bring back to Tennessee. When commercial fishermen along the river, who caught striped bass to sell to the hatchery, found out who he was and what he was doing, they would throw rocks at him when they saw him on the river. They did not want him catching "their" striped bass.

Eventually, many of the fishermen changed their attitude toward Bishop's efforts when he explained to them that if he were successful with his plans to develop a viable striper population in the state of Tennessee then the odds of the striped bass surviving as a species would be improved. He told the fishermen that they might be coming to Tennessee to get fry some day if something were to happen to the fishery on the Roanoke River.

The initial stockings of stripers in Kentucky Lake, the largest impoundment in the state of Tennessee, were unsuccessful, even though it appeared that the environment of Kentucky Lake was similar to Santee Cooper.

Dave Bishop did not give up, however, and he stocked fry in other Tennessee reservoirs where the fish grew well.

It was in the early 1960's that a fisheries biologist by the name of Bob Stevens from South Carolina developed the technique of injecting female stripers with hormones to cause the eggs to ripen in captivity, which greatly improved a biologist's ability to produce striper fry. Before the idea of injecting a female with hormones to ripen her eggs, hatcheries were dependent on commercial fishermen to catch female striped bass from the river that were "ripe," which meant the eggs were flowing from her vent and were at the stage of development where they could be successfully fertilized.

If a female, prior to the development of the hormone injections, was captured, and she was not "ripe," it did not do any good to place her in captivity, because the eggs would not ripen. When placed in a pen, an unripe female would simply absorb the eggs.

Since the use of hormone injections has been developed, a female striper with unripe eggs can be captured and placed in a circular tank with water circulating through it. She can then be injected with hormones to cause her to ovulate. In North and South Carolina, biologists check the female periodically after the injection to determine when she is ripe. When the eggs are ready, biologists manually strip the eggs from the female. The eggs are placed in a pan where they are immediately fertilized by stripping sperm from a male striper. Minutes later, the fertilized eggs are transferred to aerated tubes for hatching, where they hatch in a few days.

In Tennessee, biologists do it slightly differently. A female striper with eggs is captured from a lake and injected with hormones. She is then placed in a dark green, circular, fiberglass tank under a cover which provides shade. Bishop says a striper does not beat or bump against the insides of a shaded tank and quickly settles into a calm state.

Dave Bishop and the other biologists, who were working with him, discovered quite by accident that an injected striper will lay her eggs in the tank eliminating the need to constantly monitor her ovulation and strip the eggs from her when she is ripe.

"It all happened by accident. One spring we were working to hatch fry, and we placed several injected females into our covered tanks so that we could monitor them as the eggs ripened," Dave Bishop says.

"We were shorthanded, and after a few days, we were worn out from all the work. We forgot to check one of the females on an hourly basis, and she laid her eggs. We were surprised, because at the time, we believed that the female, even when injected, would not lay out in a tank. But she did."

The discovery was a major breakthrough in the science of hatching striper fry. Now, a biologist can place an injected female bass with eggs into a tank along with an injected male striper and leave the fish alone until the eggs are dropped and fertilized. After that, the fish are removed from the tank, and the eggs, which receive a constant flow of water through the tank, hatch in forty-five to forty-eight hours in the tank.

The method eliminates the need to monitor the injected female every hour to determine when she is ready to ovulate so that the eggs can be stripped. By not needing to monitor the fish every hour, which means capturing the fish and pulling it up out of the tank to run a needle up her ovaries to get an egg sample, the striper is not subjected to as much stress and potential injury. In fact, when the method of checking the fish until she is ready to ovulate and then manually removing the eggs is used, ninety percent of the brood fish end up dying.

Manually stripping the eggs and fertilizing them is also not as effective in terms of the number of eggs that are fertilized. When manually stripping, the rate of fertilization is fifty-five percent. When utilizing the tank spawning method, the rate of fertilization is eighty-eight percent.

"We've been using the tank spawning method since 1985, and it has really been a blessing to our program," Dave Bishop said. "We don't have the luxury of all the brood fish that North and South Carolina have, and the fact that we are able to release most of the brood fish back into the lake after they have spawned is an important improvement. We can also produce more striper fry with less personnel when using the tank method, because we don't have to monitor the fish constantly and manually strip and fertilize the eggs."

When using the tank spawning method, biologists have found that they also have to inject the male striper with hormones to get it to fertilize the eggs. Dave Bishop says that when an un-injected male is placed in a tank with an injected female that the male is "reluctant to perform" when the female releases her eggs. The hormone injection eliminates the male striper's inhibitions.

CHARACTERISTICS OF A STRIPER

A striper is very sensitive to light. Dave Bishop has noticed that even striper fry are light sensitive. Because of their aversion to bright sunlight, stripers often feed very early in the morning, late in the evening and at night when feeding in shallow water. In deeper water, the fish will use the depth of the water to reduce the light level. In deep water, stripers may feed in the middle of day, because most of the sunlight is filtered out.

Stripers are also very temperature sensitive, not as bad

as trout, but more than black bass or bluegill. The maximum temperature that a striper can tolerate for an extended length of time without suffering adverse effects is eighty degrees. On some lakes, this intolerance of high water temperatures creates serious problems for stripers. As the summer sun heats up the water nearer the surface, stripers are forced to go deeper in order to find cooler temperatures. Unfortunately on many inland lakes, because of the lack of current, decaying vegetation, manmade pollution, and other problems, there is an inadequate supply of dissolved oxygen in deeper water. So, as high temperatures in shallow water force stripers deeper, the fish cannot survive in the cooler, although deeper, water because there is no oxygen. Biologists call the situation a "thermal squeeze."

It is a no-win situation for stripers, because if they stay in the warmer water near the surface where there is adequate oxygen, they are subject to thermal stress, and if they go deeper to find cooler temperatures, there is not enough oxygen. A thermal squeeze often results in large fish kills where hundreds of stripers float to the surface dead.

There are a few freshwater lakes where stripers reproduce naturally. The reason there is not natural reproduction in most reservoirs is because most lakes do not have enough miles of free-flowing river running into the lake to allow stripers to successfully spawn.

Stripers do not build nests on the bottom and lay their eggs like black bass and bluegills. They do not spray their eggs along shoreline vegetation like crappie and white bass. A striper deposits her eggs in flowing water where they are immediately fertilized by a male striper. Then, the eggs, which are semi-buoyant, have to float along in the current for approximately forty-five to forty-eight hours at a water temperature of sixty-five degrees before they hatch. So, current is necessary to keep the fry from sinking to their deaths. After approximately ninety-six hours from when the eggs were deposited into the river, the striper fry can swim well enough to survive.

"I think that you need at least fifty miles of river with enough depth and velocity to protect the egg and the fry, while at the same time being the type of river that mature stripers can safely migrate up," Dave Bishop says. "With all the dams that have been built in the past forty years, there are only a few striper lakes that have access to a suitable river. Santee Cooper, Kerr and Keystone are the only three lakes that I can think of which have natural reproduction, but there may be a few more."

The fact that most freshwater reservoirs do not have natural reproduction of stripers is not necessarily a bad thing. When stripers are not able to reproduce in a lake, the population is totally under the control of the fisheries personnel. Biologists determine how many or how few stripers will exist in a given lake.

"On lakes with natural reproduction, the average size of a striper is smaller than on lakes that depend on stocking to sustain the striper population. The reason probably being that when there is a good spawn, a lake with natural reproduction has more young stripers in it than what a fisheries biologist would stock in the lake during a given year. The result is lots of smaller stripers that have to compete for the available forage," David Bishop says.

Lakes without natural reproduction can be closely managed to keep a proper balance between the number of stripers introduced into a lake in a given year and the baitfish and other food available for the young fish to utilize. Fisheries personnel usually stock five to ten fingerlings per surface acre. The exact number depends on the availability of the fingerlings, and the number that biologists decide that a given lake can adequately support.

"One time on Norris Lake, we doubled up the stocking and the average weight of the fish fell. We want to maintain Norris Lake as a trophy striper fishery, so now we only stock five fingerlings per acre in order to maintain a better grade of fish," Dave Bishop says.

After being released into a lake, stripers grow at a rapid rate. At two years of age, a striper will usually weigh three to four and one-half pounds and be eighteen inches long. After that, a striper may double in weight each year for the next four years.

On the average, a five- to six-year-old striper will weigh twenty pounds or so. After the sixth year, a striper will add three to four pounds a year for the remainder of its life, which may be as long as twenty years. It is not unusual for some stripers to gain as much as ten pounds in one year which means that a thirty-pounder could grow into a forty-pounder in one season. Think about that when you are deciding whether or not to release a striper.

The oldest striper that Bishop has personally aged by counting a scale's growth rings with the aid of a microscope was fifteen years old, but a small percentage of stripers do reach eighteen and nineteen years old. The fifteen-year-old striper that Bishop aged weighed sixty pounds, eight ounces and was the world-record land-locked striper at that time. The striper was caught by Gary Helms at a warm-water discharge on Melton Hill Lake in East Tennessee. It surpassed the record set by Frank Smith of Bermunda City, Arizona, when he caught a fifty-nine-pound, twelve-ounce striper from the Colorado River on May 26, 1977.

The current world record striper was caught by Ted Furnish of Los Banos, California while trolling on O'Neill Forebay, an impoundment of San Luis Reservoir. The giant fish was landed on June 30, 1988, and sagged the scales to sixty-six pounds.

At the present time, Dave Bishop and other fisheries biologists with the TWRA are working with the Chesapeake Bay strain of stripers to see how the Bay striper does in freshwater lakes. There are several reasons why TWRA is interested in the Chesapeake Bay stripers. One reason is that their eggs are more buoyant which results in a higher percentage of eggs hatching. Another reason is that Bay stripers have historically gotten very big. Many striped bass have been caught from the Bay that weighed over seventy pounds. Bishop would like to see an inland lake produce a world record striper that would be a record in both fresh and saltwater. The current world-record striper from saltwater weighed eighty pounds!

The third reason that Bishop and TWRA are interested in the Chesapeake Bay striper is that the Bay has become a victim of man's pollution and what was once fertile water for stripers, oysters, ducks and other life is now practically a barren sea. When a striper is caught from Chesapeake Bay now, it is a rare occasion.

By trying to adapt the Bay striper to freshwater, Bishop hopes to preserve the genetic pool in the event that the damage to the Bay cannot be reversed and the Chesapeake Bay striper disappears from saltwater forever. Transplanting Bay stripers to freshwater may be the only way to save the valuable characteristics and traits of this important strain of stripers.

One of the main reasons that fisheries biologists wanted to introduce stripers into many freshwater lakes is that most major impoundments have an over-abundance of gizzard shad which quickly grow six to ten inches long and are totally worthless as forage for other freshwater gamefish, including black bass. A striper, due to its increased size, has no difficulty ingesting the larger shad, so the transplanted fish helps control the shad population.

Stripers are not as bottom or shoreline oriented as black bass, catfish, crappies, and most other freshwater gamefish, so stripers were also stocked because biologists believed stripers would utilize large schools of suspended shad that spend most of their time feeding on plankton over deep, open-water areas.

When stripers were landlocked they did not lose their nomadic habits. Stripers in freshwater cover tremendous amounts of water in a day's time compared to other gamefish. Biologists have attached radio transmitters to stripers to track their movements. The studies have revealed schools of stripers moving fifty miles in a day's time.

It is probably a striper's habit of moving long distances in a matter of days that causes most fishermen to have trouble catching stripers on a consistent basis. Many

STRIPED BASS
(20 pounders common)

Tongue with two tooth patches

Stripes distinct occasionally broken

1st stripe below lateral line distinct and complete to tail

HYBRID
STRIPED BASS X WHITE BASS
(seldom exceeds 10 pounds)

Tongue with two tooth patches

Stripes distinct usually definitely broken

1st stripe below lateral line distinct and complete to tail

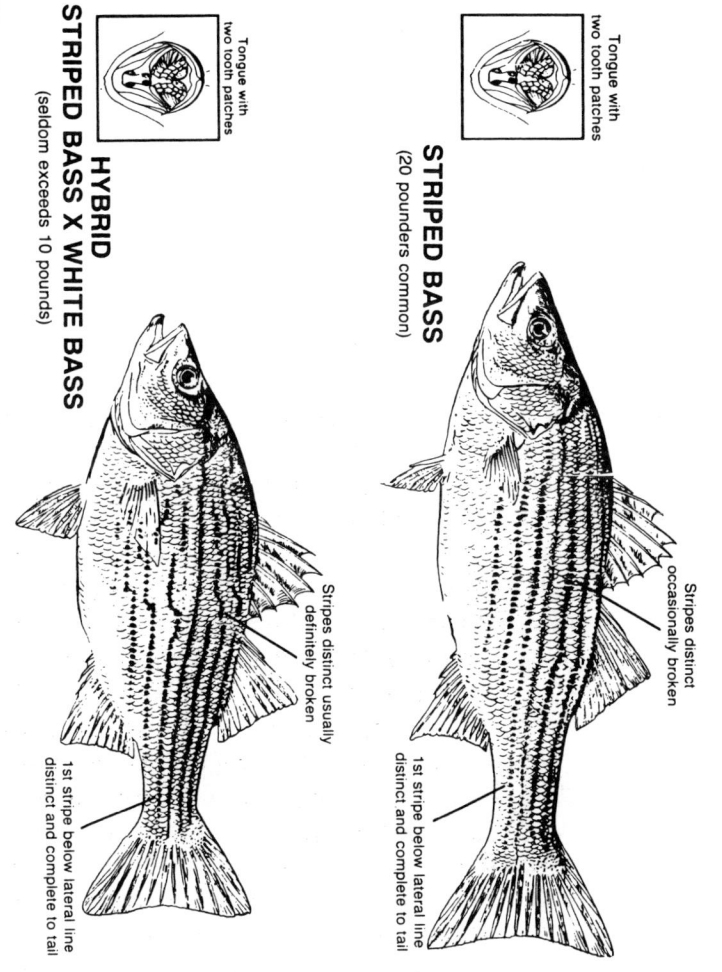

REMEMBER:

a. To distinguish white bass from striped bass and hybrid, check center tooth patches on tongue as indicated above.

b. Stripes on white bass are faint with 1st stripe below lateral line not distinct nor complete to tail.

c. First stripe below lateral line distinct and complete to tail on the striped bass and the hybrids.

NOTE: Broken lines on side does not necessarily mean hybrid. Some striped bass have broken lines.

40

11

freshwater fishermen are used to fishing for crappies, black bass and catfish, which normally do not move great distances if water conditions remain the same. Fishermen are used to catching a mess of fish off a bank one day, and then being able to go back and catch some more fish there the next day.

You may do that when striper fishing. But odds are that many times when you return to yesterday's productive spot, you will draw a blank. Inexperienced striper fishermen will blame the weather or some other factor for causing the stripers to quit biting. The fact is, however, the stripers are probably still biting, but are five miles across the lake.

In many areas of the country, a conflict has developed between fisheries biologists and striper fishermen, who want to see the freshwater striper fishery continue to grow, and anglers who concentrate on catching black bass, crappies and bluegills, who do not want fish and wildlife agencies to continue stocking striper fry into freshwater lakes. The reason for this opposition to stripers is that many fishermen believe the large saltwater transplants devour other game fish such as black bass and crappies.

In many cases, the stocking of stripers in the 1970's and '80's has been made in lakes that were very productive black bass and crappie lakes during the 1950's, '60's and early '70's. Unfortunately, a natural decline in the fishing as a lake ages was beginning on many lakes just as the striper population was beginning to receive attention from fishermen. The increased fishing pressure today for popular species such as bass and crappie along with the natural decline in many lakes' productivity has resulted in fewer and fewer bass and crappies being creeled from many lakes. For many anglers, who remember the good ole days, stripers have become the scapegoats on which to blame all their fishing woes.

All the studies to evaluate the impact of stripers on other freshwater gamefish have shown that stocking stripers does not negatively affect the number or size of other gamefish in a lake.

Stomach analysis done on thousands of stripers by fisheries biologists have revealed that stripers do not prey on black bass and crappies, but instead feed on shad and other baitfish almost exclusively.

Taxidermists, who mount hundreds of stripers a year, also report that they seldom find anything in a striper stomach other than shad or herring. A former world record striper which weighed sixty pounds, eight ounces, was examined by Dave Bishop, and it had a fourteen-inch river herring and a half-pound carp in its stomach.

Because stripers usually prefer deeper, more open expanses of water than black bass, the two species seldom have a conflict over available structure, cover or forage. It is the striper's habit of chasing shad in open water that biologists believe actually benefits many bass lakes, because stripers help reduce a part of the shad population that black bass never utilize.

HYBRIDS

After South Carolina fisheries biologist Bob Stevens developed the method of injecting female striped bass with hormones in order to get them to ovulate in captivity, he and Dave Bishop decided to try and create a cross between a female striped bass and a freshwater male white bass. White bass usually spawn earlier in the spring than stripers. But with the ability to cause a female striped bass to start ovulating, Stevens and Bishop could produce ripe striped bass eggs while male white bass still contained sperm.

In early 1965, Bishop furnished male white bass from the state of Tennessee, and Stevens provided the female striped bass from Santee Cooper. The breeding took place at the hatchery on Santee Cooper on April 18, 1965. An estimated 120,000 eggs from a twenty-pound striped bass were fertilized with sperm from three one-pound white bass. The crossing produced 80,000 fry.

Dave Bishop brought 35,000 of the fry back to Tennessee. Since there were no hatchery facilities available to place the fry, Bishop released them into the Frog Pond on east Tennessee's Cherokee Lake. The lake contains 30,000 surface acres and is used for power generation and flood control. Because of that, Cherokee has an annual fluctuation of seventy to ninety vertical feet.

The lake is located in an area of east Tennessee where large recessions have been formed in the limestone substrate. As a result of the area's geology and the annual fluctuation of the water, potholes are formed as the water level recedes during the fall.

The Frog Pond is a five hundred acre pothole that connects with the main lake through a surface channel during periods of high water. There are underground crevices in the limestone that allow the pothole to fluctuate with the reservoir. In the winter, when the water level of Cherokee is lowered, the Frog Pond empties.

When the pothole fills in the spring, fish migrate in through two large crevices. Only a limited number enter the area, however, and when the spawning season begins, the Frog Pond is under-populated. Because of that fact, survival rate of fish is usually high.

When the water level drops, most of the fish are stranded in the pothole which makes it easy to recover the fish by seining.

The two-day-old fry were released into the Frog Pond the night of April 22. They were gradually conditioned to the pH and temperature of the reservoir for thirty minutes.

The first hybrids were recovered on October 4, after water levels had dropped and the Frog Pond had divided into several smaller potholes. The potholes were seined frequently until the area completely emptied in mid-November. A total of 5,017 hybrids up to 8.4 inches in length were recovered.

Three thousand of the largest hybrids were released into Cherokee. One hundred and twelve failed to survive the seining and handling. The remainder were taken to the hatchery, where many died before injuries and parasitic infections could be effectively treated. Some were released into smaller impoundments, and four hundred were held in concrete troughs for experimental purposes.

On February 14, 1966, nine hybrids weighing up to one pound were recovered from a pothole several miles from the Frog Pond. Biologists believe that the fish had escaped from the Frog Pond during the two months of high water the previous spring.

The 35,000 fry left with the State of South Carolina all perished because there were no rearing facilities for them at the hatchery on Santee Cooper.

"Before we went to South Carolina in April of 1965, Bob Stevens had already produced two hatches of hybrids at the hatchery using white bass that he had caught from Santee Cooper. But those two hatches had all died, because there wasn't a rearing facility to raise them in," Dave Bishop says. "After we brought our fry back to Tennessee, the third hatch of fry left in South Carolina also died."

"I have often wondered if it hadn't been for the Frog Pond, how long it would have taken before fisheries biologists raised a hybrid past the fry stage."

The reason that fisheries biologists were interested in a hybrid bass was because in many freshwater lakes where striped bass had been stocked, the stripers were not doing very well. High water temperatures, inadequate oxygen in deeper water and poor water quality were all factors that limited the survival and growth of stripers in many lakes. Biologists hoped that a cross between the less tolerant striped bass and the hardier white bass would create an offspring that grew like a striper and survived like a white bass.

The hybrid seems to have lived up to the hopes that fisheries personnel had for it. Hybrids have been stocked in numerous lakes around the country and are doing well. Hybrids are particularly popular in Florida and other southern states where warm temperatures and shallower water combine to make most major bodies of water unsuitable for striped bass.

"Hybrids are more catchable, have a higher survival rate when stocked, tolerate poorer water quality, and are not nearly as susceptible to thermal squeeze as stripers," Dave Bishop said.

Hybrids have an average life expectancy of four to five years. Dave Bishop has never aged a hybrid that was over ten years old.

Most hybrids never get bigger than seven or eight pounds. But on particularly fertile lakes, hybrids weighing between ten and twelve pounds can be caught on a fairly regular basis. The world record hybrid weighed twenty-two pounds, six ounces, and was caught from the Savannah River by Jerry Adams of Augusta, Georgia, on July 27, 1986.

The locks and dams along the Savannah River near Augusta seem to attract heavyweight hybrids. Jerry Adams' hybrid is the fourth world record to be caught from the river. The previous world record was a twenty-pound, twelve-ounce hybrid landed by Stephen Bayazes, Jr. of Augusta on May 11, 1982.

During the first couple of years, hybrid bass have a faster growth rate than striped bass. According to Dave Bishop, one study was done where one hundred-twenty hybrids were stocked in a thirty-acre pothole containing only carp and goldfish. The hybrids weighed approximately a pound apiece when stocked in May. When the pothole almost dried up in August, one hundred eight hybrids were seined from the pond. Most of the fish weighed over two pounds apiece, which meant that the hybrids had more than doubled their weight in exactly three months!

Florida biologists, contrary to the hybrid projects in other states, have produced a hybrid by crossing a female white bass with a male striped bass. The hybrid is called a sunshine bass, and Florida fishermen have become avid fans of the fish. Sunshines can reach fifteen inches or more in nine to ten months and weigh two to three pounds within a year.

Bill Baab, outdoor editor of *The Augusta Chronicle*, does a lot of fishing for hybrids in South Carolina's Strom Thurman Reservoir, formerly known as Clarks Hill. Thurman is one of, if not the best, hybrid lakes in the country. Living so close to prime hybrid waters, Baab has become an excellent hybrid fisherman.

One of the major differences that Baab has noticed between stripers and hybrids is that stripers prefer deeper water than hybrids. It is not unusual to catch a hybrid in six inches of water, but you seldom find stripers in real shallow water.

"Hybrids school a lot near the surface where they attack shad and blue-back herring," Bill Baab says. "I've caught hybrids schooling on top in the summer as well as the winter."

To catch schooling hybrids, Baab uses a popping cork with a three-foot long leader attached to the end of it. To the leader, he ties The Thing, which is an oversized popping bug. The Thing is made up of a two and one-half inch long floating head with a stout hook glued in it which has feathers tied to it.

"With the popping cork, you can cast The Thing a long way. When the rig hits the water, I like to reel it back with a straight, steady retrieve," Bill Baab explains. "When you do that, The Thing bounces across the surface like a small shad."

Baab believes it is very important to use smaller lures and hooks for hybrids than you would for stripers. For live-bait fishing, he recommends a 3/0 hook and a three- to four-inch threadfin shad or blue-back herring to catch more hybrids.

The next time you catch a hybrid, take time to really look at it. A hybrid has a small head on a large body. So, even though you may be trying to catch a five- to seven-pound fish, it has a mouth smaller than a three pound largemouth bass. By scaling down the size of your artificial lures and live bait, you increase their appeal to hybrids.

During March through May, a topwater lure can entice monstrous size stripers. By learning to fish a variety of different type topwater lures, you will increase your fishing success.

Chapter 2
TOPWATER FISHING

Regardless of their favorite method for catching stripers, almost every experienced striper fisherman will tell you that topwater fishing is the most exciting way to catch the silvery-sided monsters. As Steve Baker sees it, "When a thirty- to forty-pound striper sucks a hole in the lake as it inhales your topwater lure, your knees just have to shake."

THE LURES

There are four major categories of topwater lures that Steve Baker uses. His favorite is a seven- to eight-inch long floating, shallow-lipped plastic or balsa minnow.

Before fishing a floating minnow, Baker always makes sure it has a split ring attached to the line tie. By tying the line to a split ring instead of a rigid, molded-into-the-body line tie, the minnow will have a better wobble as you crank it through the water.

Since striper-size topwater lures sport large, thick stainless steel treble hooks on them, you need to sharpen the hooks with a file before fishing a new lure.

When deciding what color to fish, Baker has only a few favorite colors that he uses. On sunny days, he fishes a lure with a chrome finish and either a blue or black back. On cloudy days, Baker does not like to fish a lure with a chrome finish, but instead prefers a gray, or as it is sometimes called, a Smokey Joe color, which has a flat finish.

When fishing a floating minnow, Steve Baker casts it out and uses a slow, steady retrieve that makes the plug wobble with the tail just breaking the surface. The "V"-

shaped ripple created by such a retrieve catches the attention of hungry stripers.

If a striper boils on a floating minnow and misses it, Baker stops the lure and gives it a couple of jerks with his rod tip. This maneuver causes the minnow to dive underneath the water a few inches and then pop back up.

When the bait rises up to the surface for the the second time, Baker resumes his slow, steady, wobbling retrieve. "After a striper misses the minnow, it will either hit the lure as I jerk it underneath or when I begin the retrieve again," Steve Baker says.

The second type of topwater lure that Steve Baker casts for stripers is a stick bait. A stick bait has a long, cylinder-shaped body and lacks a lip, concave face, spinners or other hardware to impart action to the lure. A stick bait's action is derived entirely from the type of retrieve that an angler uses with it.

To fish a stick bait, Steve Baker stands up in the boat and makes a long cast. Then, while holding the rod down, he twitches the rod tip sideways away from the lure while cranking up the slack line.

You need to develop a smooth, steady rhythm as you twitch the rod tip. Some anglers have found that it helps them to tap their foot in time with the twitches to maintain a steady cadence. As you do, the lure's design will make a stick bait dart from side to side or zigzag. Black bass fishermen refer to the retrieve as "walking the dog."

The reason a stick bait is a very effective topwater lure is that by employing a zig-zagging retrieve, you create a lot of motion on top while at the same time actually moving the lure only a very short distance. A striper gets the impression that the lure is a critically injured shad on the surface that will be easy to catch. Even a striper in twenty feet of water knows it can make it to the surface before the dying baitfish can get too far away.

Steve Baker often uses a big floating minnow when searching for topwater stripers. And if a striper just swipes at the minnow, but misses it, he immediately throws back to the same spot with a stick bait. The slow side-to-side motion of the stick bait without actually moving more than a foot or so through the water is often more than a pugnacious striper can bear.

The third category of topwater lure that Baker recommends is a seven- to eight-inch popper. While poppers are very popular with black bass fishermen, there are not very many commercially available poppers designed for striper fishing. Because of that, Steve Baker has designed his own popper made from aged cedar and weighted for balance. The lure, called a Tennessee Popper, is seven inches long, and the rear treble hook is dressed up with a white bucktail skirt. The head is cut at a forty-five degree angle and concave to produce a loud popping noise similar to the sound of a striper attacking a ten-inch gizzard shad. The Tennessee Popper has glass eyes and comes in several colors.

Baker likes to fish a popper best when there is a chop on the water. When the wind is blowing and creating a ripple on the surface, stripers are not as wary as they are when the water is slick and calm. Consequently, the sound created by a popper will readily appeal to the aggressive nature of a striper when the wind is blowing and baitfish are moving around.

To attract stripers, Baker pulls his rod tip in six- to ten-inch strokes which causes the concave head to dig into the water and produce a popping sound. Baker likes to keep the lure moving across the water as he creates various sequences of pops until he discovers what the stripers prefer on a given day. For example, he may make three quick twitches with his rod tip to produce a series of three pops, then stop the lure for a few seconds before he creates three more quick popping sounds. He may repeat the three-pops-and-pause retrieve all the way to the boat. Then on the next cast, try two pops and a pause.

"You need to try a variety of rhythms until you discover what works, but I always keep the popper working and only use very short pauses," Steve Baker says. "When striper fishing, you don't need to work a popper slow like people do with a Hula Popper for black bass."

The final type of lure that you will want to try for topwater stripers is a prop bait. A prop bait has a minnow-shaped body with a tiny propeller or spinner on each end that kicks up a surface commotion when you twitch it. Some prop baits may only have one propeller on them, usually on the back hook.

One of the problems that striper fishermen have is that there are precious few commercially produced prop baits for stripers. The majority of prop baits in the freshwater fishing marketplace come in the three and one-half to five-inch size for black bass. For striper fishermen, a bigger seven- to eight-inch size prop bait is usually best. Stripers chasing ten-inch gizzard shad are not interested in four-inch lures.

If you live near saltwater, you should be able to find some suitable prop baits designed for saltwater fishing. If you don't live near the coast, you may be able to find some big prop baits designed for muskie fishing which will attract striper.

Fishing a prop bait is very similar to fishing a popper. Use your rod tip to jerk the lure a few inches at a time across the water. The motion will cause the propellers to turn in the water and kick up a ruckus on the surface. Fish the lure with a variety of twitches and pauses until you aggravate a striper into trying to murder the injured baitfish.

TACKLE

When casting surface lures, Steve Baker employs twenty- to thirty-pound-test line depending on the size of the stripers that he is anticipating catching and the amount of cover in the water in which a striper could tangle the line.

"I don't think line size matters in surface fishing except as the diameter of the line affects your ability to make long casts. When you are properly working a surface lure, there should only be few feet of line actually touching the surface of the water anyway," Steve Baker explains.

Baker thinks that the only advantage in fishing lighter line is that you can cast twenty-pound-test line further than thirty-pound-test line, which is very important in topwater fishing where you often need to make casts of thirty to forty yards.

Unlike a surface-leaping largemouth, a striper usually does its fighting near the bottom, so you have to base your choice of line size on the amount of potential line-snapping debris on the bottom. Even when fishing a topwater lure over deep water, Steve Baker has had giant stripers fight their way to the bottom and hang the plug's hooks on roots or rocks. "I've had forty-pound stripers hit a topwater lure and race off to the bottom in seventy feet of water," Steve Baker says. "When they get to the bottom, the hooks will hang up and you'll break your line."

For casting striper-size surface lures, Baker uses a stiff, seven and one-half-foot graphite rod and a baitcasting reel. To get the maximum distance that he can from a cast, he leaves the lure hanging down from the rod tip a foot or so when he winds up to throw. Even with twenty- and thirty-pound test line, Baker will often snap a lure off during a morning's casting, because of the wear and tear on the line that long-distance casting with a heavy lure creates.

WHEN AND WHERE

Once the surface temperature of the water nudges above the fifty-five degree mark, stripers can be caught consistently on topwater lures. The warm surface water attracts shad, and the baitfish hold near the surface. In east Tennessee, where Steve Baker guides for stripers, mid-March to early May is normally prime time for topwater fishing.

In the early spring, you need to be on the water at daylight if you want to be a successful topwater fisherman. To the inexperienced angler, it may seem odd casting out a seven-inch topwater bait when the air temperature at daylight is in the thirties. But once the water temperature reaches the mid-fifties mark, stripers do not wait for the day to warm up so the fishermen will be comfortable. Before the sun illuminates the water with full force, stripers know it is easier to ambush a shad.

By nine a.m. topwater fishing is usually over for the day. Of course that is not true when stripers are chasing huge schools of shad out in the lake in what is commonly called "jump fishing." But when casting the banks in the spring for shallow-water stripers, you will find the action shuts off about the time most fishermen are dragging themselves to the lake. "Many mornings, I've been back to the dock with a guide party before eight a.m. with over a hundred pounds of stripers," Steve Baker says.

Unlike what many novice anglers believe about topwater fishing, Steve Baker does not like to see the water still and calm. He prefers a ripple or slight chop on the surface which helps to break up the penetration of light rays that can adversely affect the stripers' feeding even in early morning. "If you are fishing an area, and the water near one bank has a ripple on it and the water near the other bank is slick, you will catch the stripers on the bank with the ripple," Steve Baker says.

Baker thinks choppy water breaks up the silhouette of an artificial lure and makes it easier to fool a striper into believing that the long piece of plastic or wood with two to three huge treble hooks dangling down from it is a shad.

When fishing a point or bank, especially on some of the mountain lakes where the wind blows from all sorts of directions out of the numerous hollows, there will sometimes be a calm area near the bank for the first ten yards or so. Then as you move the lure further from the bank, you will encounter a strip of choppy water for ten to twenty yards and then the surface will become slick again between that strip and boat. "When stripers are holding in such an area, I have found that I get the majority of my topwater strikes as the lure comes through the choppy surface even though there is nothing different below the surface to distinguish the strip of choppy water from the areas of calm water," Steve Baker says. "And if the wind shifts and a previously calm area becomes choppy, then the fish start hitting a topwater lure as it comes through the newly created choppy water."

It is a very subtle thing, but you can improve your topwater success by observing even a mild breeze as it comes out of a hollow or cove and fishing any areas of choppy water that it creates. Of course, this fine tuning of where to concentrate your casts is only useful once you have located the general structure where stripers are schooling.

When guiding fishermen in the spring, Steve Baker tells them to practice their casting before they arrive at the lake so that they can comfortably cast a topwater lure thirty to forty yards. "I tell them if a forty-pound striper attacks a shad thirty yards from the boat, they need to be able to cast to it," Baker says. "That striper will only be there for a few seconds before moving on, and if a person can get a surface lure in front of it, he will be taking a trophy fish home."

Despite Baker's advice, many clients arrive at the lake without the ability to cast a topwater lure far enough. When that happens, the client often gets frustrated when Baker is placing his lure near the bank from a distance of thirty yards or more, while the client's lure is plopping in the water near the boat. When that happens, a client will often ask Baker to move closer to the bank. Baker will then explain to the client that if he moves closer to the fish, then neither one of them will get a strike. "What happens in a situation like that is that I will cast out the lure for a client and then hand him the rod," Steve Baker says.

While many fishermen dislike fog, especially when it makes it difficult to navigate the lake, fog can be a blessing to springtime topwater fishing, because it will delay the sun's appearance and extend the time of the stripers' surface feeding activity. Be careful, though, when running your boat in a fog so that you do not run up on the bank or into another boat. If the fog is really dense, try to keep the bank in sight so you can use it as a reference point. If you get out into the middle of a fog-shrouded lake, you will not be able to tell in which direction you are headed unless you have a compass. I have seen veteran striper guides on Santee Cooper's lower lake use a compass to run across the eleven-mile-wide lake in fog so thick you could not see twenty yards ahead of yourself. With incredible accuracy, they would stop their boat within yards of a favorite hole.

Likely places to lure a striper into attacking a topwater bait are long, sloping sand, gravel and mud bars and points that extend into deeper water. In the spring, the water in the feeder creeks will warm up faster than the water in the main lake, so points in creeks are excellent places to fish topwater baits. "After a heavy spring rain, the water temperature in a creek will rise several degrees, but the rain will also color up the water. The best striper fishing usually occurs a few days after a heavy rain, when the water begins to clear up," Steve Baker says.

While stripers, typically, never stray too far from deep water, the term "deep water" is a relative one, which on some bodies of water may mean fifteen feet and on others seventy feet. In the spring, you can catch trophy stripers in eight to ten feet of water as the fish feed over shallow bars, flats and points near deeper water, but not necessarily near the deepest water, such as the inundated river channel. On deeper lakes, springtime stripers will often be found holding on secondary points off the river channel or in major creeks near bars and points where the water drops off into forty or fifty feet instead of a hundred feet like it does off the main channel structure.

"Striper fishermen are programmed to think structure near deep water when searching for schools of fish. Eighty to a hundred feet of water is often the kind of depth you find adjoining productive striper structure," Steve Baker says. "When I'm searching for stripers in the summer and winter, I don't get too far away from the main river channel.

"But in the spring, especially during the topwater season, I believe that a lot of veteran striper chasers are overlooking schools of big fish because they still confine their searches to structure on the main channel. In the spring, stripers may be across the cove from a main river

Swimming Minnow Bait

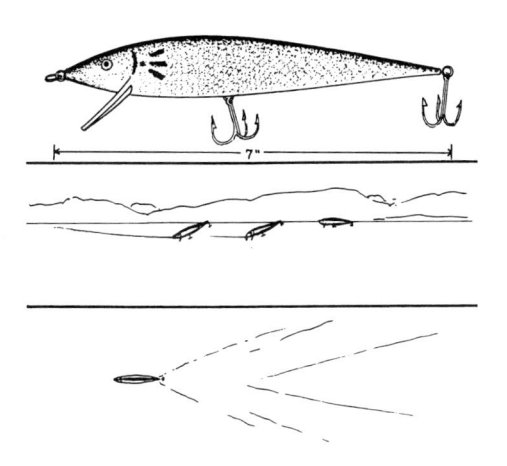

The swimming minnow type bait is extremely productive with a slow steady retrieve that creates a V-type wave behind the lure. These lures work best when the surface has a slight ripple. Large lures up to 7 or 8 inches long work better when surface temperatures are holding above 50°. Remember stripers feed on very small baitfish during cold water conditions. The larger lures are better choices during late March and April.

Prop Bait

Use your rod to twitch a prop bait across the surface with a stop-and-go retrieve to simulate an injured shad. By varying the length of the twitch, you increase or decrease the amount of surface disturbance that the lure creates.

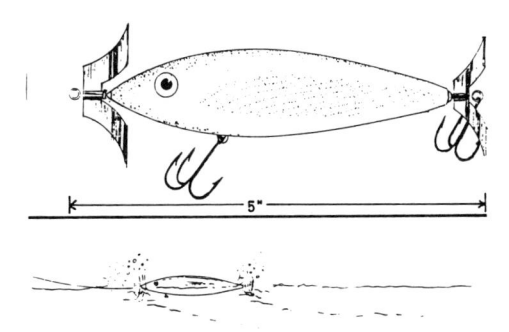

Stick Bait

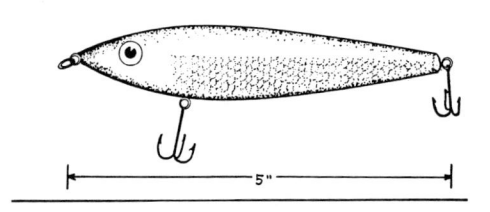

Stick baits have proven themselves better in calm, quiet, slick water conditions. With no lip on the nose, these lures must also be worked with a jerk-and-pause. This produces a back and forth "dogwalking" type motion. Some lure companies build a rattle chamber directly into the body of their baits. The soft rattling sound often drives a striper crazy and will bring on an instant strike. Color seems to be a secondary factor with these lures. Clear see-through lures are often productive when worked with the proper retrieve.

Popper Bait

The noisy popper type lure must be retrieved with a fast jerk and wind type motion. Poppers work best during periods of high wind that creates rough surface conditions. Stripers seem to strike a popper type lure out of anger instead of thinking of it as a quick and easy meal. Long high quality bucktail on the trailer hook will give a pulsating effect that often makes just that little extra difference. Keep your eye on these lures in choppy water. Look for a slight disturbance on the surface behind the lure that will allow you to brace for a strike.

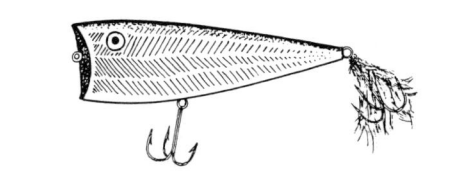

point on a bar in ten to fifteen feet of water that only drops to forty feet deep into a secondary channel or hollow instead of the main channel."

Of course, Baker still fishes structure adjoining the main channel in the spring, but he does not hesitate to check out secondary structure that may be a mile or more from a channel, if the structure drops off into water in excess of ten feet or more.

As an example of off-channel structure, there is a cut-through or opening between two small islands jutting up out of Norris Lake near Steve Baker's home. Norris Lake is maintained by TVA to help alleviate flooding, and the water is often drawn down as much as fifty feet or more during a year's time. In the spring, the passageway between the islands is fifteen to twenty feet deep. By late summer, the opening will not have any water over it. The islands themselves have forty to fifty feet of water around them during the spring, but there is not a submerged creek or river channel in the area.

"During April and May, the two island points on each side of the cut-through are magnets for stripers, including fish in the forty-pound class," Steve Baker explains. "In the spring when the water is high, schools of shad use the cut-through as a short cut around the islands. The stripers know that and hang around the opening waiting for the baitfish."

By casting a topwater lure across the points, Baker has caught stripers off the spot for two weeks or more before the stripers move out.

When looking for likely structure to catch stripers on topwater lures, Baker does not have to see fish attacking shad before he will stop and try a place. "It's good to see shad activity near the top and, of course, if you see stripers busting shad, you know fish are there, but I don't necessarily have to see either one in order to stop and make a few casts."

By fishing practically every day in the spring, Baker usually knows an area where he can find some active fish. But when fishing an unfamiliar lake, Baker will fish as many as forty, fifty, or sixty points in the two and one-half to three hour period between daylight and nine a.m. He will pull up to a likely-looking point or bar and make ten to fifteen casts across the structure. If he does not get a rise, Baker cranks up and moves to the next spot. He may cover as much as thirty to forty miles of lake when topwater fishing in the spring.

"When you're searching for fish in the spring, you have to keep traveling until you find an area that is holding some stripers. When topwater fishing on a lake, I figure I have approximately a three-hour fishing day, so I have to make my time count," Steve Baker says. "When I do find a point, shallow hump, or bank where the stripers are feeding, I will keep fishing back and forth across it until the stripers quit feeding. Many times, I catch four to six stripers in the fifteen to thirty pound class from one spot."

When approaching a potential topwater spot, Steve Baker approaches the area as quietly as possible. He shuts his outboard motor off before he reaches the prospective striper hang-out, so that waves created by the big motor do not wash across the area.

Baker warns not to drop your electric motor into the water, but to ease it over the side. He then uses his electric motor to maneuver within casting distance of his chosen location. "When stripers are near the surface, they are very spooky. So I try to sneak up on them, because big fish are hard enough to fool anyway without warning them in advance," Steve Baker cautions. "Early in the morning, you have a good chance of being the first boat to work a school of stripers that day. So make it count."

When casting topwater lures for stripers, Steve Baker often places a couple of rods in holders on the stern of his boat with a free-swimming shad hooked on them. Many times the free lines will catch the heaviest striper of the day, because an eight- to twelve-inch gizzard shad swimming near the surface is more than most surface-feeding stripers can resist.

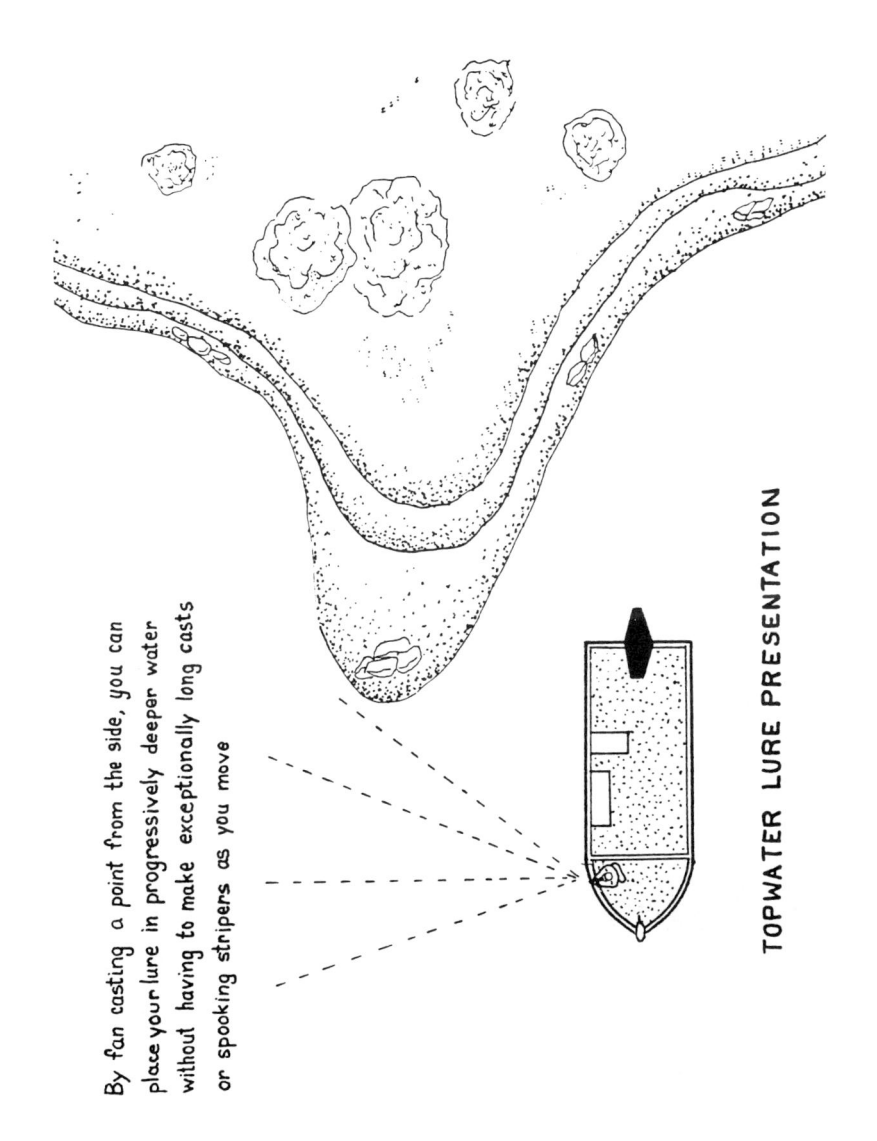

By fan casting a point from the side, you can place your lure in progressively deeper water without having to make exceptionally long casts or spooking stripers as you move

TOPWATER LURE PRESENTATION

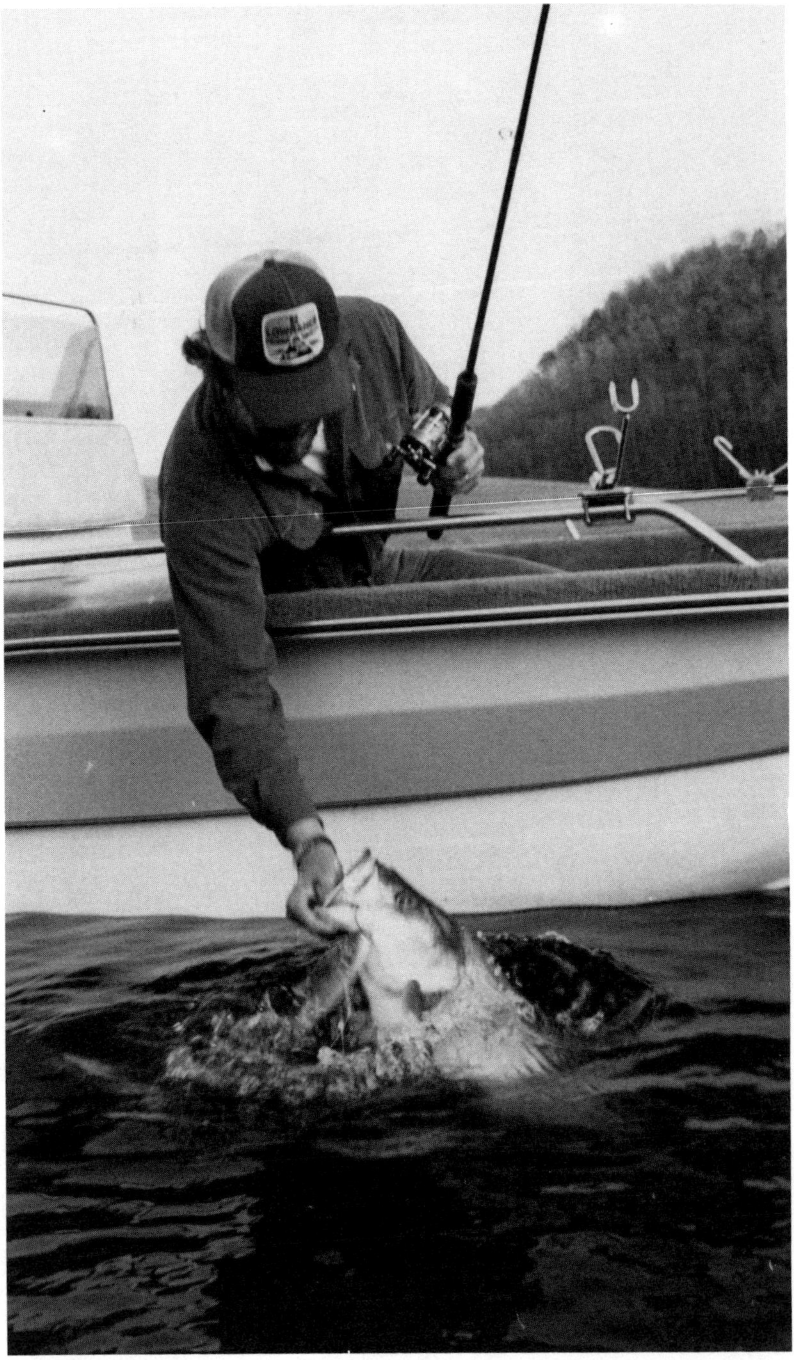

Chapter 3
CATCHING AND CARING FOR SHAD

Steve Baker's number one lure for catching a striper in excess of thirty pounds is a live shad. Shad are found in virtually every striper and hybrid lake in the country, and in most waters, shad make up the bulk of a ravenous striper's diet. Shad are ideal forage for stripers because the baitfish school in vast numbers and cruise open water in search of microscopic organisms in the water called plankton.

There are two major species of shad found in most lakes. A threadfin shad is a small, streamlined baitfish that can be readily identified by the tiny, black dot located in back of each gill cover. A threadfin shad reaches a maximum length of five to six inches long which makes it ideal forage for a variety of different size fish.

A gizzard shad has a more plump appearance than a threadfin shad, and it is not unusual for a gizzard shad to grow more than a foot long. Such big shad are unsuitable as forage for the majority of smaller fish, and therefore many lakes have an overabundance of gizzard shad in excess of eight inches long. This is one of the reasons that fisheries biologists favor stocking stripers because the larger predators can control the gizzard shad population.

"A shad bigger than seven or eight inches is virtually useless as forage for black bass," fisheries biologist Jerry Buynak with the Kentucky Department of Fish and Wildlife says. "A bass will eat a shad that is a maximum of half the bass' size. So, when you have an eight-inch shad, it takes a fifteen- to sixteen-inch bass to eat it. And the majority of bass in a lake will be under that length."

Both species of shad spawn in the spring when the surface temperature rises to sixty degrees. Shad do not build nests, but randomly scatter their eggs in shallow creeks and along shoreline cover.

Gizzard shad normally start spawning three to four weeks before threadfin shad. Studies have revealed that in the central United States, gizzard shad begin spawning in early April while threadfin shad do not begin their spawning ritual until early May. All shad do not spawn at the same time, and studies by fisheries biologists have found both gizzard and threadfin shad spawning into July.

After spawning, and as the water temperature climbs into the high seventies, shad move from the shallows into deeper, open water where they often suspend from five to twenty feet deep. In the summer and fall, the location of schools of shad can change daily and is highly influenced by the wind. Many fishermen believe that a stout wind blowing into a cove or point pushes shad in to such areas. While you will find shad concentrated in such a situation, it is not because the wind forced the shad into the area, but because the wind swept plankton into the area. Shad are simply there to take advantage of a concentration of food.

NETS

The most versatile means of catching shad is a cast net. Cast nets come in a variety of sizes, but the most common size for catching bait in fresh water is a four- to twelve-foot net made from three-eighths to five-eighths inch mesh. For the occasional weekend fisherman, a four-, five-, or six-foot net is the best choice, because it does not take as much skill to cast the smaller size nets.

Manufacturers size their nets by the distance from the center of the net to the outside edge. So a six-foot net is actually twelve feet in diameter. Any net eight feet or bigger takes a lot of practice to learn to cast, and anytime you throw it you will work up a sweat.

Cast nets are made from either strands of nylon or monofilament. Steve Baker prefers a soft monofilament net, because monofilament sinks faster than nylon.

Nets are available in different mesh sizes, and the size mesh that you choose depends on the size baitfish you want to catch. When casting for gizzard shad in the eight to twelve inch size, or when trying to catch smaller-size shad in deeper water, Baker prefers a one-half or five-eighths-inch mesh net, because it will sink faster than a smaller mesh net.

For catching gizzard shad and other baitfish in the six-inch size range and smaller, Steve Baker switches to a three-eighths-inch mesh net, because the smaller baitfish get their bodies stuck in the wider mesh, which kills a lot of the bait.

PRESERVING LIVE SHAD

One of the most difficult problems that an angler has to deal with when fishing live shad is keeping the bait alive and healthy, especially during the hot summer months. Shad are very fragile and die a lot easier than shiners and other types of bait fish.

A well-designed bait tank is needed to effectively hold shad. Steve Baker recommends a circular tank with two inches of injected insulation in the top, bottom and sides. Insulation is very important, because it helps keep the water temperature cool during the summer. A poorly insulated tank sitting in your boat on a scorching July day will heat up like a tea kettle, and no matter how hard you try, you will lose plenty of shad. When inspecting a tank's insulation, make sure the lid is also insulated. If the lid is not insulated, the tank is like a refrigerator without a door.

The shape of the tank is not as important as the insulation, but a circular-shaped tank prevents baitfish from crowding into one corner where they will be constantly bumping against each other. Shad often swim in circles, in sort of a follow-the-leader type response, so a circular tank keeps shad swimming around and prevents crowding up on any one side.

Tanks come in a variety of sizes with the most common

ranging from twenty-five to fifty gallons. Steve Baker uses a thirty-gallon tank which he says will easily keep three to four dozen shad measuring six to nine inches very lively for a day's fishing.

A bait tank with slick inside walls is also a feature to look for when buying a tank. Some of the better tanks are gel-coated, and the smooth inside walls help prevent shad from knocking off their scales as they bump against the tank.

In order to keep four dozen shad alive, a tank must have an adequate aeration system. Steve Baker's bait tank is equipped with a long, tubular-shaped agitator system that consists of a brass paddle with a mesh covering to prevent shad from getting caught in the paddle. As the paddle turns, it keeps the water constantly churning which mixes oxygen from the air into the water.

Baker's bait tank has a circular hole cut in the top for the agitator to fit down into. The agitator draws one and one-half amps per hour, so with a standard 105-amp marine battery, you can run the agitator for two days before you need to recharge.

Even with a quality tank and agitator system, you still have to take additional steps to keep shad alive. In the summer months, the biggest killer of shad once you place them into a tank is high water temperatures. Warm water cannot hold as much oxygen as cold water. So, even with an agitator running constantly, warm water will be more oxygen deficient than cold water. In the summer, you need to ice the water in the tank down to sixty degrees. If the water temperature climbs above seventy degrees, shad will get the "red nose" and die.

When you catch shad from water that is in the seventies and eighties, which is common in the summer, you have to slowly temper shad to the cooler water because shad will go into shock if subjected to a sudden temperature change in excess of fifteen to twenty degrees.

While you ultimately need to lower the water temperature in a tank down to the sixty degree mark to maintain four dozen shad for a day's fishing, you should initially dump the shad into water that is within twenty degrees of the temperature of the water from which you caught them. Then, slowly begin to add ice to the tank in order to reduce the temperature.

Steve Baker recommends filling plastic bread bags with water and freezing them for use in cooling down your bait tank. You will need several bags for a day's fishing.

For example, when you fill you bait tank in the morning, empty the ice from a bag and place it in the water to begin lowering the temperature. Once you add shad to the tank, allow them to become accustomed to the water for a half hour or so, then add another bag of ice to the water to continue the cooling process.

It is a trial-and error method as you learn how fast to cool down the water by adding ice without killing the shad. A small hand-held thermometer will allow you to measure the water temperature in the tank to help prevent cooling down the water too fast.

If you buy your ice or freeze it from tap water, there is a good chance it contains chlorine, since almost all water systems are treated with chlorine nowadays. This will kill your shad, and, therefore, when adding ice to your tank, you need to use chemicals that remove chlorine from the water.

Jungle Laboratories' Baitsaver or Baitcycle made by Boatcycle Manufacturing are two of the best chemical solutions for treating water in a bait tank. Not only do the two solutions remove chlorine, they also help lower the ammonia in the water. Ammonia is created when baitfish pass waste into the water. When you confine three to five dozen gizzard shad in a thirty-gallon tank for a day, the fish put out a lot of waste. If the water is not treated, the ammonia level in the water could rise to a lethal level and kill the shad.

Baitsaver and Baitcycle also improve the water's ability to hold oxygen, and the chemicals add valuable electrolytes to the water. Both bait treatments turn the water blue when they dissolve, and as shad swim in the treated water, the chemicals harden the skin and scales on the baitfish, which helps reduce fungus and tailrot. When you are going to use all of your shad up in one day, the benefits of treating shad with chemicals are not as important as when you have dozens of shad that you need to keep alive for several days.

Besides a bait saver solution, Steve Baker adds a white, milky liquid to his water, called foam kill, made by either Boatcycle Manufacturing or Jungle Laboratories. If you have ever handled a shad, you know it is a very slimy fish. When you get a few dozen shad swimming around in a tank, they create plenty of slime, which rises to the top as a foamy scum. The build-up on the surface reduces the agitator's ability to mix water with air, and the oxygen in the water decreases. Foam kill helps reduce the build-up of slime, so the agitator can create an adequate supply of oxygen. Baker uses one tablespoon of foam kill to thirty gallons of water.

Rock salt also helps to keep baitfish alive and healthy. Salt reduces the growth and spread of fungus and other infections that shad are very susceptible to in captivity. Baker dumps one cup of rock salt into a thirty gallon tank, and he uses the rock salt in addition to a bait saver solution.

After you have worked hard to catch your bait and gone to considerable effort to keep it alive, do not waste all that time and trouble by mishandling the shad when you hook it on your line. If you start with a perfectly healthy shad in your tank and end up with a severely injured shad on your hook, you have failed.

For removing shad from a tank, Steve Baker uses a short, aluminum-handled net with a fine, soft webbing. The soft webbing prevents a shad from knocking off its scales or tearing its fins as it flops around in the net.

When catching a shad in a tank, Baker recommends that you lower the bait net into the water and slowly move it until you feel a shad bump the net. When it does, lift up on the handle and you will have a shad. "Don't chase shad around the tank with a net trying to scoop one up. It just scares the bait and causes them to injure themselves as they dart against the walls of the tank," Steve Baker warns.

Because the treated water in bait tanks contains rock salt, which is highly corrosive, rinse your agitator off in fresh water when you are finished with it. Also, try not to get the treated water on your reels, rod holders, depth finders and other equipment, because it will cause anything that is not stainless steel to rust.

WHERE TO CATCH SHAD

Once you learn to use a cast net, you have to learn where to find schools of shad that are suitable for striper bait. The size shad that you are searching for will obviously depend on your personal preference. But when fishing for stripers in a lake, Steve Baker prefers a gizzard shad measuring six to ten inches long.

If you do much live bait fishing, you will discover that even though most lakes are full of shad, the majority of bait-fish will be under five inches long. So, in order to catch enough suitable bait, you will find yourself constantly searching for schools of big gizzard shad.

One of the most consistent places to catch shad is in the very back end of a creek. Every major impoundment has a number of feeder creeks running into it. In the hot summer months when the water temperature registers in the eighties and the clarity of the water is such that you can see the bottom in ten feet of water, it gets very difficult to catch shad on the main lake.

By running ten to fifteen miles up a creek, you will often find shallow, dingy water that is five to ten degrees cooler than the main lake. Gizzard shad will school up in such areas, because a creek is a constant source of food, and the dingy, cooler water allows shad to remain comfortably in shallow water where a cast net is most effective.

Shad in the back of a creek will be near the bank or over any shallow flats running out from the bank. Look for shad flipping on the surface in the dingy water in order to decide where to throw your net. Most of the time, you will be throwing into three to five feet of water, since shad in the creeks do not have any reason to go deeper.

"I have caught nets full of ten- and twelve-inch gizzard shad in July and August by running up a major creek until it narrows down into the original creek banks," Steve Baker says.

In order to catch suitable size shad from the main lake during the summer months, you often have to catch your bait at night. A method that Steve Baker uses to catch eight- to twelve-inch long gizzard shad in the summer months is to place a couple of lights near the surface of the water in a boat slip or stall that is situated over deep water. He lets the lights burn all night. Then, a couple of hours before daylight, Baker, with the help of another person, stretches a twelve-foot cast net across the slip and drops it into the water.

The net Baker employs has a forty-foot-long rope on it, and he lets the net fall the length of the rope before he hauls it up. A five-eighths-inch mesh net is best, because it sinks fast.

Usually, a boat slip will produce four to six big gizzard shad on the first drop. "The best drop I ever made netted five dozen gizzard shad between eight and twelve inches long," Baker says. "I took those shad that same morning and caught fourteen stripers ranging from twenty-seven to forty-eight pounds apiece."

Baker advises not to get greedy and light up several boat slips. Usually, this will not attract more big gizzard shad, it will just scatter the ones that are present. Instead of concentrating a half a dozen big shad under one slip, you will end up with one or two under four or five slips.

"I'll leave the lights burning over the slip for a week at a time. And every morning before daylight, I will drop a net over it," Steve Baker says. "I usually won't catch but three or four big gizzard shad, but if I can net just two lake shad in the ten- to twelve-inch size range, that's all I need to catch a thirty-pound striper when they're schooled up over deep-water structures. "I've seen times in June and July that I would have paid twenty dollars for one giant gizzard shad."

At Clarks Hill Reservoir in South Carolina, fishermen often use a similar tactic for catching shad and blue-back herring. They tie their boats up to bridge piers and put out lights to attract the baitfish. When they think the lights have drawn up enough bait, the fishermen extinguish their lights and cast their nets. The reason for turning out the lights is that the fishermen believe it prevents the baitfish from seeing the net as it drops into the water and as a result fewer fish escape the net.

Threadfin shad on top. Gizzard shad on the bottom.

A cast net is the most effective way to catch live bait.

INSTRUCTIONS FOR THROWING 8 FT. TO 12 FT. NET

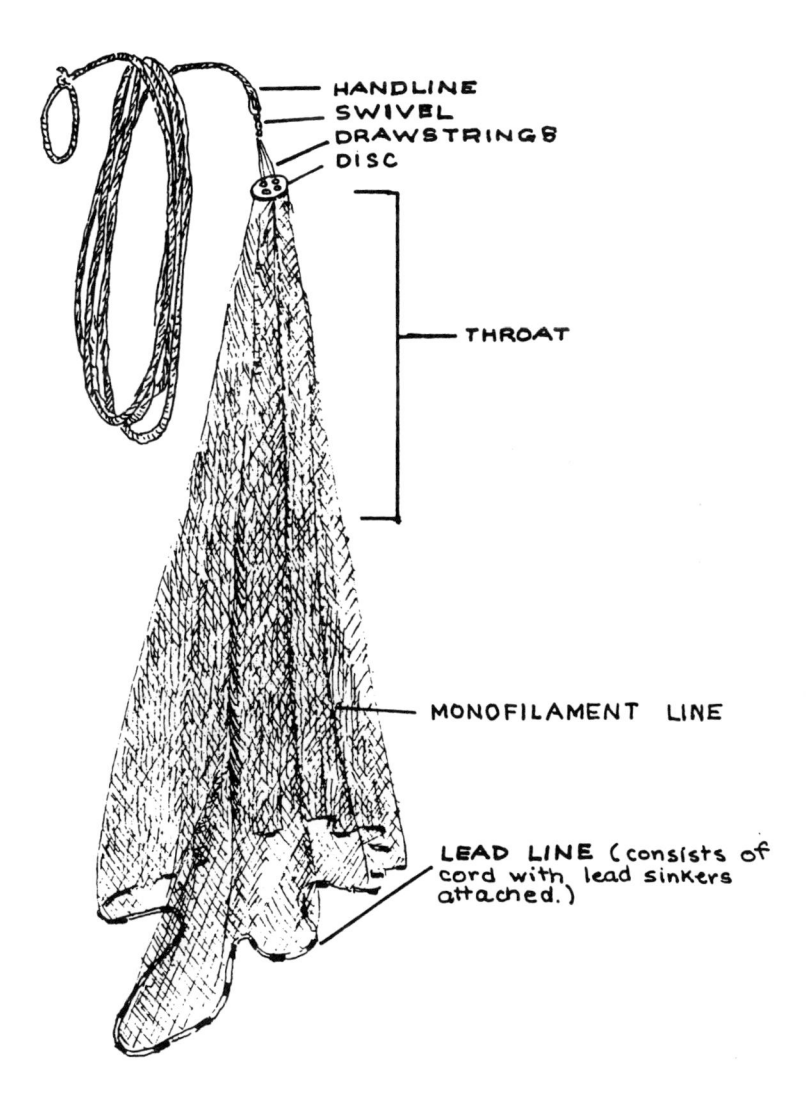

- HANDLINE
- SWIVEL
- DRAWSTRINGS
- DISC
- THROAT
- MONOFILAMENT LINE
- LEAD LINE (consists of cord with lead sinkers attached.)

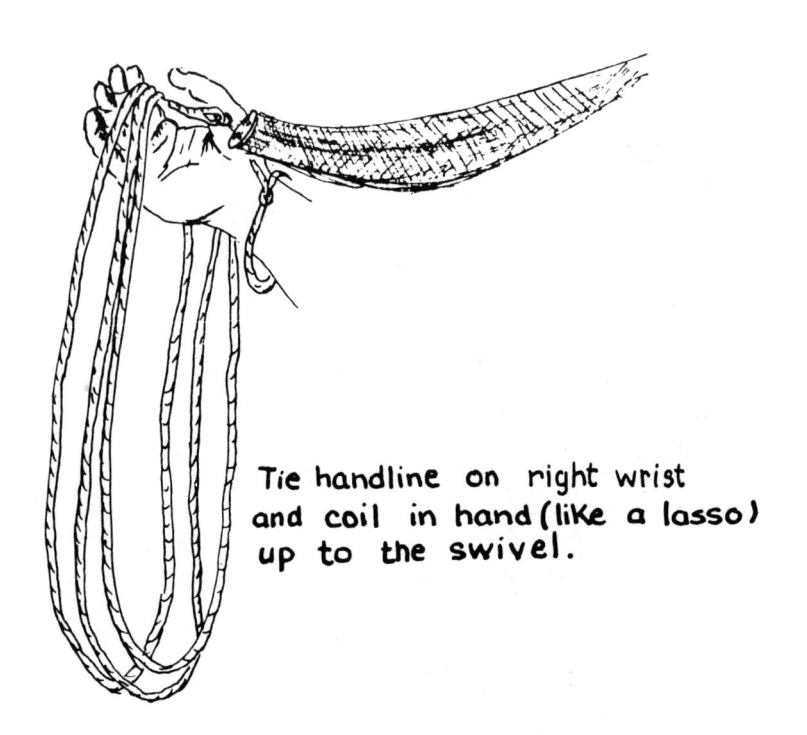

Tie handline on right wrist
and coil in hand (like a lasso)
up to the swivel.

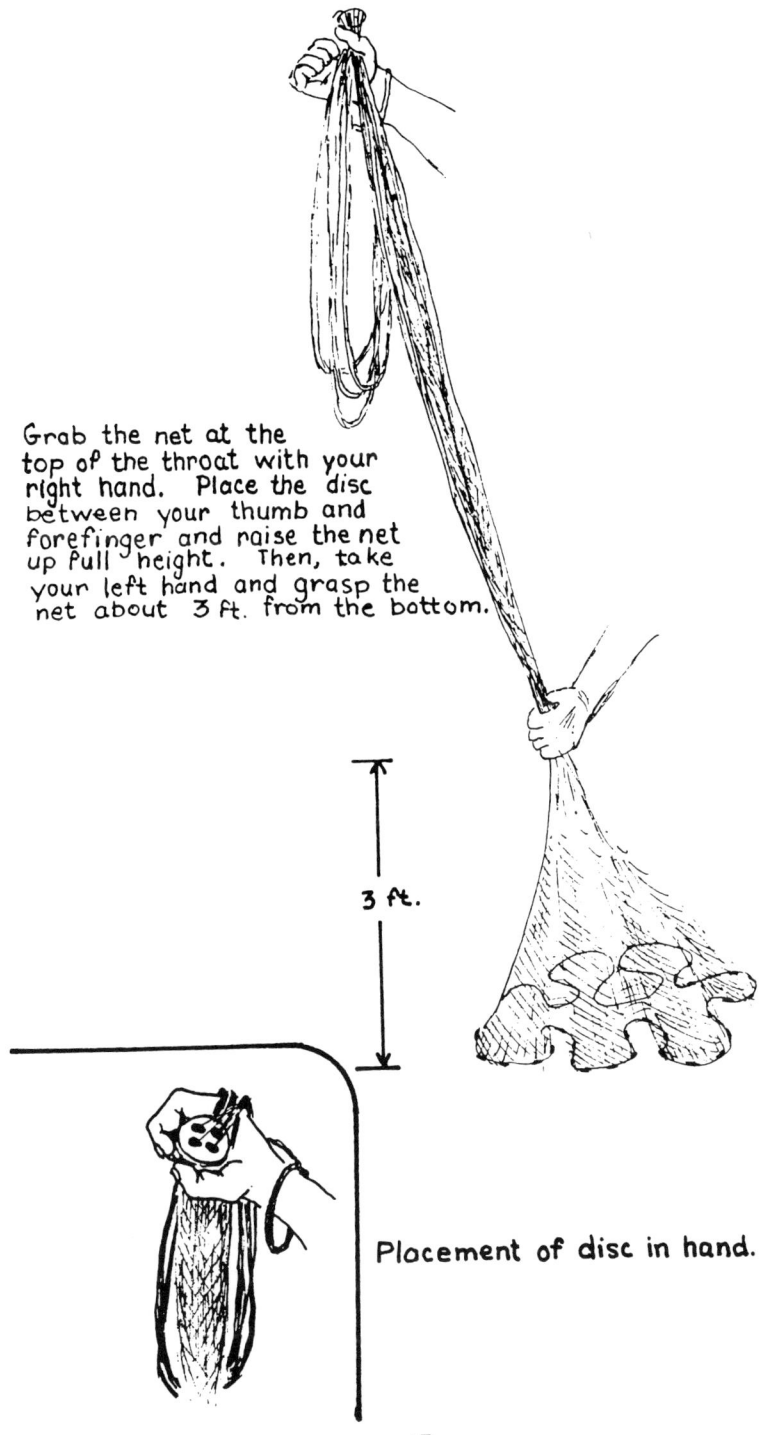

Grab the net at the top of the throat with your right hand. Place the disc between your thumb and forefinger and raise the net up full height. Then, take your left hand and grasp the net about 3 ft. from the bottom.

3 ft.

Placement of disc in hand.

Place the net from left hand to right hand.

Hold excess net in same hand as handline.

(outside edge of leadline.)

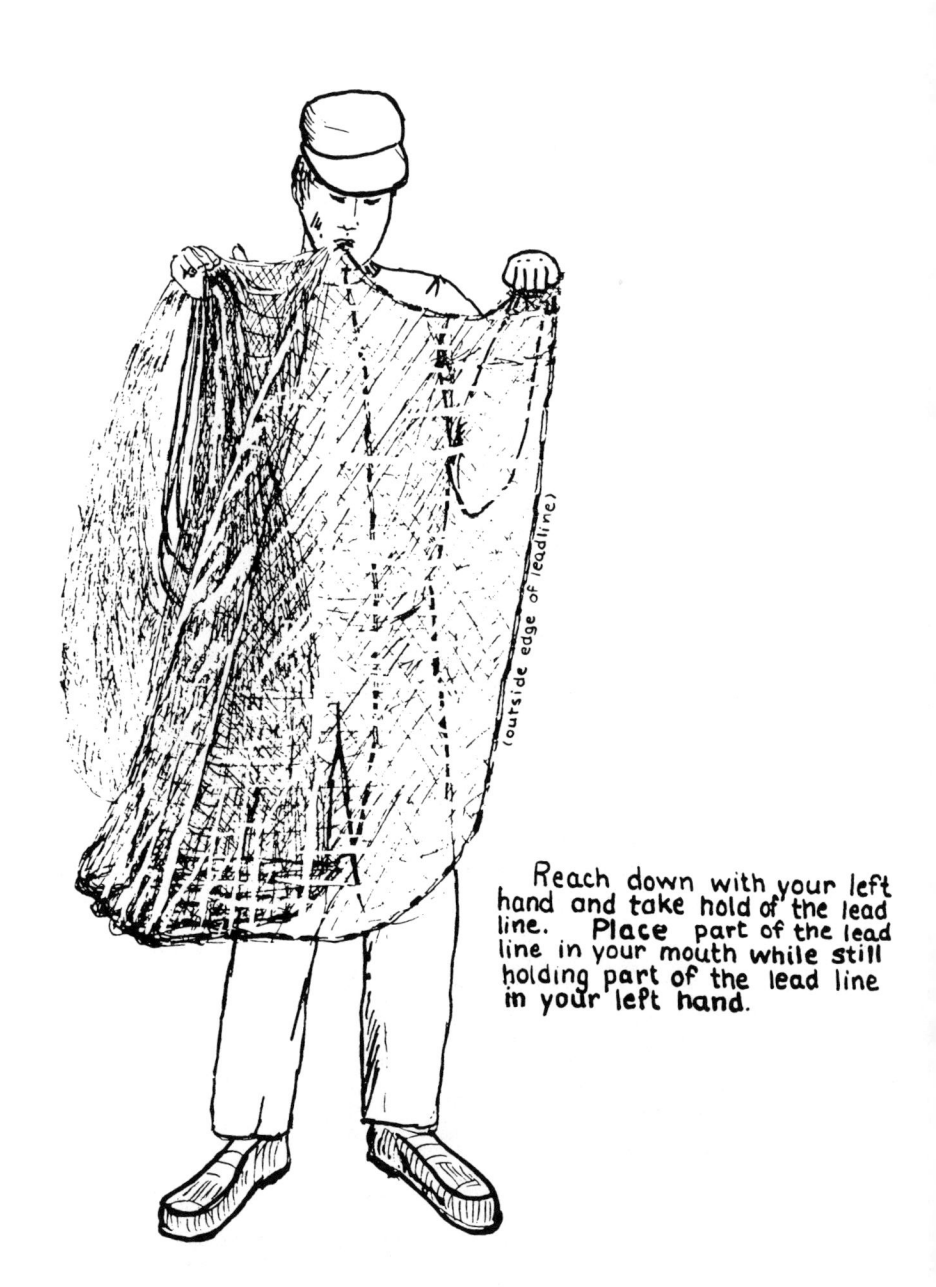

Reach down with your left hand and take hold of the lead line. Place part of the lead line in your mouth while still holding part of the lead line in your left hand.

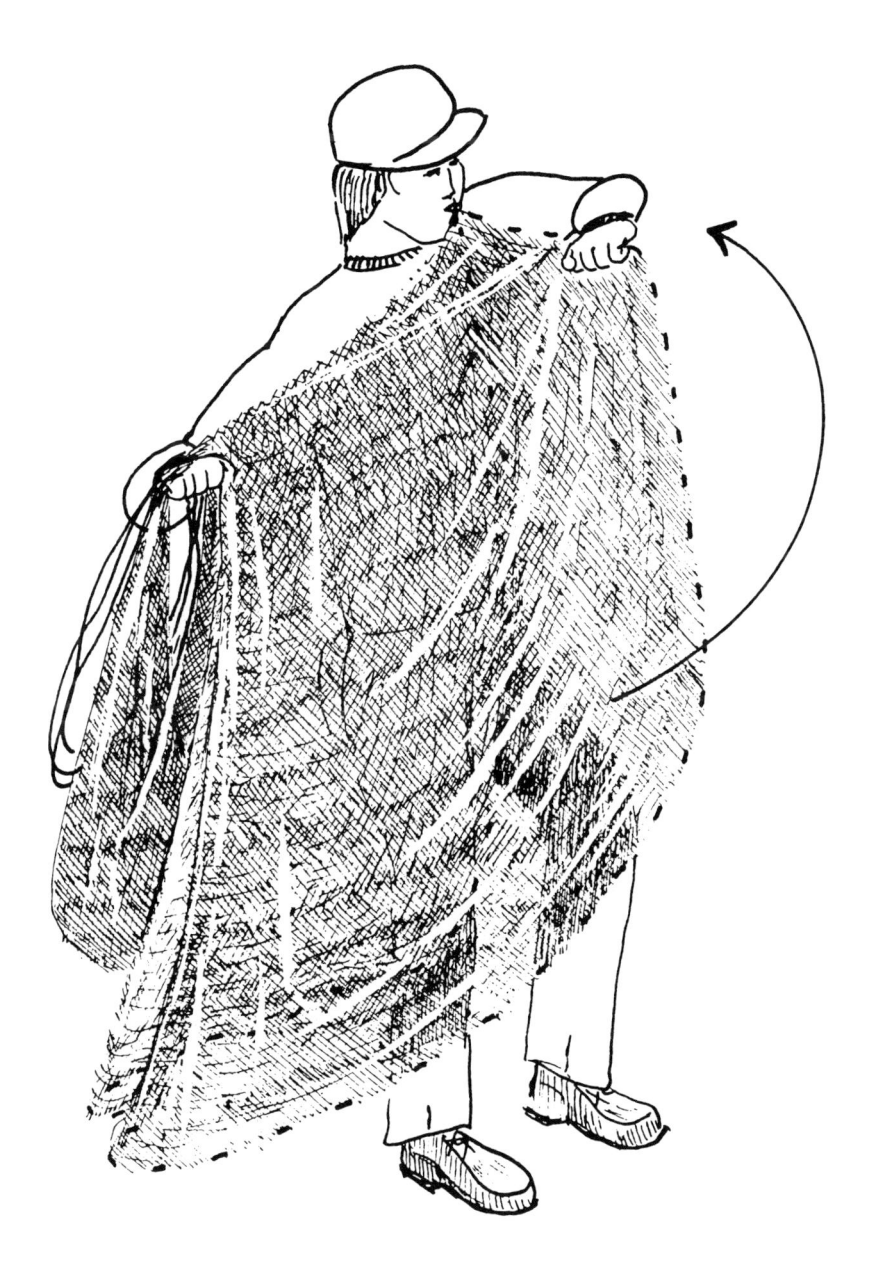

Pivot your body to the left, and turn your body in a complete spin.

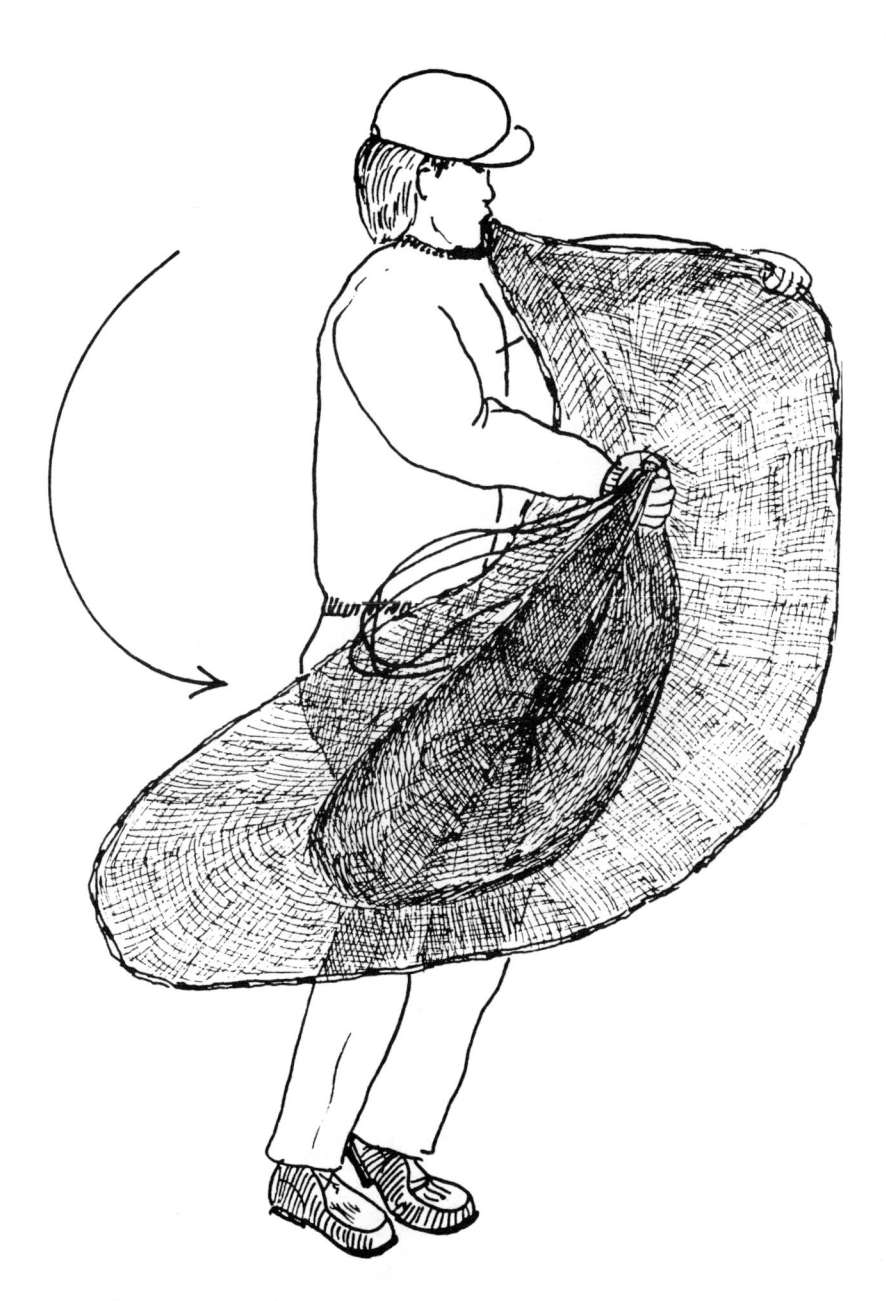

As you complete your turn, the net should be on the outside of your body as the centrifugal force pulls the net upward and out.

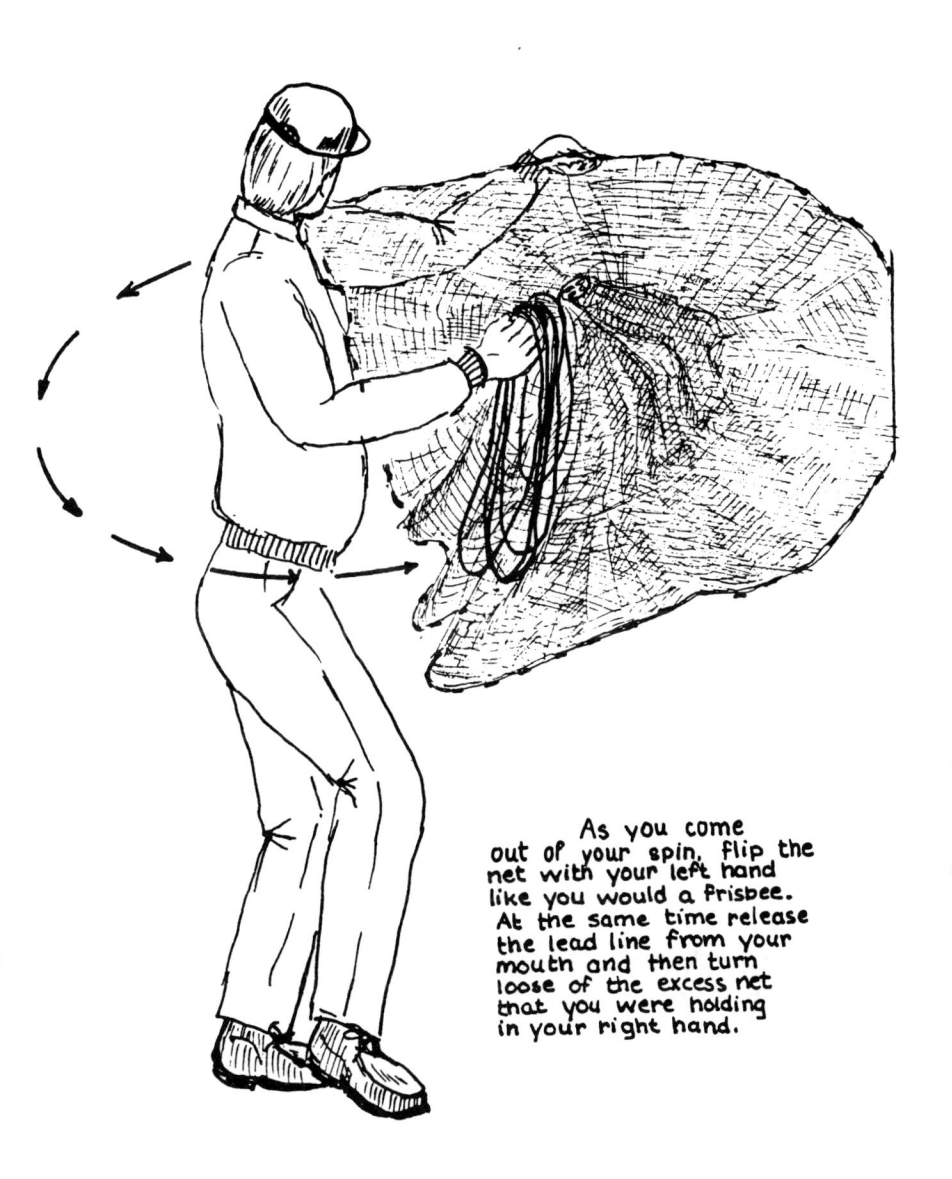

As you come out of your spin, flip the net with your left hand like you would a Frisbee. At the same time release the lead line from your mouth and then turn loose of the excess net that you were holding in your right hand.

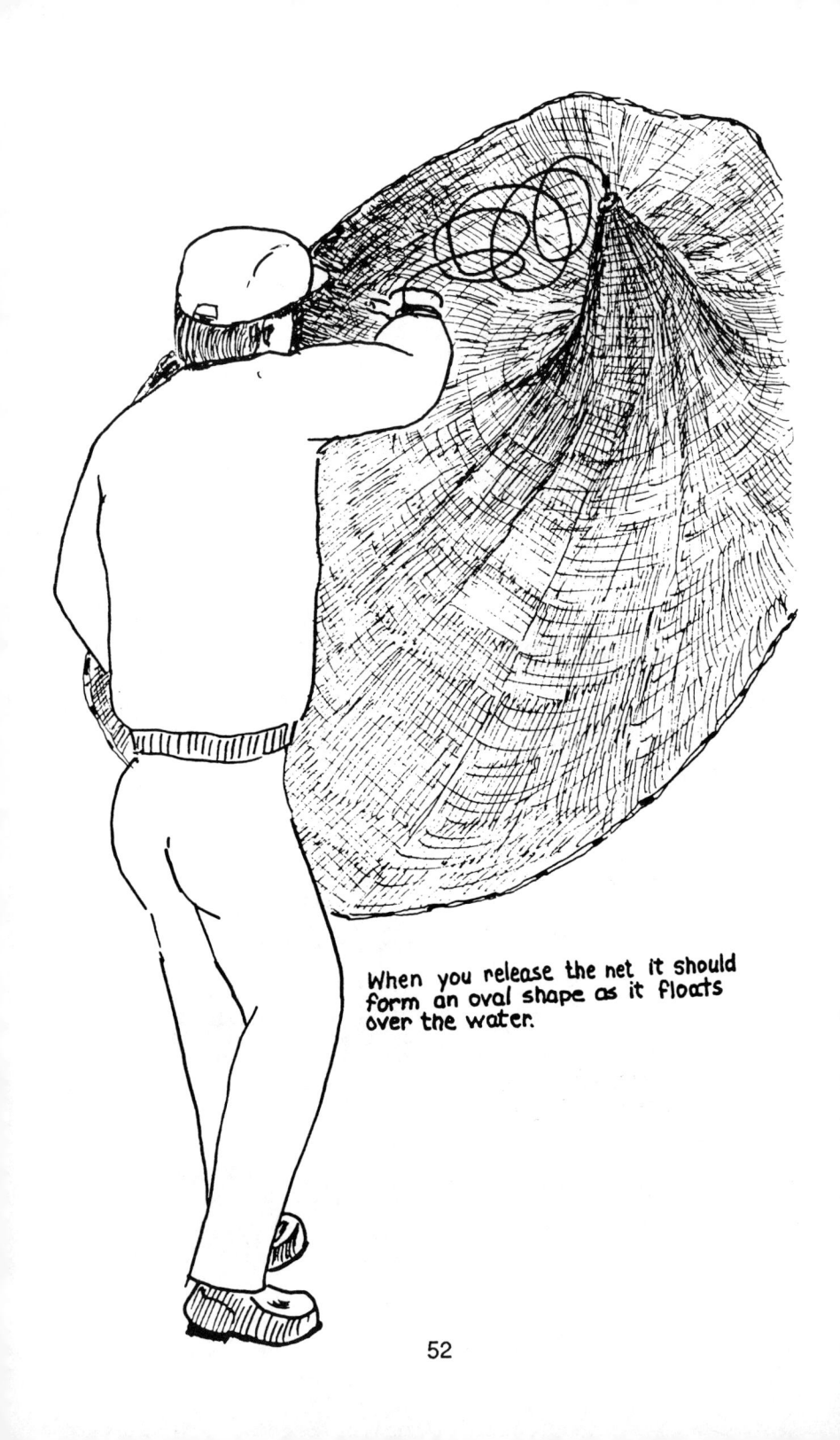

When you release the net it should form an oval shape as it floats over the water.

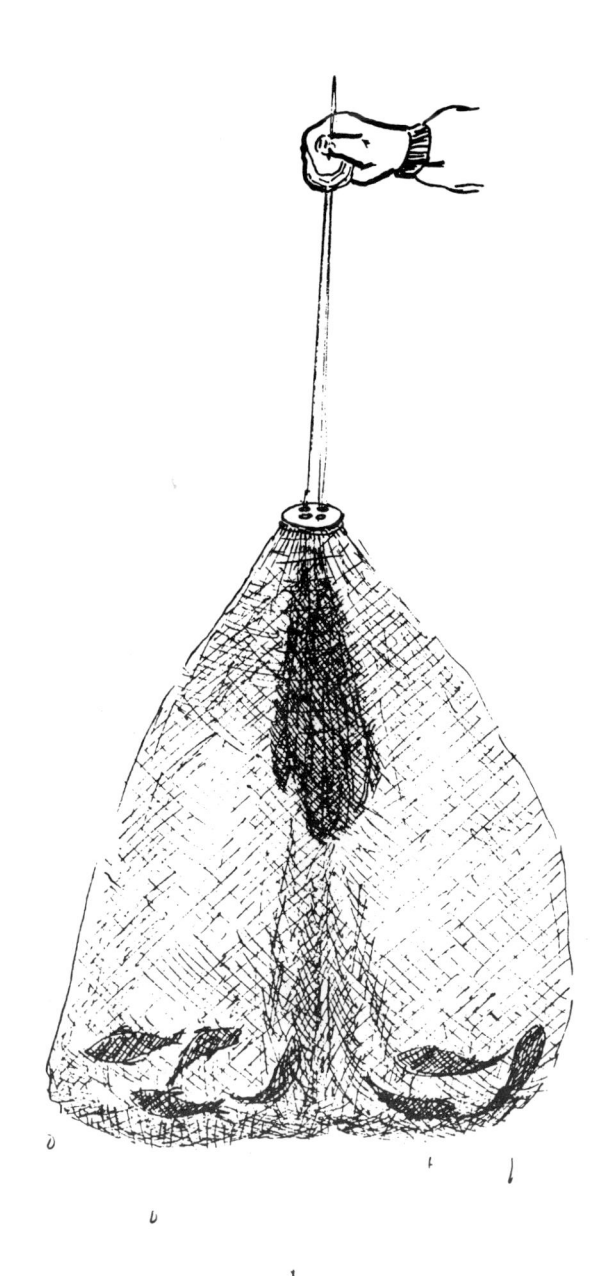

Pull handline in slowly, holding the line only.

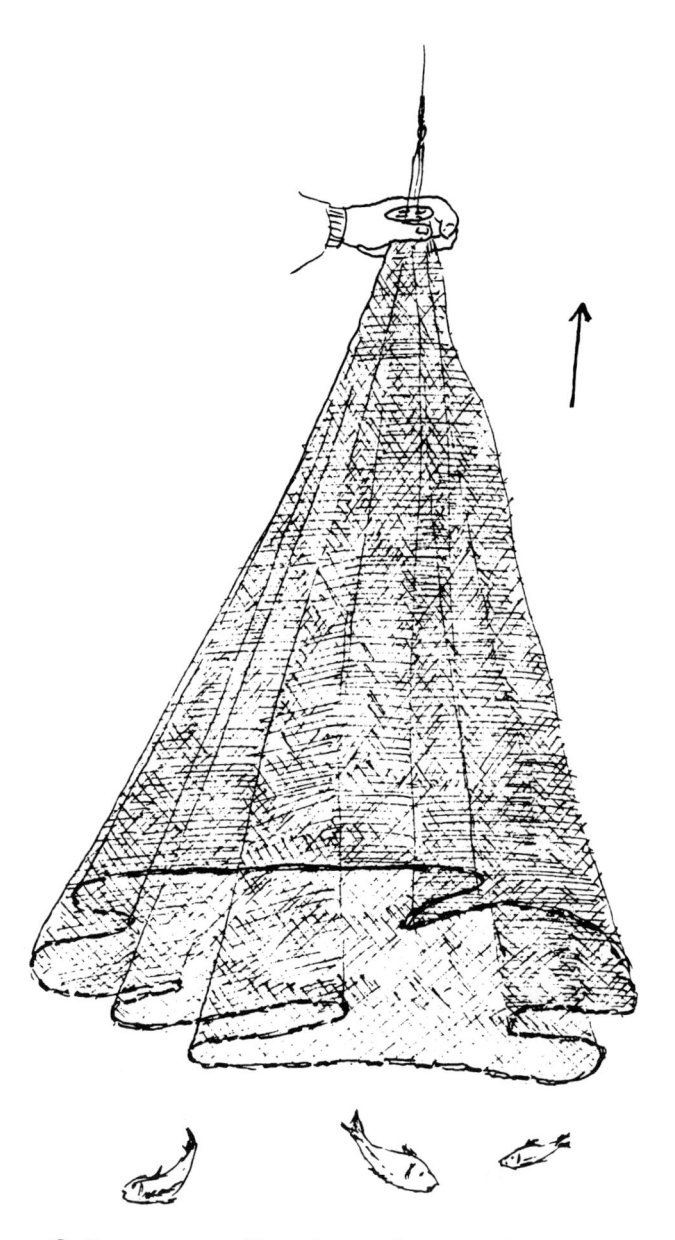

Pull up on disc to release live bait.

Chapter 4
LIVE BAIT FISHING

Of all the ways to catch a trophy striper, there is not a more effective method than fishing live bait. While some fishermen consider fishing with live bait less challenging than angling with artificial lures, consistently boating thirty- and forty-pound stripers on live bait requires as much skill and know-how as any method of angling.

Regardless of how shallow or deep the water is, how hot or cold the temperature is, or how slow or fast the current is, live bait will consistently dupe the heaviest stripers in the lake if you know how to properly use it.

EQUIPMENT

For fishing live bait, Steve Baker uses a seven and one-half foot medium-action rod. The definition of "medium action" can vary from one rod manufacturer to the next, but Steve Baker defines it as "a rod with a good backbone and a medium soft tip."

Baker believes that a rod with a soft tip will result in more hook-ups than a stiffer action rod when fishing live bait. "When a striper or hybrid initially takes a shad, a soft tip offers little resistance during those critical few seconds when a fish is inhaling the bait," according to Baker. "By the time a striper feels the resistance of the rod, it is already streaking off with the shad in its mouth and the odds for a solid hook-up are a lot greater."

Baker cautions that when he recommends a rod with a soft tip, he is not referring to a buggy-whip type action, where the whole rod bends like a willow switch. Instead, he is describing a rod built with a tip that has a lighter or "softer" action for the first twenty-four to thirty-six inches

Steve Baker fishes gizzard shad on down rods to catch summertime stripers.

before changing to a medium-action backbone.

A fiberglass rod is fine for bait fishing. While graphite and boron rods are lightweight and offer increased sensitivity, those factors are not important when you are placing the rod in a holder. Since a live-bait fisherman will often fish four to ten rods at a time, the lower-priced fiberglass rods make it financially possible to carry an arsenal of rods.

The most popular reel for fishing live bait is a baitcasting reel with a "clicker" on it. Several reels on the market now have a clicker which when engaged produces a "clicking" sound as the line is pulled off the spool. "A clicker acts as an alarm system," Steve Baker says. "When you have six to twelve rods in the water at a time, a clicker can be a big help, because you can't watch all the rods at the same time."

On a baitcasting reel, if you do not turn the reel handle to engage the gears that turn the spool, the reel is in free spool and the line will revolve off the spool. If the reel has a clicker, you can engage the clicker without turning the reel handle, and the minor tension exerted by the clicker will keep the reel from free spooling.

By setting the clicker without engaging the reel, you make it possible for a fish to pull line off the reel without feeling any pressure other than minor tension from the clicker. In certain live-bait fishing situations, that feature is very important, because there are times that you need to let a striper or hybrid run with a bait before setting the hook.

A rod holder that is attached, either temporarily or permanently, to the side of the boat is necessary for live-bait fishing. Depending on the size of the boat, most fishermen will have six to twelve rod holders on their boats. By utilizing more than one rod, an angler can experiment by fishing live bait at different depths.

For fishing live bait in lakes, Steve Baker casts ten- to fourteen-pound test line, especially in deep, clear lakes. The lighter line is less visible to stripers than seventeen- and twenty-pound test line. The ten- to fourteen-pound test line also does not impair a baitfish's swimming ability as much as heavier line.

When striper fishing in a lake, where he normally uses bigger shad than he does in a river or tailrace, Steve Baker prefers a size 3/0 or 4/0 style 42 Eagle Claw hook. "Always match your hook size to the bait. When fishing shad from four- to seven-inches long, I prefer a 3/0 hook. For shad over 7 inches long, I switch to a 4/0," Steve Baker says.

In live-bait fishing, there are two ways that you can fish the bait. You may fish the bait on an unweighted line, which is often called a "free line" or "flat line." This set-up is the most natural way to present live bait to a wary striper and is used a lot in the spring and fall when stripers are not very deep and roaming a variety of depths as they prowl for food.

In hot weather, when stripers seek the cooler, more oxygenated water found in a lake's deeper water, a weight is needed to get a baitfish down to the stripers. A weighted line suspended off the bottom is called a "down rod."

When fishing a down rod Baker uses a one and one-half ounce elongated-shaped sinker, listed in some catalogs as a trolling sinker, that features a swivel on each end. A hooked shad swims in circles and will twist your line unless your sinker is equipped with swivels.

To rig up a down rod, pull off a five- to seven-foot length of line from your reel and clip it off to create a leader. Next, tie the line from your reel to the swivel on one end of the sinker. Then, tie one end of the leader to the swivel on the opposite end of the sinker. After the leader is tied to the sinker, tie the hook to the other end of the leader.

When fishing a down rod for suspended stripers, Steve Baker does not vary the weight of his sinker. Regardless of whether he is fishing fifteen feet deep or forty feet deep, Baker sticks with the one and one-half ounce sinker. The reason for the heavy sinker is that a seven- to twelve-inch gizzard shad is a powerful swimmer, and if you use a weight that is too light, a shad will swim up out of the zone where the stripers are suspended. For example, assume you spot a school of stripers in twenty-five to thirty feet of

LINE FROM REEL

1 1/2 OZ. ELONGATED SINKER
(TENNESSEE BAIT WEIGHT)

5 to 7 ft. LONG LEADER

EAGLE CLAW STYLE 42 HOOK

BAKER'S SETUP FOR FISHING LIVE BAIT

water over a sixty-foot deep river channel bend. You lower a shad down to the twenty-five-foot range and when the gizzard shad eyes that school of stripers, it will try its best to avoid them. If you do not have enough weight on your line, a shad will swim up into ten to fifteen feet of water where most stripers suspended in twenty-five feet of water are not going to bother it. While the shad fins around in ten feet of water, you sit in your boat and wonder why you have not got a strike, because you know you lowered the shad into twenty-five feet of water.

Through trial and error, Baker has found that a one and one-half ounce sinker will keep a seven- to twelve-inch gizzard shad down at the depth where he places it. Of course, if you are using smaller-size shad, you could switch to a lighter sinker.

"Keeping that shad from swimming up is very important, especially in the summer when stripers get very lethargic and won't chase a baitfish very far," Steve Baker says. "In the summer, if the stripers are suspended in thirty feet of water, you need to keep that shad swimming around and around in a circle at the thirty-foot mark and not swimming up to twenty feet, then back down to thirty, then up to fifteen and so on. To get a finicky striper to bite, you need to keep a shad swimming around and around in its face until that striper decides it can't pass up such easy prey."

While many live-bait fishermen prefer a sliding egg-shaped sinker instead of a fixed sinker, Steve Baker sees no advantage in using an egg sinker on a down rod when fishing for suspended stripers.

When fishing live or cut bait on the bottom, Baker will switch to an egg sinker. When a sinker is lying on the bottom, an egg sinker offers the advantage of allowing the line to pass freely through the core of the sinker so that a striper does not feel the weight of the sinker until you are ready to set the hook. But when fishing suspended bait, the drag of an egg sinker on the line is going to be felt just as quickly as a fixed sinker.

Many of the striper guides on Santee-Cooper use one-to two-ounce wrap-around sinkers with tiny "ears" for crimping the weight to the line when drifting shiners for stripers suspended over main-lake bars and flats.

BAIT

The live bait that Steve Baker uses most when striper fishing in lakes is a gizzard shad measuring six to ten inches. During the summer months, when the water temperature climbs into the eighties and nineties, catching the proper-size shad often becomes the hardest part about live-bait fishing.

While Baker will often drive one to two hours to catch gizzard shad from a tailrace and then transport the bait back to a lake, he prefers to catch shad from the lake. "A lot of gizzard shad that you catch in the lake will be fatter and have a golden tint to their backs instead of the more streamlined shape and darker back that you find on a gizzard shad from a river," Steve Baker says. "If you can catch a big, lake shad with a golden color to it and drop it down near a forty pound striper, I guarantee the striper will eat him for lunch!

"You can use a threadfin shad for bait. But in a lake, it is hard to catch any threadfins over three inches long," Steve Baker explains.

Usually, if Baker uses threadfin shad for lake fishing, it is five- to six-inch threadfins that he has caught from a tailrace. But even when he can catch the bigger threadfins, Baker is not real fond of using them when fishing for lake stripers. "A threadfin shad has two speeds--wide open and dead," Baker says. "When you put a threadfin on a down rod, it will swim hard for ten to fifteen minutes. Then it is worthless."

A gizzard shad is a lot hardier than a threadfin, and a gizzard shad can swim around on a hook all day. "A gizzard shad has all kinds of speeds. It will even stop and rest for awhile, then start swimming again," Steve Baker states.

When fishing a gizzard shad on a down rod, the rod tip

Fishing quality live bait on a down rod will consistently produce stripers.

will just occasionally twitch as the shad swims around. But if you see the rod tip start to twitch up and down at a faster pace, get ready because a striper is making that shad very skittish.

To hook a shad, place the point of the hook between the shad's nostrils and work the point back and forth to cut the hook through the nose and out the underside of the shad's mouth. This cutting motion does less damage to the fragile baitfish than jerking a hook through its nose like most anglers do when baiting up.

When you are ready to fish, do not just throw the shad into the water. Instead, gently lower it into the water and get it down into the deep, cool water immediately, because hot surface water will kill a shad. Remember, the livelier the shad, the better your odds of attracting a striper or hybrid.

Besides trying to keep the shad on your hook as active as possible, remember that keeping shad alive in a bait tank during June, July and August requires a constant effort to properly maintain the water as described in Chapter Three. If you want to catch trophy stripers in the summer, you have to have healthy shad. "I would rather have a dozen shad in good shape than three dozen half-dead shad," Steve Baker believes.

DOWN-ROD TECHNIQUE

To fish shad on a down rod, you need to vertically position your boat over the stripers. When you lower the bait, it is important to measure out just enough line to place the shad right above the stripers. For example, assume that you have spotted stripers swimming in twenty-six to thirty feet of water over a forty-foot bottom. On most rods, the distance from the reel to the first line guide is approximately two feet, but you should measure your rods to check the distance. Assuming the span is two feet, hold the line in front of the reel with your thumb and forefinger while the reel is still disengaged. Pull the line down the rod until your fingers reach the first guide. You have now lowered the shad two feet down into the water. Repeat this sequence, counting by two, until your shad is near the twenty-six foot depth where you marked the stripers.

Once the shad has reached the desired depth, turn the reel handle to engage the reel. Place the rod into a rod holder and set the clicker, which acts as an alarm system.

Baker keeps the drag on his reels set so that it will slip on a medium pull. Having the drag properly adjusted and checking it periodically to insure that it is not locked up is very important, because when the reel is engaged, the drag has to be adjusted to give a striper some line when it first hits the live bait.

Many live-bait fishermen do not engage the reel when they place the down rod in the holder, but simply flip the clicker on. The clicker will keep the weight of the sinker from free spooling to the bottom. When a striper hits the live bait, the fish will be able to take out line until you engage the gears in the reel by turning the handle. Fishermen who fish this way feel like you need to give a striper additional line before you set the hook.

"I believe that engaging the reel and adjusting it for a medium drag before you set it in the rod holder will increase your percentage of hook-ups," Steve Baker says. "When a striper hits a live shad, it doesn't need a lot of line before it has that shad engulfed in its mouth. By using a medium drag, a striper can take off with the bait. But when it starts pulling line off the reel, it is doing it with some pressure on the line which I believe helps set the hook."

If stripers or hybrids are not very aggressive, especially in the winter months, Baker may fish his live bait without the reel engaged and only the clicker set to keep the reel from free spooling. But even then, he will leave his reel out of gear only if he has had several runs and missed the fish on an engaged reel set with a medium drag.

When a striper takes a shad, the fish may streak off with the line. When that occurs, do not touch the rod in the rod holder until the second or third line guide from the tip goes into the water. It takes some restraint not to grab the rod when the line first takes off. But if you will wait until the rod goes down, you will increase your hooking percentage.

At times, you may notice the rod tip bounce up and down several times before a striper takes off with the shad. When that happens, once again be patient and do not pick up the rod until the tip goes down into the water.

When stripers are not biting real aggressively, you will even have fish pull the tip down and then just as quickly turn the shad loose. There is not anything that you can do to prevent those missed strikes. When a striper is serious about eating a shad, it does not miss!

When you take the rod from the holder, you may want to set the hook by pulling back on the rod one time, but really you do not even need to set the hook. When that striper takes off with the bait, it usually hooks itself and all you need to do is hang on. "Many times, fishermen break their lines when they try to set the hook two or three times while they're battling a striper," Steve Baker states. "If you want to set the hook, one time is plenty."

If you have adjustable rod holders, adjust a down rod so that it is horizontal to the surface of the water. That position helps to eliminate a lot of above-water slack from gathering in the line, especially on a windy day.

CATCHING SUMMERTIME STRIPERS

Steve Baker's favorite time of the year for fishing live bait on a down rod are the months of June and July. Every year Baker and his guide parties catch a number of thirty and forty pound stripers during the summer months.

Instead of being scattered all over the lake and feeding at a variety of depths, summertime stripers are usually congregating at a specific depth in or near the deep, open water of the main lake. Warmer water temperatures and a lack of dissolved oxygen content often confine stripers to a relatively few areas of a lake, which makes it easier to locate the fish.

A lot of major impoundments stratify during the summer and this process will determine how deep the stripers will be located. Stratification begins in late spring as the sun warms the surface water and creates a layer of water that fisheries biologists call the epilimnion. This layer contains the warmest water temperatures and increases in depth as the sun continues to warm the water near the surface.

Below the epilimnion is a narrower zone of rapid temperature change called the thermocline. In fact, the thermocline has a temperature change of at least one-half a degree per foot of depth. Because of cooler temperatures and a greater supply of dissolved oxygen, stripers prefer the thermocline to the rapidly warming water of the epilimnion.

Below the thermocline is a colder, less oxygenated layer of water known as the hypolimnion. On some lakes, the hypolimnion is devoid of oxygen in the summer, because of bacterial decomposition from dead organic material that sinks down from the upper layers and a lack of photosynthesis which is responsible for producing oxygen in the upper layers. On many lakes, however, especially deep, clear lakes, the hypolimnion does not become oxygen deficient, and stripers utilize the hypolimnion to escape from bright sunlight.

Summertime stripers usually congregate in the thermocline or just below it in order to take advantage of the cooler temperatures and higher oxygen content. You can locate the thermocline by lowering the probe of a temperature gauge into the water and noting when the temperature starts to change at a rapid rate. The cable to the probe should be pre-measured so that the depth can be determined when the temperature begins to fall sharply.

Even without a temperature gauge, you can find the thermocline by observing at what depth the majority of fish, including baitfish are suspended. On a paper chart recorder, the thermocline will even show up as a light gray band.

Once you have determined the depth of the thermocline, you need to suspend the live bait on your down rods near that depth range, because that is where the greatest concentrations of active fish will be. By using the thermocline as a depth guide, schools of stripers will be easier to find. Remember, stripers may be located below the thermocline, but they will seldom be located above it, because they cannot tolerate the higher water temperatures for a sustained period of time. So, if you use the location of the thermocline as the minimum depth where you will find a school of summertime stripers, and keep an open mind as to how deep the fish will go below that, you will be more successful.

"On my home lake, Norris, the thermocline will normally be twenty-four to thirty feet deep in June and July," Steve Baker says. "By August and September, the thermocline drops down to forty, fifty, even sixty feet deep."

Baker often sees stripers by way of a video screen streak up from below the thermocline and take a shad that he has suspended in the thermocline. He believes that even though the thermocline may have comfortable temperatures, adequate oxygen and concentrations of bait-

Locating the thermocline and fishing live bait in it will result in trophy fish like Steve Baker is unhooking.

fish, stripers often go below the thermocline on clear-water lakes to escape the harsh, summer sun. "The bulk of the baitfish will be in the thermocline, but don't always expect stripers to be there," Baker says.

Since a striper will never go down to take a bait, but it will swim up a considerable distance to attack a baitfish, you can lure stripers up from deeper waters by suspending your live bait in or just below the thermocline. Steve Baker recommends fishing a number of rods at various depths until you locate the most productive depth for that day or particular location.

After he has determined the depth of the thermocline, Steve Baker begins his search for stripers in the summer by cruising the middle to lower end of a lake in a hunt for structure at or below the thermocline.

Stripers are not a bottom-oriented fish and will readily cover miles of open water in their hunt for baitfish. Steve Baker believes that the importance of structure is that baitfish relate to structure and cover, even using it as a hiding place.

"A striper is a transplanted saltwater species. Because of that, it is an open-water fish that will travel great distances without ever venturing near the bank," Steve Baker relates. "I think that the reason you often find stripers schooled up near a channel ledge or point is because that is where the baitfish gather."

Baker points out that on Norris Lake, which was impounded in 1933, a lot of the points are comprised of bare sand and clay, which the local fishermen refer to as a "slick" point. In various areas of the lake, you can find six or eight "slick" points running out into the lake within close proximity. Sandwiched in between all those "slick" points will be a point with a rubble of broken rocks on it.

A majority of the time, you will find shad schooled up on the "rough" point and nothing relating to the "slick" points. Of course, any stripers in the area will also be suspended near the "rough" point.

"A school of stripers will usually be suspended at twenty-five to thirty feet deep out from the point. So, I don't believe it matters to stripers if the point is sandy or rocky," Steve Baker says. "I believe that it is the shad and other baitfish that prefer a rocky or stumpy point over a slick point in the summer, and the stripers just follow the bait."

Baker's theory is supported by scientific facts. Shad feed on plankton which are microscopic organisms of either the plant or animal family. The plankton of plant origin is called phytoplankton, and it floats around in the lake in whichever direction the winds and currents take it.

Plankton of animal origin is called zooplankton, and it can either be free floating or equipped with cilia (hairlike fibers) which allow it to swim in the water. Zooplankton with the ability to swim attach to wood and other debris on the bottom and are called periphyton. Therefore, where there is cover on the bottom, there is usually periphyton attached to it. Shad are then drawn to the cover because of the periphyton.

Whatever the reason for stripers showing a preference for structure with a rough bottom or cover on it, you can use that behavior to help narrow the search down when faced with miles and miles of potential structure. For example, if you find a bar extending out into a lake with a mile or more of good drop-off along it, try to find the area on the drop with some sort of cover on it, such as rocks, mussel shells or stumps.

"Even though a school of stripers may be suspended twenty or thirty feet off the bottom, I still seem to do better when there is some sort of irregular feature on the bottom which makes the spot stand out from the surrounding terrain," Steve Baker says.

Points and underwater ridges that drop off into the river channel, humps and channel bends are all likely places to connect with deep-water stripers.

"You can find a lot of baitfish suspended over open water in the summer, and sometimes you can catch stripers suspended under the bait," Steve Baker says. "But over the years, I have noticed that a school of baitfish located near some sort of structure is more likely to attract a school of stripers than the open-water baitfish. Maybe stripers use the structure to help corral the bait."

If the thermocline is thirty feet deep, Baker does not look for structure at the thirty-foot mark. Instead, he searches for a hump, channel bend or other structure in forty to sixty feet of water. "A striper is not a bottom-oriented fish, and I have better luck finding stripers where they can suspend in or near the thermocline over structure that is considerably deeper than the thermocline. I believe stripers like to have a lot of water between them and the bottom."

When fishing deep-water structure with down rods, many anglers prefer to anchor and keep their baits suspended directly over the structure. It is a productive way to fish and, sometimes, the best way.

If possible, however, Steve Baker prefers to suspend his baits directly under the boat, and then use an electric trolling motor or slight breeze to slowly work his baits across a long point, channel ledge or hump. He believes this method allows him to present his baits to a larger number of stripers in a day's time.

FISHING A FREE LINE

In the spring, fall, and winter, fishing live bait on a hook without a weight is one of the best, if not the best, ways to catch a trophy striper. Live bait swimming on a free line is the most natural lure a striper will ever see.

When fishing a free line, which he does a lot, Steve Baker prefers to use an eight to twelve inch gizzard shad. The reason Baker chooses bigger shad is that he has found smaller shad in the four to six inch size range will not swim as deeply as the bigger shad when they are hooked.

When hooking a shad on a free line, Baker runs the point of the hook crossways through one of the shad's nostrils and out the other nostril. Some anglers prefer to run the hook through the fleshy part of the back in front of the dorsal fin.

For fishing an eight to twelve inch shad, Steve Baker uses a 3/0 or 4/0 hook and twelve to twenty pound test line depending on the amount of cover in the water. On deep, relatively debris-free lakes, Baker prefers fourteen pound test line.

To fish a free line, Baker lowers his shad into the water and lets out sixty to seventy feet of line before he flips on the clicker. The clicker will prevent additional line from free spooling off the reel. But when a striper hits the shad, it will be able to take line freely, because the reel is left out of gear.

"Unlike when I am fishing a down rod, I believe it is best to leave the reel out of gear with the clicker on when you are fishing a free line," Steve Baker says. "When a striper hits a shad on a free line, the fish will be in four to fifteen feet of water, and that striper will be going out and not down when it takes the bait. In a situation like that, I believe it is important to let a striper take some line before you set the hook."

After the shad is hooked on a line trailing sixty to seventy feet behind the boat, Baker places the rod and reel in a rod holder mounted on the stern of the boat. The rod holder is adjusted so that the rod is positioned up at a thirty-degree angle to the surface of the water instead of being set straight out on a horizontal plane with the water like Baker recommends for a down rod. Positioning the free line at such an angle allows a bow to form in the line which makes it easier to keep track of the free-swimming shad as it drifts or is pulled along behind the boat.

By watching the line, Baker can tell how deep the shad is swimming. If there is a long bow in the line, the shad is finning around near the surface. If the line angles sharply into the water, the shad is down deep.

When a striper hits a shad on a free line, the line will go screeching off the reel. Do not break any rods in your rush to get to the rod with the striper on it. "I know it is not easy to do, but don't get in a big hurry, take your time getting to the rod," Steve Baker advises.

When you reach the rod, pick it up and turn the reel handle to engage the gears. Reel up the slack and set the hook hard. Unlike a down rod, where a striper usually sets the hook itself, you need to set the hook hard and on a tight line when using a free line.

For catching stripers shallower than seventeen feet deep, Baker does not use down rods, but instead relies on a free line to lure wary stripers to the hook. The cooler water temperatures of spring, fall and winter often draw stripers into water less that seventeen feet deep, which makes a free line an excellent way to fish live bait during those seasons.

Shallow points, humps, ridges and channel ledges are the best places to catch stripers on a free line in the spring, fall and winter.

In the spring and fall, wind can often be an important factor in locating stripers. Wind-blown mud and clay banks near deeper water as well as pockets and coves with the wind blowing into them are prime spots for spring and fall stripers. The wind piles up the warmer surface water in such places during the spring which attracts both stripers and baitfish. During the fall, wind colors up the water as it blows into the bank which makes stripers less wary than in clearer water. "If the wind blows into a cove and colors up the water, you can often catch stripers in the dingy water all day long as opposed to just early and late in clearer water," Steve Baker says.

PROPER BOAT CONTROL

Controlling the boat correctly is a must when live bait fishing. In the spring and fall months when the stripers are shallow, a big gizzard shad is deadly when worked properly on a free line. It is very important to set up and get all the baits in position before moving into a potential feeding area.

If Steve Baker is fishing a point, he likes to swing the boat wide across the point or breakline using only an electric motor to prevent spooking the stripers. Then he cuts the boat sharply to the inside. This maneuver pulls the free line over the area of the point that the boat has not crossed.

If Baker has had a striper strike a topwater lure near the bank several times without a hook-up, he will put out one rod with a big shad for bait and position the boat very close to the area where the fish is feeding. If there is any wind, he allows the wind to drift the boat silently over the shallow water near the bank.

When fishing live bait over deep-water structure, such as a river ledge or hump, it is important to control your boat in a manner that allows you to fish both the deep-water drop-off and the shallow flat adjoining the drop-off. To do this, Steve Baker uses his electric motor to move the boat in a zig-zag pattern. On a given day, stripers may be feeding on the high side of a ledge or hump and also over the deep-water side. A zig-zag pattern enables you to fish both areas.

When pulling a free line fifty or sixty yards behind the boat over deep structure, it is important to know how to move the boat in order to fish the shad at different depths. To work the shad shallow, simply pull the boat straight ahead with the electric trolling motor. This movement will pull the shad upward into shallower water.

If you want the shad to go deep, turn the boat to the left or right slowly, which allows slack line to form between the rod and the bait. When given slack line, a large shad will slowly swim deeper. Repeat this maneuver as you work the shad along.

One of the most common mistakes that striper fishermen make is not considering the speed at which they are pulling or drifting their live bait. It is extremely important to keep a down line almost perpendicular to the rod as you use an electric motor or the wind to move across a likely striper location. If the boat speed is too fast, the drag created on the lines will pull the shad up from the desired depth by ten feet or more.

If the wind is blowing too hard to keep the lines straight down as he drifts across a piece of structure, Steve Baker either pulls the boat into the wind with the aid of an electric motor in order to slow down the drift or adds extra weights.

BOAT POSITIONING AND CONTROL

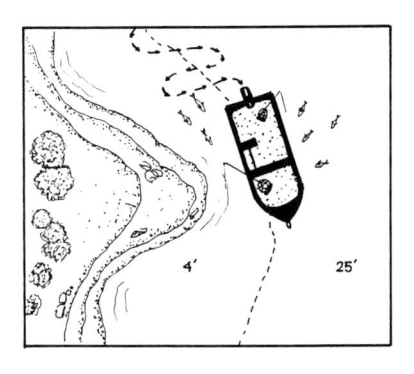

When fishing a breakline or drop-off with live bait or trolling, a zigzag pattern will produce fish from both the shallow break and deep water area.

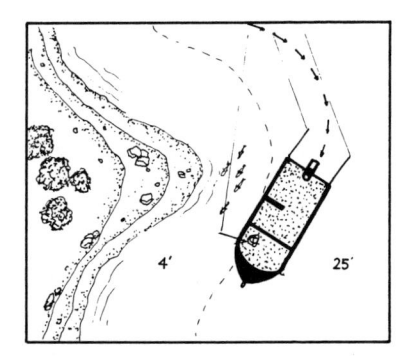

Swinging your boat wide across a point then cutting sharply toward the inside will swing a free-line or balloon rig over the feeding area without spooking the fish.

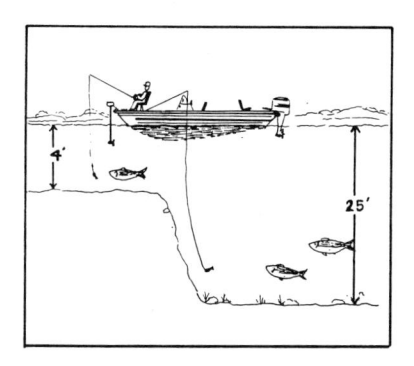

By positioning your boat near a shallow water break, you can cast up on the flat or fish a down rod in deep water where stripers may suspend.

Proper boat speed must be maintained to keep your weighted lines perpendicular to the rod for exact depth control.

In most cases, he prefers to work into the wind because he has more control over the boat.

Once a school of fish has been located, it is best to pull the free lines in and work over the school with only down lines. Maneuver the boat in tight figure-eight patterns to keep your lines moving through the school. Be careful, however, when making tight turns. Go slowly in order to keep the lines straight down to prevent tangles.

If you locate a school of stripers while drifting with the wind, don't crank up and run directly over the fish to make another drift. Wait until the boat is a good distance from the school. Then start the engine and make a wide circle to line up for another drift. Most anglers will get excited after catching the first striper from a school and run directly over the top of the feeding fish. This kind of careless boat positioning will often scare a school away.

If stripers are situated near a river ledge or creek channel, it is best to position the boat near the top of the ledge. In this position, you will be able to cast live bait, cut bait or artificial lures across the top of the ledge. At the same time, you will be able to fish live bait on down rods in the deeper water directly beneath the boat.

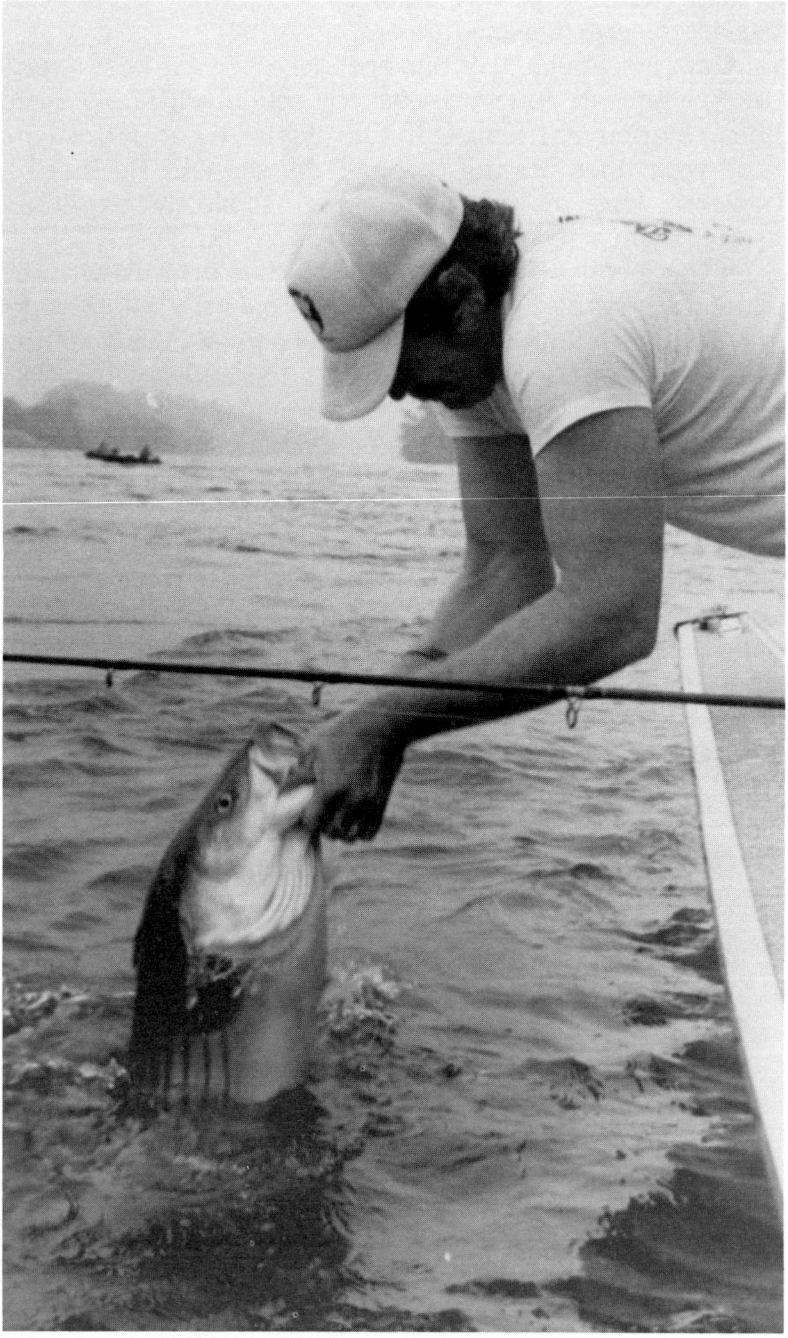

Chapter 5
TAILRACE FISHING

The water immediately below a dam, commonly called a tailrace, can produce some of the fastest striper and hybrid action that a fisherman could ever hope to experience. Numerous tailraces across the country attract huge schools of stripers and hybrids, including the tailraces below the dams that form Chickamauga, Nick-A-Jack, Melton Hill, Fort Loudon, Cherokee, Watts Bar, Pickwick and Percy Priest Lakes in Tennessee; Guntersville, Yates, Wilson and Martin Lakes in Alabama; Richard B. Russell and Seminole Lakes in Georgia; Texoma, Eufaula, and Keystone Lakes in Oklahoma; Murray and Santee-Cooper in South Carolina; Kerr and Leesville in North Carolina; Whitney in Texas; and Mohave in Arizona.

Tailraces are a feeding ground for stripers, especially from July to September when warmer water temperatures slow down striper activity in the main lake. Usually, dams with productive striper fishing are equipped with turbines for producing hydroelectricity. Since the water released below the dams is being pulled from near the bottom of the reservoir to turn the turbines, the water is often ten to twenty degrees cooler than the surface water. The cooler water draws summertime stripers up the river to the tailrace.

The constant flow of water through the turbines and the agitation of the water as it is forced from the turbines also increases the dissolved oxygen in the water, just like an aerator adds oxygen to a bait tank or livewell. Stripers seek the oxygenated water found in tailraces because

Tailraces offer some of the most productive striper and hybrid fishing available.

water with a high level of dissolved oxygen is very important to a striper's survival during hot-weather months.

The cooler, oxygenated water also attracts massive-size schools of baitfish which congregate in tailraces. With an abundance of food in such a concentrated area, it is no mystery why stripers and hybrids reside in tailraces all summer long.

Normally, you will not catch as big a striper in a tailrace as you will in the main lake itself, but tailraces will yield a tremendous number of stripers in the six- to twenty-pound range, with an average size of three to twelve pounds. As an example of the productivity of tailraces, Steve Baker's guide parties boated seven- to eight hundred stripers in one summer of tailrace fishing.

"I started fishing tailraces about seven to eight years ago in order to combat the slow striper fishing that the lakes offer in the dog days of August and September," Steve Baker says. "Because I had guide parties that wanted to fight stripers and not listen to excuses, I had to find some hot-weather striper action. Tailraces are the answer."

EQUIPMENT

For fishing tailraces, Baker uses a seven to eight foot heavy-action rod with a sensitive tip. He prefers a graphite or boron rod, because of its increased sensitivity when compared to a fiberglass rod. Some of the rods designed as "flippin' sticks" for bass fishing work well for tailrace fishing. A "flippin' stick" is generally seven and one-half feet in length and has a flexible tip for the first foot or so of the rod's length, before it changes to a stiff, powerful action.

Since heavy line is necessary for striper fishing in tailraces, a heavy-duty baitcasting reel is the best choice below dams. Spool the reel up with twenty to thirty pound test line. The bottom below many dams is extremely rough and rocky. With a strong current constantly forcing your line downriver, rocks quickly abrade monofilament line.

"You need to keep a hooked striper up off the rough bottom," Steve Baker says. "It takes twenty to twenty-five pound test line to deal with a striper in swift current."

When you hook a striper in a tailrace, the fish will often run upstream. It is not surprising for a river striper to strip off fifty to seventy-five yards of line as it heads upstream. The fish will then turn and run downstream just as quickly. You need to crank up the slack line as fast as possible when the striper heads downstream, because the current will immediately push any slack line down and your line will get tangled up on bottom debris.

A trick that Steve Baker uses when a striper hangs up on the bottom is to start up the outboard and head upstream. When you get above where the line is hung, raise up on the rod. Many times the line which has become caught in a crevice will pop free.

When fishing tailraces, Baker uses live bait the majority of the time. For fishing live bait, he ties on an Eagle Claw style 42 hook in a 1/0 size. A medium-size shad, measuring three and one-half to six inches long, is the best live-bait choice for tailraces, and a 1/0 hook matches up well with that size shad.

To rig up for fishing live bait in tailraces, Baker threads a three-quarter ounce to one and one-quarter ounce egg sinker, the size depending on the strength of the current, on his line. Then he ties on the hook. Sliding the egg sinker up the line from the hook for a distance of two to two and one-half feet, Baker slips a toothpick into the sinker to peg it to the line.

With such a set-up, Baker can quickly get his live bait down in a powerful current and keep it bouncing along the rough bottom.

LIVE BAIT

When fishing tailraces, you are likely to encounter three species of shad. Gizzard shad are found in abundance below the dams and readily grow to twelve or fifteen inches long. Threadfin shad are narrower and more streamlined in shape than gizzard shad and normally reach only four to seven inches long. Threadfin shad can be easily identified by the small black dot situated behind each gill cover. The third species of shad is a herring which is often called a hickory shad. It has a green or blue-tinted back and easily grows ten to fifteen inches long.

Unlike gizzard and threadfin shad, a herring is carnivorous. Because of that, herring can be easily caught by anglers casting small jigs which imitate tiny minnows.

For catching tailrace stripers, Steve Baker prefers a threadfin shad measuring three and one-half to six inches long. "Gizzard shad are usually the most numerous species of shad found in tailraces, but I have found stripers prefer the less abundant threadfin shad," Baker says.

While Baker regularly captures gizzard shad from tailraces and transports them back to the lake for bait, he does not use gizzard shad at all when angling tailraces.

Tailrace stripers often feed heavily at daylight before the majority of anglers arrive on the scene. About an hour or two after daylight, a crowd begins to gather and the stripers' feeding activity starts to slow down. "I'm sure that the increased boat activity in such a confined area spooks some stripers, but I believe what really slows down the action is that suddenly dozens of shad are being dragged down in front of their noses," Steve Baker says.

To combat the increased fishing competition, Baker will bait up with a drum or bluegill measuring three to six inches long. Many times the switch will allow Baker to catch several more good-size stripers, before the morning feeding spree usually ends around nine or ten o'clock.

To catch shad from a tailrace, throw a cast net in the slack water along the dam wall and near the bank. Use a six or eight-foot cast net instead of a bigger 10- or 12-foot cast net that you might throw in a lake, since the current makes throwing and retrieving a net more difficult.

"Be extremely careful when using a cast net in tailraces, because the current is very unpredictable below a dam. The amount of water being released through the turbines varies and it causes surges in the strength of the current," Baker explains.

When you throw a cast net into a tailrace, even in the slack water areas, the current quickly forces the net down. If there should be a change or surge in the current, a net can be swirled up in the current and pushed to the bottom.

If the cast net should become hung on the irregular bottom, you could be in danger of having the current pull you into the turbulent waters.

Steve Baker advises anyone using a cast net in a tailrace to keep a knife handy for cutting off the rope attached from the cast net to your wrist in case a net does hang on the bottom and the current starts to pull you in. "You've got to remember that rope usually consists of twenty strands of eighty-pound test line. You're not going to break it by pulling on it," Baker says.

To minimize the odds of hanging a cast net on the rough bottom, Baker shortens the rope attached to the net and does not let the net sink more than a few feet before he starts pulling it up. The water where you throw your cast net is usually not more than five or six feet deep, so you do not need to let it sink very long.

For catching bait in tailraces, Baker throws a cast net with a three-eighths inch mesh instead of the wider one-half and five-eighths inch mesh nets. The reason for this is that for tailrace stripers, Baker uses three and one-half to six inch threadfin shad instead of the larger gizzard shad that he fishes in the lakes. These medium-size threadfin shad will injure themselves by getting their bodies stuck in a wider mesh net.

Tailraces contain a potpourri of fish and when you toss in a cast net you may haul in a number of fish species. On one throw, you may catch threadfin, gizzard and river herring, drum, catfish, white bass, gar and bluegill.

Besides a cast net, many anglers use a dip net equipped with fine mesh to scoop up shad as the baitfish congregate along the walls of the dam and in the eddy water near the bank. You can use a dip net from either the bank or a boat to catch shad.

An especially good area for utilizing a dip net is where a swift current swirls back to form a pool of smoother water near the bank or a concrete wall. The current's action washes shad into the eddy, and you can scoop them up as the shad are pushed into the pool.

To capture shad that are forced against the wall of the

dam by a swift current, Steve Baker has designed a special "V"-shaped basket net consisting of a metal frame covered with one-half inch mesh screen wire. A rope tied on each end of the basket allows it to be lowered down the side of the wall from the bank. The basket is submerged until a school of shad swims over the basket. Then you quickly pull up on the ropes and trap the shad in the basket.

The basket is very useful at dams with such turbulent boils and current that you cannot safely get a boat against the walls. In such situations, lower the basket down the wall and into the water as you stand above the wall. Periodically, as the water boils up from the turbines, the surge will throw dozens of disoriented shad against the concrete wall. Then you can easily scoop them up in the basket.

You cannot always anticipate where along a wall a surge in the current will force shad. If the current forces a school of shad against a wall, but up or down the wall from where you have your basket submerged, drop the front or leading end of the basket a few feet below the back, or trailing end, and walk the basket down the wall to the shad. By lowering the front end, you reduce the drag of the basket, and it is easier to move it through the swift waters.

Regardless of how you choose to catch shad from tailraces, you need to quickly place the fragile baitfish in a live-bait tank equipped with an adequate aeration system and filled with water that has been treated with the proper chemicals for keeping shad alive.

"Sometimes, it is hard to catch bluegill in the tailraces. So, if I want to be sure and have a few bluegill in case the stripers get finicky, I catch bluegill from the lake and carry them to the tailraces," Baker advises.

The proper-size drum for tailrace stripers can also be difficult to catch. Most of the drum that you catch in a net will be too big. However, if you can capture some small drum, say three to six inches long, you can catch some nice stripers on them.

LIVE BAIT TECHNIQUE

To catch tailrace stripers and hybrids, Steve Baker will often run his boat to within twenty or thirty yards of the dam itself. As water is released from the turbines, it shoots up off the bottom and "boils" or mushrooms, like the blast from an atomic bomb, as it heads to the surface.

When fishing the boils, Steve Baker will not position his boat directly in front of a turbine, because the water is too swift and the boat would be swept downstream too fast. Instead, Baker will position his boat slightly to the side of a turbine where the water is not as turbulent.

For example, say there are four turbines running at the same time. On his first drift, Baker may position his boat between turbines number one and two. By lining up the boat with the bow pointed upstream between the two turbines, Baker will not drift downstream as fast, and more importantly, he will be in position to get his bait to bottom.

What Baker tries to do is drop his heavy egg sinker and shad into the ring around the edge of the boil or mushroom, because the water around the outside edge of the boil is being sucked back down to the bottom. By dropping the bait into the edge of the boil, you will get it to go down to the bottom instead of being washed up in the current.

If you position your boat between two running turbines, you will also discover that besides the down wash created by the boils themselves, you also have a down wash created where two powerful currents merge. "Where two strong currents meet, they can't wash over each other, so they create a downward pull that I use to pull my bait to the bottom," Steve Baker says.

Where the currents fold back downward, a foam line of tiny bubbles appears on the surface. An experienced tailrace fisherman looks for such a place and drops his bait into it, because he knows his bait will reach the bottom instead of being swept up in the current.

When the bait hits the bottom, let the sinker "peck" along the bottom as the current pushes the boat downriver. Normally, Baker drifts for a hundred to two hundred yards below the dam before he cranks up and heads to the boils again. Depending on how much water is being released, a drift may only last a few minutes before you are out of the productive water.

"The water below most dams is not as deep as people think. The bottom usually varies from ten to twenty feet deep," Steve Baker says. "What makes it tough to keep your shad on the bottom is the tremendous amount of current."

To keep the bait down as you drift and also to minimize hang-ups, you need to keep the line almost vertical beside the boat. If you allow the sinker and line to drift out horizontally from the boat, the current will push the bait up off the bottom or the line will snag in a crevice on the bottom.

The best way to quickly get your shad to the bottom is to make a short, underhanded pitch cast so that the bait and heavy sinker land fifteen to twenty feet from the boat. When the sinker hits the water, immediately raise the seven and one-half foot rod back to the one o'clock position while the reel is still disengaged. This maneuver will release enough additional slack line to let the sinker swiftly fall to the bottom, assuming the bottom is fifteen to twenty feet deep.

Engage the reel and lower the rod back down toward the surface of the water as the weight of the sinker and shad pull out the slack line.

It is very important that you get the bait to the bottom as fast as possible, because the current will sweep the boat rapidly downriver as soon as you shut off the outboard. If your shad is not near the bottom, you may drift over the top of stripers or hybrids without getting a strike.

Unlike some species of fish, stripers and hybrids prefer a swift current when feeding. Many times you will catch stripers right at the edge of the boils, where the water is moving so fast that your bait is swept down river in a matter of seconds.

As the boat drifts downriver, you want to feel the pegged

egg sinker occasionally "pecking" or bumping along the bottom. If you are getting your shad down to the bottom where it needs to be in order to catch fish, you will get hung up a lot! Two people will often break off fifty to seventy-five hooks a day and almost that many egg sinkers. Steve Baker goes through a five-gallon bucket of sinkers during a season of tailrace fishing.

After you have fished the tailraces for a while, you will learn to lift up on the line to "walk" the sinker over rocks, but you will still get snagged dozens of times a day. "The combination of a powerful current and a rocky bottom makes it impossible to completely control your line. Sometimes, I'll make three drifts and break off three times," Steve Baker says. "However, I've also made eight drifts and caught eight stripers!"

If the size of your boat allows you to safely stand up and fish as you drift the tailrace, you will be able to control your line better. With a long rod and sensitive feel, you can anticipate when the sinker is about to hang and move the line sideways so that the current washes the bait around the potential snag.

When you hook a fish, you can also control it easier if you are standing up. By standing, you can walk the line around the boat if the fish runs underneath the boat.

When a striper or hybrid takes a shad as you are drifting down river, you do not really need to set the hook. The fish will grab the bait and take off with it. Since the reel is already engaged, all you need to do is to lift up on the rod tip and hang on until the striper slows down.

Even though you are using twenty-five-pound test line, keep the drag adjusted to where it will yield line on a medium-heavy pull, because a tailrace striper is faster and more powerful than a lake striper. If you do not let the fish take some line against the drag when it hits, you will break off a big striper or rip the hook out of its mouth.

When you shut the motor off to begin a drift down the tailwaters, you want the bow of the boat to be facing the dam. Pitch your line off to the side of the boat and hang on as the current swiftly forces the boat downriver again.

Since the speed and direction of the current is so unpredictable, the boat will spin around and change angles as it drifts downriver. As it spins around, use the rod to move the line around the boat so that your rod and line are always off to the side of the boat or on the upstream side of the boat. If you do not and the line gets snagged, the boat will drift right over the top of your rod as you try to get it unhung. When that happens, the rod will get in a bind and break as the boat rolls over it.

To be a successful tailrace fisherman, you have to learn to read current. The speed of the current does not remain constant throughout the day. The gates releasing the water are adjustable and the amount of water varies as the gates are opened and closed.

"The gates not only control the speed of the current, but also its direction," Steve Baker says. "On a four-turbine dam, if one turbine is shut off, it completely changes where the eddies are formed and where the stripers and hybrids will be located on the bottom."

Each turbine will create its own boil when the water shoots up off the bottom. As the water mushrooms out near the surface, a current will be created. The speed of that current will depend on the amount of water that is being released to create that boil or mushroom. The exact direction of the current will depend on how many other boils are being created and mixed with that boil.

You may start out the day drifting a shad with a three-quarter ounce sinker. As the day progresses and demand for electricity increases, you may have to switch to a one-ounce sinker to keep the bait down as more water is released from the turbines.

Likewise, if only two turbines are running, an edge or break in the current will be formed where the swift water from the turbines meets the slack water formed in front of the idle turbines. You may catch stripers all morning from the boils created by the two turbines. But when turbine number three is kicked on, the fish may relocate in front of turbine number three due to the change in the current.

"When fishing a tailrace, you have to locate the stripers

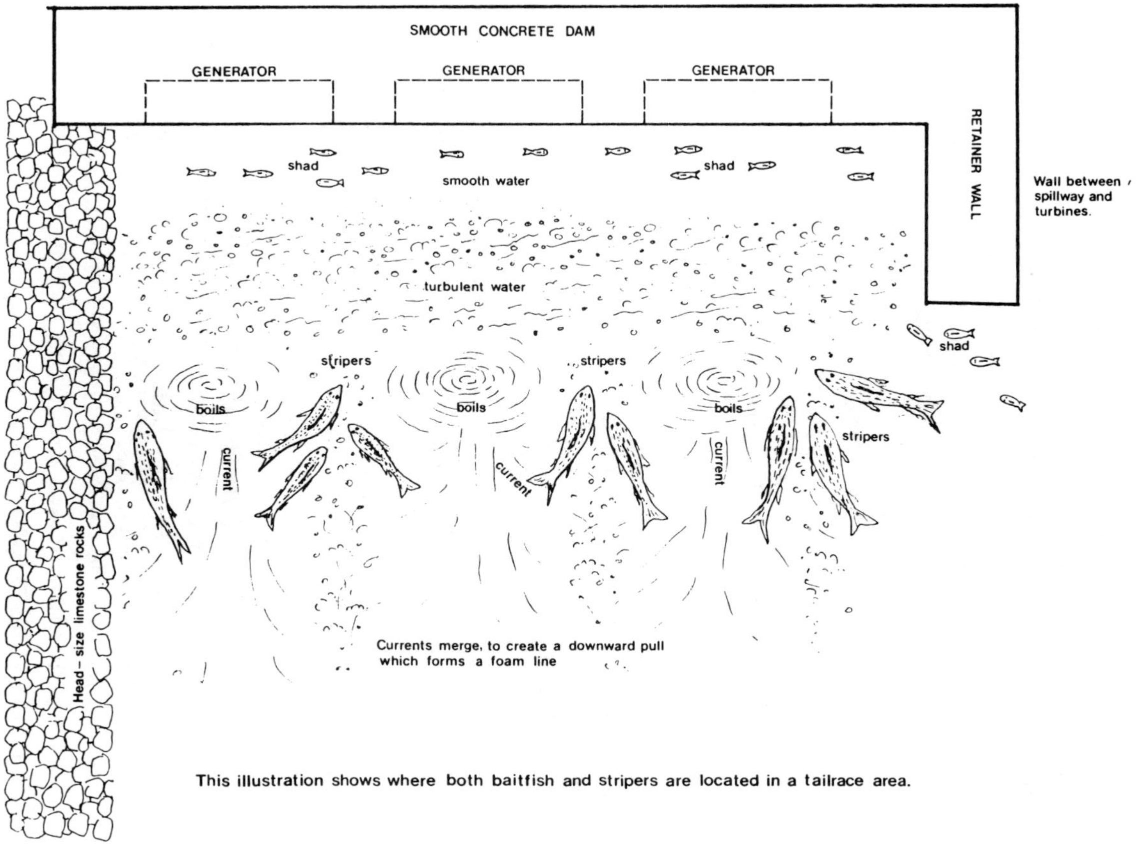

This illustration shows where both baitfish and stripers are located in a tailrace area.

just like you do in a lake," Steve Baker says. "When I first get on the water, I'll make three or four drifts between turbines one and two. If I don't do any good, I'll make three or four drifts between turbines two and three. If I still don't find the fish, I'll move to the next turbine, and so on, until hopefully, I catch a striper."

Although tailrace stripers like fast water, they will often lie on the bottom where the water falls off to form a slightly deeper hole or pocket. After you fish a particular tailrace for awhile, you will learn where the holes and ditches are situated. A clue that you have drifted over a deeper hole is when the heavy egg sinker quits pecking steadily along the bottom. When that occurs, let out a little more line to get the sinker back on the bottom.

"Stripers will sometimes relate to the downstream side of a bar or ditch, because it breaks up the current's flow," Steve Baker says.

Do not count on your depth finder or graph recorder to help find depth changes, because the water near turbines is full of air bubbles which interfere with the depth finder's operation. Of course, the further downstream you fish, the more useful a depth finder becomes.

Since the current is so strong and the bottom is so rough, a hooked shad does not hold up very long. Swimming in the current wears a shad out in a hurry and bouncing off the rocks knocks a lot of its scales off. If you do not hang up and break off, Baker recommends that you hook on a fresh shad after every two or three drifts. It is not unusual for one of Baker's guide parties to use two hundred shad a day.

When you hang up in swift water, immediately clamp down on the spool of your baitcasting reel with both thumbs and pull back on the line to break it. If you let the boat drift too far before you try to break off, the stretch in the line will make it even harder to break.

Clients often ask Baker why he does not anchor in the swift water and drift shad from a stationary boat. He explains to them that he has tried that, and he does not catch as many fish as he does when he lets his boat drift with the current. Baker is not sure why he does better fishing from a moving boat, but he suspects that the bait obtains a more natural drift as it moves with the boat.

If a lot of water is being released through the turbines, the current can sometimes become too swift for even stripers. When that occurs, stripers will move downstream from the dam a distance of one- to two-hundred yards, depending on the force of the current.

"When the stripers are not in the real turbulent water, I will sometimes put a sliding cork on my line and fish the shad out to the side of the boat, instead of underneath it," Steve Baker says.

The reason for using a cork to drift the shad out to the side of the boat is to keep from spooking stripers located in the calmer water, especially on sunny days.

If you hook a big fish in a tailrace that does not make a long run, but instead refuses to budge from the bottom, then do not be surprised if you land a twenty-pound drum or catfish. With such a variety of fish in a tailrace, you are liable to hook into any kind of fish.

ARTIFICIAL LURES

Besides live bait, artificial lures also account for plenty of the stripers taken from tailraces. In the spring and fall, large swimming minnow plugs fished near the surface can be very productive on feeding stripers. "In the spring, it seems like I can catch stripers just casting a minnow lure across likely looking spots, such as an eddy or a backwash," Steve Baker says. "But in the fall, I have to see a striper chasing a shad near the surface before I can get a fish to hit the lure."

When a tailrace striper does hit a topwater bait, you do not have to worry about it swiping or swirling at the plug without taking it solidly like the fish often do in a lake. When a tailrace striper hits a topwater lure, it explodes on it and all you have to do is hang on for the fight!

For casting swimming minnows in tailraces, especially from the bank, Steve Baker often spools up with thirty and forty pound test line. He uses a seven and one-half foot rod and tightens the drag on his reel practically all the way down. "When I'm casting from the bank and a striper hits, I just plant my feet in the rocks and hang on tight," Steve Baker says.

Baker does not let a hooked striper take any line against the drag, and often he does not even crank his reel handle to take up line. He simply holds on and lets the current push the striper downstream against the rocks. "When you hook a thirty or forty pound striper, the rod will squeak and groan under the strain. But just hold on, it won't break," Steve Baker advises.

Eventually the powerful current, heavy rod and stout line will get the best of most fish, and when the striper lets up, the swift current will wash it up against the bank. "In most tailrace situations, there will be someone on the bank to net it or gaff it for you when the fish is pushed in against the rocks," Steve Baker says.

The reason for the strong-arm tactic is that if you start chasing after a hooked striper on foot, you will never keep up. A striper will run you for a mile or more down river if you give it a chance. Moving down the bank with a striper is a great way to break your ankle in the rocks, and backing off on the drag to give it line is just increasing the odds that the fish will tangle up your line on an underwater obstruction and break off.

"Most of the time, when you catch a tailrace striper on topwater, it will hit the lure as you bring the lure through an eddy or slack water," Steve Baker explains. "So when that fish runs out of that eddy, it is in trouble. Because the current is so swift, a hooked striper can't fight it long."

Bucktail and other synthetic hair jigs are the most popular artificial lures for fishing in tailraces, because jigs will catch stripers year-round under a variety of changing conditions. The most productive size jig to use depends on the amount of current. Since the velocity of the current below a dam may change several times a day, you need to carry a variety of different size jigs, ranging from one-half ounce to four ounces or more.

Steve Baker with a 28-pound striper caught from a tailrace in September.

To catch stripers from a tailrace consistently on a jig, you need to bump the artificial lure along the bottom. Use the lightest jig you can as long as the lure gets down to the bottom in the swift water. You will lose a tremendous number of jigs. But if you are not getting the lure on the bottom, you are fishing above the majority of stripers.

Baker advises increasing the size and action of the jig by dressing it up with a plastic worm or grub. The most popular combination for stripers is a white jig and a white plastic worm or grub with a ribbon or swimming type tail to it. Do not be close-minded about colors, however. In some of the tailraces that Baker fishes regularly, a white jig and a six-inch purple plastic worm with a white twister tail is the most effective color combination.

When fishing a jig in swift water, the lighter the line you use, the better the jig will sink. Thick-diameter line has more buoyancy in water and will not allow a jig to sink as fast. Choose your line size based upon the size of stripers that you will probably hook, and the amount of underwater debris that the line will come into contact with. In some situations, you may be able to use seventeen or even fourteen-pound test line, and under different circumstances, you may need twenty-five and thirty-pound test line.

When fishing from the bank, cast your jig into the edge of the boils created by the turbines and let the current bounce the lure downstream. If you are fishing from a boat, Steve Baker advises you to pitch a jig into the edge of a boil just like you would with live bait and let the jig bounce along the bottom as the boat drifts downstream.

"If you don't have to cast, don't," Steve Baker advises. "When you make a cast, it puts a lot of line into the water, and the swift current will pick the line up and keep a jig up off the bottom just like it will live bait when you make a long cast.

"You will catch more stripers on a jig if you keep it bouncing along almost vertically under the boat."

Crankbaits will also catch tailrace stripers. While crankbaits are not effective in really swift water, shad-imitating plugs can dupe some of the heaviest stripers in a tailrace when cranked through the calmer water near the banks and across eddies formed in the current. A Poe's number 300 or 400 series crankbait in a green-back-with-pearl-sides pattern is an excellent lure for matching the size and shape of threadfin and gizzard shad that congregate in tailraces.

A crankbait will have more action and dive deeper on fourteen and seventeen-pound test line as opposed to twenty and twenty-five pound test line. So, whenever possible, use lighter line when fishing a crankbait.

CABLED AREAS

At many dams across the country, authorities have placed a cable across the river below the dam to prevent people from running their boats up to the dam. The distance from the cable to the dam may vary from one hundred to three hundred yards depending on what state you are in and what power company controls the dam.

Obviously, with a cable in place, you will not be able to move your boat over top of a boil and drop your bait vertically, into the water. When dealing with a cabled-off tailrace, you have to change your tactics to reach the stripers. When fishing from a boat, anglers often tie up to the cable and use surf casting rods, which measure ten to eighteen feet long, to hurl their lures toward the dam. Because of the extremely long casts needed to reach the boils and other fast water below the dam, anglers use two- and three-ounce jigs and similar size topwater lures.

For fishing live or cut bait, striper fishermen will use a four- to eight-ounce bell-shaped sinker tied to a leader approximately twelve to sixteen inches long. The leader is then attached to the ring on a three-way swivel. A second leader, two to three-feet long, is then tied to the second ring on the swivel and a hook attached to it. Next tie the main line from the reel to the third ring on the swivel and the rig is complete except for hooking a live shad or piece of cut bait to the hook.

When you cast the rig into the current, the bell sinker bumps along the bottom on one leader, and the leader with the hook and bait floats two to three feet above the bottom to reduce hang-ups. Some fishermen use a lighter-size line when tying the bell sinker to the three-way swivel. This way, when the sinker becomes lodged in the rocks, and it will, you can break the sinker off without running the risk of also breaking the line above the swivel and losing the whole set-up.

When you are forced to make long casts in a tailrace, the number of hang-ups will increase dramatically. It is not unusual for an angler to break off fifteen pounds of sinkers or more in a day's fishing, especially when he is losing four to eight ounces of lead each time he hangs up. Because of the vast amount of terminal tackle that they break off, most veteran river fishermen own sinker molds and pour their own sinkers.

Jig fishermen will also use the three-way swivel rig to help them reach the water near the dam. Instead of tying a hook on the leader, you tie a one-half- to one-ounce jig to the line. The bell sinker increases your casting distance and bounces across the bottom while the jig, usually dressed up with a plastic grub or twister-tail worm, swims tantalizingly along above the debris-ridden bottom.

When fishing a cabled-off tailrace, fishing from the bank may allow you to reach areas near the dam that anglers in a boat cannot reach. Depending on local regulations, you are often allowed to fish from the bank above the cable which obviously makes casting a lot easier.

"One advantage to fishing a tailrace is that a boat is not necessarily needed. Many anglers cast from the bank with artificial lures and live bait, and I have seen days when bank fishermen would catch three times as many stripers as fishermen using a boat," Steve Baker says. "There have been a few days where I parked my boat and fished from the bank to catch nice limits of stripers."

Anglers fishing from both the bank and a boat have devised some innovative ways to get their lures and live bait to stripers in a cabled tailrace. In eddy areas, striper fishermen will use a large balloon attached to their line with a clothespin. When the balloon is cast into an eddy area, the water will carry it back toward the dam. The fisherman feeds out loose line as the balloon drifts back upriver. When the balloon reaches a likely-looking area for a striper to be feeding, the fisherman gives the line a jerk to free it from the clothespin and his lure or bait which was dangling under the balloon tumbles to the bottom.

Another even more sophisticated, as well as expensive, method of reaching the boils in a restricted area is the use of a miniature, motor-powered boat controlled by remote control steering. The boats are very popular with hobbyists, who build them for racing.

Ingenious river fishermen have attached clothespins or similar release devises to the boats in order to hold their line in place as the anglers steer the tiny boats into the treacherous boils and other swift currents below a dam. When the boat reaches its chosen destination, the line is jerked to free it from the clothespin and the boat is driven back to the boat or bank for the next drop! One enterprising hobbyist in Missouri is selling all the miniature boats that he can build in his spare time to tailrace fishermen.

SAFETY

Because of the powerful and unpredictable currents in a tailrace area, it is imperative that you keep personal safety in mind at all times, even when fighting a twenty-five pound striper.

One rule that veteran river fishermen always observe is to stay away from a "dead hole." A "dead hole" is the water in front of an idle turbine. The danger lies in the fact that when a turbine is turned on, a lot of extra air is mixed with the water being released. The initial release of air and water will often shoot fifteen feet straight up into the air. After a few minutes, the water will settle down. But if you happen to be over the "hole" when it is turned on, your boat could be swamped. "When a turbine is first turned on, it sounds like a giant commode flushing," Steve Baker says.

As mentioned earlier, if your boat is stable enough to allow you to safely stand up in turbulent water, you can control your bait better as it bounces along the bottom and often work it over potential hang-ups. When standing up, it is advisable to always wear a life vest. Tailrace water is cold and swift. Even an excellent swimmer would have a difficult time staying afloat. With today's lightweight, comfortably fitting vest, there is no reason not to wear a vest in the dangerous waters.

Always be careful when navigating a tailrace, because there are usually boulders and bars that could ruin a prop or lower unit. One of the factors that makes boating in the tailraces tricky is that the water level varies with the number of turbines turned on and off. The water can fall as much as three feet when one turbine is turned off. Obviously when the water drops, a bar that might have been deep enough to safely motor over a few hours earlier is now a navigational hazard.

SUMMARY

Tailraces offer some of the most productive striper and hybrid action in the country. Fishing the fast, turbulent waters does not require a boatload of sophisticated equipment and tackle. What tailrace fishing does require is plenty of hard work. Constantly cranking up the outboard and running back up near the dam to start a new drift in fast waters that may only last a few minutes before you have to start all over again is work! Standing up in the boat and trying to keep your bait from getting snagged while the current spins the boat around leaves the muscles in your back, arms, and legs sore after a long day. Tearing up a fifty dollar cast net when it catches on the rocky bottom as you are attempting to catch some bait tries the patience of even the most dedicated striper angler.

"I know plenty of striper fishermen who won't fish tailraces, because the waters are dangerous and the fishing, even at its best, is hard work," Steve Baker says.

"A lot of fishermen don't want to break off fifty to seventy-five times a day, and they don't like the constant activity of drifting a stretch of water and then having to run back up the river and start over again."

What keeps Steve Baker coming back to the tailraces is the sheer number of stripers and hybrids concentrated in such a small area.

Chapter 6
SEASONAL PATTERNS
LATE WINTER AND EARLY SPRING

Late winter and early spring finds a large percentage of a lake's striper population located up the rivers and major creeks that empty into a reservoir. Many of the fish have been there since late fall when cooling water temperatures attracted stripers from the main lake.

In February and early March with the water temperature ranging in the high forties to low fifties, stripers are not very aggressive and their feeding activity is sporadic. At this time of year, stripers are often feeding on threadfin shad measuring from an inch to two inches long. In the cold water, one of Steve Baker's favorite lures is a plain bucktail jig weighing from three-eighths to one-half ounce. He does not add a plastic grub or any other type trailer to the jig, because he wants to keep the lure small to match the size of the baitfish that the stripers are feeding on.

Instead of the larger surface lures and crankbaits that striper fishermen traditionally use, Baker will switch to a number 11 Rapala, which measures four and three-eighths inches long, or a similar size plastic-bodied minnow. It takes lighter line and equipment than is normally used for striper fishing to effectively cast the smaller lures. But with patience and a properly adjusted drag, it is not difficult to wear down a thirty-pound striper on ten- to eight-pound test line.

"In the spring when the water temperature is still below fifty-five degrees, I often see stripers just dimpling the water as they feed on small threadfin shad," Steve Baker says. "I'll cast out a small Rapala or similar minnow-like lure and just start slowly winding it across the surface.

"If there is a chop on the water, a forty-pound striper won't even make a ripple as it engulfs the lure. All you will feel is just a bump or tick and the Rapala will disappear as your line starts peeling off."

A lure set-up that Baker also uses a lot in the early spring is a poppen spoon. The poppen spoon consists of a wooden popper body approximately seven inches long with a line tie in the front and a snap attached to the back. The popper itself does not have any hooks attached to it.

A leader of ten- to fourteen-pound test line measuring three to four feet long is tied to the snap. A one-half ounce single-hook spoon measuring three and one-eighth inches in length is attached to the end of the leader.

To fish a poppen spoon, use short, steady jerks of the rod tip to produce a popping sound with the wooden body. The sound attracts a striper's or hybrid's attention as it simulates the noise produced by a fish as it attacks a shad near the surface. In cold water, a striper or hybrid may not be aggressive enough to hit a surface lure. But when it sees the small spoon fluttering down behind the popping body, the fish will often strike what appears to be a shad in the two to three-inch range.

"Sometimes, even in the early spring, you will get a striper or hybrid that will attack the popper body. But at that time of year, the majority of stripers and hybrids want a lure that resembles a small threadfin shad, Steve Baker says.

"I have added hooks to the popper so I could catch the occasional fish that strikes it. But the leader gets caught in the hooks when you cast it and tangles the whole thing up. So, I gave up on that idea."

Baker first started using the poppen spoon on Norris Lake. It was the middle of April, and stripers were feeding on the surface in the same areas every morning and afternoon. Baker had thrown everything from a plastic minnow to a bucktail jig without a single hook-up. Some of the stripers would roll at a topwater lure, but they would not take it. On the third morning, Baker stopped on a schooling spot, and a big striper exploded on the surface, spraying threadfin shad, measuring about two inches long, into the air. Until then, Baker had not realized that the shad were so small.

So he tied a very small bucktail jig on ten-pound test line and cast into the area where he last saw the feeding fish. Cast after cast was made without even a tap.

Steve Baker studied the situation and tried to recall some past experience that might be of help in trying to attract the stripers. He remembered a rig called a poppen cork that a friend in Georgia had shown him. The poppen cork is a styrofoam cork about four inches long that had a hollowed-out area in the front to produce a popping noise when jerked across the surface. A small bucktail jig is attached about thirty inches behind the cork. The rig works real well in attracting hybrids on Georgia lakes.

Baker searched his tackle box and came up with a poppen cork that his friend had given him. Looking for a lure to imitate the small threadfin shad, he found a Tony Accetta spoon in a one-half ounce size. The flashy chrome finish and natural life-like wobble of the spoon resembles to perfection a small threadfin shad or blue-back herring.

As Baker tied the small one-half ounce spoon to the seventeen pound leader, another striper chased a school of threadfins to the surface. He made a long cast behind the baitfish, and worked the cork with a fast action, popping it every foot or so. On the first cast, a fifteen-pounder swallowed the small spoon so deeply that Baker just cut the line once he got the fish into the boat. He would get the spoon loose when he filleted the fish.

Figuring that any lure can get lucky once, Baker tied on another spoon and caught a twelve-pounder on the next cast. The rig continued to catch stripers for the next several mornings until the school moved on.

Since that time, a poppen spoon, as Baker dubbed it, has become one of his deadliest weapons in both spring and fall. He has caught stripers up to thirty-one pounds and hybrids up to fourteen pounds on the rig. One advantage that Baker likes about the poppen spoon is that a school of surface-feeding fish does not have to be present for the rig to produce. He simply works likely-looking points, humps and other areas that stripers and hybrids prefer when feeding, and the sound of the poppen spoon rig will often lure fish up to the surface.

When Baker first started making poppen spoons, he cut up broom handles to make the poppen bodies and screwed in metal eyelets for attaching the leader. He has since refined the poppen spoon and produces a commercial model that is available from Baker Enterprises, 128 Dogwood Trail, Maynardville, Tennessee 37807.

MID- TO LATE SPRING

As the water temperature begins to rise in the spring, creeks warm up faster than the main lake. Because the influx of warm water from spring rains runs directly into a creek and because a creek is a smaller, more confined area than the main body of the lake, the runoff quickly raises a creek's water temperature several degrees higher than the surface temperature found on the main lake.

The upper end of a reservoir where the lake begins to narrow down into a river-like environment will also warm up faster than the lower end of the lake. Tributaries along a major river immediately empty spring runoff into the river, and being similar to the narrow confines of a major creek, the upper end of the lake warms up faster than the wide open expanses of water near the dam.

The warmer water temperatures found in major creeks and up the river attract both stripers and shad in the spring. Spring is a time of year when you do not need a graph recorder or downrigger to catch trophy stripers, because stripers and hybrids migrate into the shallows near the headwaters of major tributaries. Stripers weighing thirty to fifty pounds can be taken in water less than ten feet deep.

Studies conducted by the Kentucky Department of Fish and Wildlife on Lake Cumberland have verified that big stripers congregate in the creeks during the spring. "A majority of stripers move from the main lake into the creeks as winter sets in, and they remain in the creeks right on through late spring," says fisheries biologist Benjy Kinman.

On Kentucky's Lake Cumberland, known for producing stripers in the thirty- to forty-pound range, the majority of stripers do not make a run to the lake's headwaters like the fish do on many lakes, but instead confine their heaviest migration to the major feeder creeks. The reason offered by Kinman is that because Cumberland is over a hundred miles long, the stripers find enough suitable habitat in the the creeks without any need to travel a considerable distance up the river.

On other lakes, however, such as North Carolina's Kerr Reservoir and Tennessee's Norris and Cherokee Lakes, headwaters are one of the most popular springtime striper fishing spots.

Besides warmer water temperatures, many fishermen believe that stripers and hybrids are drawn to the rivers and creeks because of the instinct to spawn in moving water. Stripers in the ocean travel up freshwater rivers to deposit their eggs. Unlike black bass or bluegills, stripers do not build a nest on the bottom. Instead, the female randomly drops her eggs into the current and the male fertilizes the eggs as they wash downstream. Once in the water, the eggs absorb water and expand until they are semi-buoyant. The moving water of a river or creek is needed to keep the eggs afloat until they hatch. If not, the eggs sink to the bottom and smother in the silt.

A few lakes such as Kerr Reservoir and Santee Cooper have natural reproduction of stripers in their rivers, but the vast majority of lakes do not have enough miles of undammed river with a sufficient current to carry the eggs for the three to six days needed for incubation. Even on lakes without suitable spawning waters, however, stripers and hybrids still make spawning runs up the tributaries in an attempt to propagate.

Threadfin and gizzard shad also prefer moving water when depositing their eggs. As the water temperature approaches the sixty-degree mark, shad pack into the creeks and rivers to spawn.

So in the spring a number of factors result in a large percentage of the striper and shad population congregating near the banks of major creeks and up the rivers. The situation limits the areas that you have to search for stripers and hybrids, so your odds of catching a trophy fish are greatly enhanced.

"When the water temperature reaches the mid-fifties, stripers begin to consistently hit a topwater lure and I use a topwater bait a lot for stripers in late March to mid-May," says Steve Baker.

Baker lets springtime stripers tell him when to reach for the topwater lures. As the water warms, instead of seeing stripers dimpling the water as discussed earlier, you will see ten- and twelve-inch gizzard shad leaping out of the water as a "V"-shaped wake pursues them. In the early morning light, you will jump as a sound like a cannonball hitting the water breaks the stillness. When you see and hear that type of aggressiveness, it is time to put away the small jigs and spoons and tie on a seven-inch topwater lure.

Sloping points, gradually falling banks situated in the creeks and river, cuts between islands and shallow humps are all prime spots to cast a topwater lure for springtime stripers.

Crankbaits such as Poe's number 300 series crankbait and one-half ounce bucktail jigs dressed up with six-inch curly-tail worms should also be fished in such locations.

"Sometimes, I will spend my time in feeder creeks near the middle of the lake, because the headwaters get so much fishing pressure in the spring," says Steve Baker.

Baker likes to fish a feeder creek that is fairly long with plenty of deep water and lots of points in it when he is searching for springtime stripers. "There may not be as many fish in a creek as there are in the main river, but often times there will be a lot less fishing pressure," Steve Baker advises.

By late April to early May, the water temperature, in

most of the striper lakes in the central and southern United States, will be in the high sixties to low seventies at any location in the lake. When that occurs, you can find active stripers almost everywhere that there is adequate baitfish and structure. In late spring, Steve Baker has caught a limit of good fish one morning in the upper reaches of the headwaters, and turned around the next day and caught a limit within site of the dam on the lower end of the lake.

Since the water temperature is in a comfortable range for stripers everywhere on the lake, the fish will not be as concentrated in the creeks and rivers as they were earlier in the spring. The mouths of feeder creeks as well as shallow humps and sandbars situated on the main lake become prime areas to fish during April, May and early June.

Many striper fishermen like to fish the bends in the inundated river channel when fishing during late spring. When you find a bend in a submerged river channel, you will normally find shallower water on the inside turn and deeper water on the outside bend where the current has cut away the bottom.

Anchor your boat, using anchors on both ends, near the inside bend and fish both live and cut bait across the shallower water formed by the inside bend. "Almost every time you find a sharp turn in the river channel, there will be shallower water on the inside turn. And, in some cases, a sand bar will be formed by the inside turn," a North Carolina angler told me. "After years of fishing inside bends, I have found spawning stripers love sand bars."

When fishing in the spring, look for shallow-water structure, such as a ridge, hump, or flat, adjacent to a submerged river or creek channel. By fishing live and cut bait in water varying from three to twenty feet deep, you can catch springtime stripers from numerous lakes around the country.

After the stripers have made their run up the rivers and major feeder creeks, the fish will begin to migrate back down into the main lake as the water temperature moves into the low seventies.

With water still in the comfortable range near the surface, stripers will not be in a hurry to move into deep water. At daylight, you can still catch some stripers and hybrids on topwaters during late May and early June.

When the sun pops out around nine a.m., fishing shad on a free line that allows the baitfish to scoot around in one to fifteen feet of water will catch stripers over structure near deep water.

SUMMER

By late June, the stripers have left the shallows and are schooling up over deep-water structure, such as channel bends, humps and points. The late June and July period is Steve Baker's favorite time of the year for striper fishing. He loves to dunk a gizzard shad into twenty-five feet of water and watch the rod double over as a thirty-five pound striper streaks off with the bait.

Statistics compiled by the Tennessee Wildlife Resources Agency show that more stripers in excess of twenty pounds are caught in June and July than any other period of the year. Fishermen who think the best fishing is over after May are definitely wrong. If a person is willing to spend some time on a lake studying a depth finder or graph, he will locate some massive schools of stripers congregating in deep water as the fish prowl the lake in their search for shad.

Many lakes stratify during the summer, and the stratification limits the area where you will find hot-weather stripers. The process involves a warmer layer of water forming near the surface called the epilimnion.

Underneath the epilimnion, a cooler, well oxygenated band of water develops called the thermocline. The thermocline has a temperature change of at least one-half degree per foot of depth, which makes it easy to locate with a temperature gauge.

For the striper fisherman, the thermocline is important because the majority of stripers in a lake will be located in the comfortable zone formed by the thermocline, which will be pushed deeper and deeper as summer progresses and the warmer water of the epilimnion continues to expand.

Below the thermocline is the hypolimnion, a colder, oxygen-deficient layer of water that extends to the lake's bottom. The hypolimnion is not a suitable environment for stripers to spend much time.

So, on lakes that stratify during the hot-weather months, fish for stripers at the depth where the thermocline forms and you will be spending your time in the most productive water.

While live shad are Steve Baker's favorite lure for summertime stripers and hybrids, trolling minnow-imitating lures on down-riggers to get the lures into the thermocline is also a very productive method. The biggest advantage of trolling with downriggers is that you can cover a tremendous amount of water in a day's time, which greatly increases the odds of your finding a school of feeding stripers.

Trolling with downriggers is also more effective than live bait when a school of stripers is moving. Trolling allows you to relocate the stripers quicker and easier than when live bait fishing.

By late summer, the thermocline is often fifty to sixty feet deep on many of the deep, mountainous lakes. In August and September, stripers that were in the headwaters in the spring have often swum over fifty to sixty miles in order to reach the deeper waters near the dam. The deeper water allows stripers to locate the cooler, well-oxygenated water that the fish need to survive the heat of summer.

On some lakes, however, the deep water with cooler temperatures lacks sufficient oxygen to sustain stripers, which often results in fish kills during periods of extreme heat. During one study conducted by biologist Dave Bishop on East Tennessee's Cherokee Lake regarding the effect of high water temperatures and a low dissolved oxygen content on stripers, Bishop tracked one striper

LIKELY LOCATIONS FOR STRIPERS AND HYBRIDS

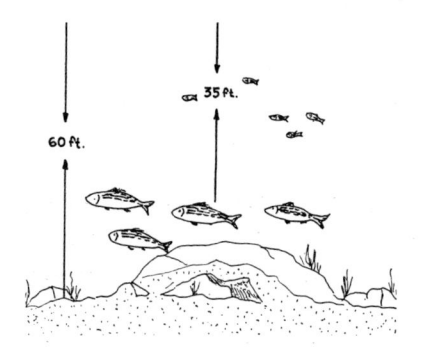

Stripers and hybrids can be located over humps throughout the year.

Big stripers tend to be loners. Ditches and old creek beds will hold fish on both sides of the ditch as well as in the bottom of the depression.

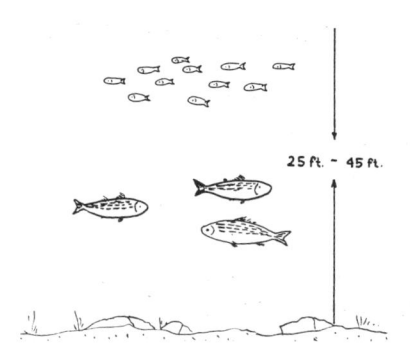

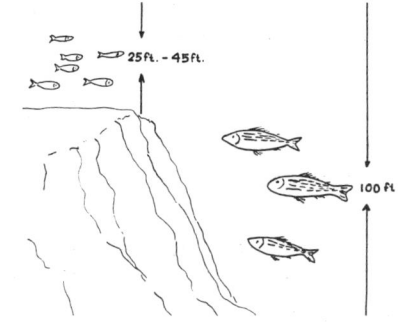

Always be on the lookout for schools of baitfish suspended over deep water. The stripers and hybrids won't be far away.

Underwater ledges are a favorite structure for both hybrids and stripers. Baitfish are also attracted to this type of structure.

equipped with a radio transmitter for several days as it swam back and forth along the bed of a submerged creek channel in thirty-two feet of water in order to take advantage of the coolest water in the lake that still had a sufficient amount of dissolved oxygen for the fish to survive.

FALL AND EARLY WINTER

When the water begins to cool, stripers begin to move back up into shallower waters. The fishing will continue to improve as the water temperature drops into the sixties and then the fifties.

Down rods with live shad are still effective as the lethargic stripers of summer begin to feed heavily with the cooling temperatures. Structure that held fish in the early summer will begin to attract stripers again.

By late fall, shad fished on free lines near shallow bars, rocky humps and mud flats will attract shallow-feeding stripers. Stripers began to head for the major creeks as schools of shad that spent the summer suspended in the main lake migrate toward the heads of the creeks.

Casting bucktail jigs and crankbaits to mud flats that gradually slope out and then drop into a creek channel is a great way to hook a trophy striper in November and December. Shad congregate over mud flats in the creeks, and hungry stripers follow. The last two Kentucky state record stripers were caught during the first week of December exactly one year apart and in the same creek on Lake Cumberland!

Overcast days with a wind that keeps the water choppy are the best times to catch late fall and early winter stripers when casting the banks. The rough water reduces light penetration, and stripers may feed all day in water less than fifteen feet deep.

When casting artificial lures for stripers in the fall and early winter, don't give up if you go several hours without a strike. Keep moving and casting every likely looking piece of structure in a creek. Stripers in shallow water can move rapidly from one bank to another as they search for shad. If you keep moving and casting, you will find a point, bank or bar where a school has moved up to feed, and you will hook, land and break off more stripers in fifteen minutes than you thought were in the whole creek.

Chapter 7
CRANKBAIT FISHING

Crankbaits are excellent lures for stripers, because crankbaits can imitate shad and other large baitfish which make up the primary forage of stripers.

While smaller crankbaits are sometimes needed, the larger size crankbaits, measuring four to seven inches long, are usually the best choice for stripers. In this chapter we will be discussing the use of crankbaits with diving bills on them, which enable crankbaits to run as deep as twenty feet or more while casting.

"Casting crankbaits for stripers is a lot of fun," professional fisherman David Fritts of Lexington, North Carolina says. "When you're casting, you've always got something to do and that keeps up your interest."

EQUIPMENT

When casting for stripers, David Fritts uses a seven and one-half foot flippin' stick and a baitcasting reel. He states that you will land more stripers on a fiberglass rod than you will with a graphite or boron rod when crankbaiting.

According to Fritts, the increased sensitivity of graphite or boron allows a fisherman to detect a strike quicker than with a less sensitive fiberglass rod. While such an advantage may be desirable when fishing live bait, jigs, spoons and other similar lures, the increased sensitivity often causes a fisherman to set the hook before a striper has a solid hold on a crankbait.

The reaction time of a graphite versus a fiberglass rod is also important. When you set the hook with a graphite rod, the graphite material responds quicker so the crankbait is affected by the rod's movement faster. A fiberglass rod reacts slower. So when you set the hook, it takes longer for

David Fritts with a 30-pound striper
caught on a deep-diving crankbait in December.

the crankbait to be affected. As a result, many crankbait fishermen believe a fiberglass rod gives the fish more time to take the lure solidly.

"The disadvantage of a fiberglass rod is that it is heavier than graphite and after a few hours of crankin', it will wear you down faster than a graphite rod," David Fritts says.

To take full advantage of a crankbait's diving ability, David Fritts fishes with ten-pound-test line. Many veteran striper fishermen scoff at the idea of using such light line, but Fritts has caught fish up to thirty pounds on the lighter line. In order to land a striper on a ten-pound-test line, you need to have a properly adjusted drag. David Fritts sets a very light drag. In fact, the drag is adjusted so light that it slips when the crankbait hits an obstruction on the bottom.

"A lot of fishermen believe that you need a tighter drag setting in order to set the hook properly," David Fritts says. "But when a striper hits a crankbait, you don't need to set the hook like a bass fisherman does when he is fishing a plastic worm.

"All you need to do is pull up on the rod and hang on. When a striper hits a crankbait, it will hook itself. If you keep trying to set the hook, you will break the line or help the striper pull the hooks free."

In order to land a striper hooked on light line, you have to let the hard-streaking fish make its initial long run before you start to turn it. You may even need to follow a particularly big fish with the trolling motor in order to keep from getting too much line between you and the striper.

Once the striper slows down, start putting pressure on the fish by pulling back on the rod. Remember, do not try to retrieve line while a striper is pulling out line against the drag. Instead, let the striper fight the resistance of the drag and the rod as it tries to swim away.

It is only when a striper slows down that you want to lower the rod and quickly crank up some line. Then, raise the rod back up to put pressure on the striper again. If the fish does not go streaking off, lower the rod and crank up some more line.

As a striper gets tired and you work the fish closer to the boat, remember to keep the rod tip pointed up unless you are taking up line, so that the fish has to fight against the bend in the rod.

David Fritts' favorite crankbait for stripers is a Poe's Super Cedar 400 series crankbait. The lure is a cedar-bodied crankbait made in northern California. It has a clear, two-inch diving bill, and on ten-pound-test line the crankbait will dive ten to eighteen feet deep.

Poe's crankbaits are available in a variety of colors. For stripers, Fritts has found the grey shad, green-back-with-pearl-sides and spook, which is white with grey stripes and metallic sparkles, to be very attractive colors to stripers.

Why is a Poe's crankbait so productive? "A Poe's crankbait has a tighter wobble than other crankbaits, and that seems to make a Poe's more effective when the water is cold, which is when most stripers and hybrids are caught casting crankbaits," David Fritts explains.

A very important part of every crankbait fisherman's equipment should be a quality plug knocker. Plug knockers come in numerous sizes and shapes. In general, a plug knocker consists of a heavy piece of lead that you thread onto your line and lower via a piece of string, tied to the top of the plug knocker, down to a snagged lure in order to dislodge the bait by bumping it with the lead. Sometimes, you have to bounce the lead up and down over a snagged crankbait several times before you dislodge it from a stump or other obstruction.

Some styles of plug knockers have short pieces of chain, heavy metal coils or other similar additions attached to the lead to help free a fouled hook. When the lead cannot jar a lure loose, a chain or coil will sometimes catch on a hook and pull the crankbait free.

Remember to have enough string tied to a plug knocker so that you can reach a deep-diving crankbait in fifteen to twenty feet of water. Some anglers use an old reel to store the string on so that it does not become tangled. To use their plug knocker, they simply disengage the reel and lower the line with the plug knocker attached over the side of the boat.

CRANKIN' FOR STRIPERS

Casting a crankbait can be productive whenever there are stripers in twenty feet of water or less, which is usually anytime of the year, except for the middle of summer.

While stripers are thought of as deep-water fish, they often move up into ten to fifteen feet of water to feed. Where a river or creek channel curves in near a point or bar to create a shallower ledge is a prime area for stripers. A creek channel may be thirty to fifty feet deep. But when it swings in against a point, the creek channel bank or ledge may jump up as shallow as ten feet or less. Shad and other baitfish will often congregate around the shallow shelf, especially if there are a few stumps or rocks situated along it.

Stripers will migrate up and down the deep channel as they hunt for food. When they reach a shallower ledge, stripers will move upon it to dine on the baitfish.

"Ledges or drop-offs in twelve to eighteen feet of water are my favorite spots for catching stripers," David Fritts says. "I may fish a dozen good ledges before I pull up on one that has a school of feeding stripers on it."

When fishing a ledge, David Fritts holds his boat over the channel itself and makes a long cast past the ledge. He then begins a slow, steady retrieve that brings the crankbait across the ledge and into the channel. By throwing beyond the ledge, the crankbait has time to reach the bottom before it reaches the ledge.

If a striper does not inhale the shad imitation as it bounces across the ledge, a striper will often hit the crankbait as it clears the ledge and swims into the channel. "Many times, stripers will be suspended a few yards off a channel ledge, and a fish will hit the crankbait as you crank it across the deeper water," David Fritts says. "When that happens, I back my boat out a little further so that I don't spook the suspended fish."

A ledge or drop-off does not need any cover, such as stumps, logs or rocks, to attract a school of stripers. If you find a good drop, and there are baitfish around it, then

Casting a deep-diving crankbait on 10-pound-test line produces plenty of stripers for David Fritts during the fall and winter.

This striper completely inhaled a shad-shaped crankbait.

odds are you will find stripers. Remember, stripers do not relate to the bottom as much as black bass do. Instead of using stumps and rocks to hide in when they feel threatened, stripers will use deep water.

"Sometimes, I have found stripers relating to brush. But most of the time, they will be situated on the edge of a drop-off, where they can escape into deeper water," David Fritts says.

On North Carolina's Kerr Reservoir, where Fritts does plenty of crankbaiting, submerged roadbeds are good places to catch stripers. It does not matter whether the road is paved or unpaved, as long as it has a ditch on one or both of its sides, stripers will frequent the area. Apparently, a ditch creates a steeper drop that stripers prefer.

Many of the channel drops, roadbeds and points where

David Fritts catches stripers are also prime areas to catch largemouth bass. It has been Fritts' experience, however, that when you find a school of black bass on a drop, you do not catch any stripers. Likewise, if you find a school of stripers on a choice piece of structure, you will not catch any black bass. "In the summer, there are several drops where I catch lots of largemouth. But when the water cools down, I don't catch anything but stripers off the structure," Fritts says.

Fall and early winter are Fritts' favorite times to crankbait for stripers. In September and October, the fish move up into ten and twelve feet of water on Kerr Reservoir. Crankin' in the creeks and upper end of the reservoir seems to be best in the early fall.

As the water continues to cool, Fritts cranks the structure near the mouths of the creeks and on the lower end of the lake. The fish will move down into fifteen and eighteen feet of water by December.

Fishing crankbaits is often a very productive way to catch numbers of ten to fifteen pound stripers because once you find a school of active stripers, you can catch them very quickly on a crankbait. When you get a striper to hit a crankbait, it seems to trigger a feeding response from the rest of the fish in the school. If you are lucky, you and your partner can catch several fish before the school spooks. David Fritts and his father-in-law, Webb Brinkley, have caught over twenty stripers a day by crankin' ledges on Kerr Reservoir with the fish averaging ten to twelve pounds apiece. On ten-pound-test line that is a lot of fun!

When crankbaitin' for stripers, a slow, steady retrieve seems to be the best. You want the crankbait to bump along the bottom across potential striper-holding structure. Stripers are bad, however, to hit at a crankbait without getting hooked. If that happens and you are cranking the lure back to the boat, the impact of the strike will knock slack in your line. When that happens, David Fritts stops crankin', because a striper will often come back and inhale a stalled plug which appears to be a stunted baitfish.

Chapter 8
JIGS AND SPOONS

THE JIG AS A STRIPER LURE

If someone conducted a national survey to determine the most frequently used artificial lure for stripers and hybrids, a jig would probably be the winner. Jigs have proven to be very productive lures for fresh-water stripers, because a jig can be fished from the surface to as deep as you have the patience to let it sink. By fishing a jig by itself or dressing it up with a plastic or pork trailer, you can imitate a shad from one inch long to ten inches long. The versatility of a jig makes it a year-round striper getter.

TACKLE

When casting a jig in a reservoir, Steve Baker uses a seven- to seven-and-one-half foot stiff-action, graphite or boron casting rod outfitted with a fast retrieve baitcasting reel. The sensitivity of a graphite or boron rod is very desirable when you are trying to detect the light "tap" that signals a striper has inhaled your jig. A reel with a high gear ratio is also helpful because when a striper takes a jig, the fish will often head straight toward the boat and deeper water. A high-speed reel allows you to keep the slack out of your line as the striper runs toward you.

For casting a jig in a lake, Steve Baker uses twelve- to fourteen-pound-test line. The lighter line gives you more sensitivity than seventeen- or twenty-pound-test line. "With twelve- and fourteen-pound-test line, you have a better feel of what your jig is doing," Steve Baker says. "Heavier line reduces your sense of feel when you are swimming a jig through the water."

A myriad of different types of jigs will catch stripers, but the most popular, especially in the South, is a bucktail jig. Steve Baker prefers a one-half to three-quarter ounce jig head with a three- to three-and-one-half inch long bucktail skirt.

In late winter and early spring, Baker casts the jig by

Steve Baker swims a bucktail jig with a plastic trailer attached to catch trophy stripers in the spring.

itself. But as the water warms up in late spring and early summer, he adds a six-inch plastic twister-tail worm to the jig in order to increase the size of the bait. "When the water is warmer, stripers and hybrids feed on the bigger shad, so you need to use a bigger bait," Steve Baker explains.

During the fall and early winter when the majority of shad have grown to at least several inches long, a jig and trailer measuring four to six inches long is needed to imitate the size of the baitfish.

Deciding what color lure to use is not a difficult decision for Baker, since he casts a white jig and white trailer about ninety percent of the time. The other ten percent of the time, he opts for a chartreuse-colored jig and either a white or chartreuse-colored trailer.

"Stripers feed on light-colored baitfish the majority of the time, and a white jig and trailer seems to be the most productive for me," Steve Baker says.

Baker has tried dark-colored patterns as well as red- and gray-colored jigs, but white seems to be the most attractive to stripers, even when fishing at night. He does believe, however, that a white jig tied with red thread is better than a jig tied with a different colored thread. Apparently, the red thread imitates the color of a shad's gills.

Choosing what size jig to cast depends on the depth of the fish, the amount of current and the wind. For fishing in a lake when the stripers are in ten to twenty feet of water, Steve Baker prefers a one-half to three-quarter ounce jig. To anglers who often fish for black bass, crappies and bluegills, that may seem like too heavy a jig, but the jig sinks a lot slower than many people realize. "When you make a thirty to forty-yard cast with fourteen-pound-test line and a one-half ounce bucktail jig dressed up with a six-'nch twister-tail worm, that jig doesn't drop as fast as you would think," Steve Baker says.

The resistance of the water against the monofilament line, the three and one-half inch bucktail skirt and the plastic twister-tail slows down the descent of the one-half ounce leadhead considerably.

Besides a bucktail jig, a plain jig head rigged with a plastic body is also very popular with striper and hybrid fishermen. Plastic shad-imitating bodies come in dozens of different shapes. One of the most effective bodies is a four and one-half to six-inch plastic grub with a twister tail. Another popular lure shape is a flat, plastic body with a boot tail.

A plastic-bodied jig creates a lot of action, especially when you swim it through the water. With the wide array of different sizes and colors of plastic bodies that lure manufacturers are now making, it is easy to duplicate the appearance of almost any baitfish that the stripers are preying on.

One of the biggest advantages of a plastic-bodied jig over a bucktail jig is price. You can buy a bulk size bag of plastic bodies along with a bag of leadhead jigs and create a striper-catching lure for a lot less than the price of a bucktail jig. Of course, you can also tie your own bucktail jigs for a considerable savings.

At times, stripers and hybrids will hit a plastic-bodied jig better than a bucktail jig and vice versa. So in order to be prepared for the fickle nature of a fish, be sure and carry a large assortment of both types of jigs.

FISHING A JIG

Unlike largemouth bass and walleyes, stripers and hybrids do not spend a lot of time on the bottom, but instead suspend at various depths above the bottom, depending on the water temperature and clarity as well as the location of baitfish.

Since stripers spend most of their time suspended, you need to keep your jig swimming above the depth where the stripers are located. A striper will swim up several feet to strike a lure, but the fish will almost never swim down to take a lure. So if the fish are situated in fifteen feet of water, you need to keep your jig swimming along in ten to twelve feet of water.

Many successful striper fishermen advocate a straight,

steady retrieve when fishing a jig for stripers. They claim that a striper, unlike a largemouth bass, does not like an erratic retrieve.

While a slow, steady retrieve is certainly effective, Steve Baker disagrees with many experienced anglers who believe that it is the only type of retrieve to use. When fishing a jig, Baker uses a sweeping motion to trigger strikes from suspended stripers.

To illustrate the retrieve, assume that stripers are twelve to fifteen feet deep over a bar that is twenty to thirty feet deep. Steve Baker positions his boat off the side of the bar and casts across the bar. He lets the jig sink eight to ten feet deep, then he begins to slowly swim it back toward the boat. After the jig has swum a few feet, Baker raises his rod tip straight up to the twelve o'clock position which causes the jig to dart up four or five feet.

Baker then lowers the rod back to the ten o'clock position, cranking up the slack line as the jig falls back to ten feet deep. Once the rod reaches the ten o'clock position, Baker retrieves the jig for a few more cranks, before he sweeps the rod back up to the twelve o'clock position again.

He then repeats the same sequence as before, allowing the jig to fall back to approximately eight or ten feet deep. Baker repeats this sweeping-type retrieve all the way back to the boat, which results in the jig darting up and falling back several times as the lure crosses the bar.

For Baker, the up-and-down motion of the sweeping retrieve results in more strikes than the conventional, straight retrieve used by many striper fishermen. On many occasions while guiding, Baker has caught several stripers using the yo-yo maneuver while a client using a straight swimming retrieve failed to get a bite.

When fishing a jig in a lake, Baker has found that a strike will often feel like just a light tick on the end of the line as a striper sucks the jig in. When you feel that tick, set the hook, because a striper will blow a jig out faster than a black bass will. If you hesitate, you will miss the fish.

While using the sweeping-type motion described earlier, you will sometimes feel a striper tick the jig when the rod is at the twelve or eleven o'clock position. Before you can drop the rod and crank up the slack line to set the hook, the striper will have blown the jig out.

If that happens, don't make another long sweeping motion. Instead, drop the rod tip and just make a couple of short twitches to move the jig a couple of feet. Many times, the same striper will come back and get the jig again. If you make a long sweep, you will pull the jig several feet away from the fish, and it may not be interested in chasing a jig that far.

Steve Baker relies heavily on a bucktail jig from mid-May to mid-June. At that time of year in his part of the country, the water temperature near the surface is in the low seventies and rising. The topwater action of early spring is about over as the majority of stripers are moving into deeper water.

With the water temperature still in the comfortable range, Baker has found that stripers aren't in a big hurry to leave the shallow-water areas for their summertime roles. Instead the fish suspend fifteen to twenty feet deep near the same points, bars and humps where Baker catches stripers earlier in the spring on topwater lures.

"After the fish quit hitting topwater lures early in the morning during late spring, I use my sweeping-type retrieve to swim a bucktail jig ten to twelve feet deep in the same places that I fish topwater lures," Steve Baker explains.

Earlier in the spring when stripers are hitting topwater lures early in the morning, Steve Baker has found that he can extend the morning action by casting a six inch plastic-bodied grub on a one and one-third ounce leadhead after the sun pops out and the stripers refuse to take a lure from the surface.

The plastic grub will sometimes continue to produce strikes from stripers for a half hour to an hour after the topwater action stops. The stripers don't go far from the easy pickings of shallow water when the water tempera-

Stripers and hybrids can be caught from deep water on jigging spoons.

ture is cool. By fan-casting the plastic grub around structure that has produced some topwater action earlier in the morning, you can sometimes pick up a few more stripers that won't rise to a topwater lure once the sun is up.

SPOONS
WINTER

Cold-weather vertical jigging is not always the answer to a fishless day. But if the proper lures and techniques are used, it can sure beat sitting at home watching television. Vertical jigging works best when stripers or hybrids are down past the forty-foot mark. In the cold winter months, schools of stripers will travel in tight groups on the lookout for large schools of shad that are seeking refuge from the cold, frigid water. In the winter months, stripers in almost every lake will be feeding on the smaller threadfin shad rather than the larger gizzard shad. The first chore is to pick the right size lure in order to match the size baitfish that the stripers are feeding on. A white- or chrome-colored Mann-O-Lure in the two-ounce size and the Hopkins spoon in a two-ounce size are Baker's two favorite baits. Because they not only get down quickly to the desired depth, they also simulate the action of a dying or injured shad drifting toward the bottom.

There are two techniques to use when vertical jigging and both work extremely well. The first method is to drop the spoon down below the fish and make long upward sweeping motions with the rod. Then, let the lure fall back through the feeding fish. One mistake a lot of anglers make is not maintaining contact with the sinking spoon as it flutters back down through the fish. Baker uses fourteen-pound test line when jigging a spoon. The heavier lure and lighter line will enable you to keep contact with the lure as it falls, and you will be able to detect even the slightest tap. Most of the strikes will occur as the spoon falls, it is very rare for a striper to hit a spoon on the up stroke.

The second method is similar to the first. After dropping the lure to the desired depth, instead of pulling the lure upward with a sweeping rod motion, you use what guides call, "burning the bait." After the spoon falls just below the suspended stripers or hybrids, crank a high-speed reel in gear and reel as hard as you can for twenty feet or so. Stop, and then crank the spoon up for a few more feet. On certain days, this method drives finicky feeding fish wild.

When using both methods, Baker likes a seven-foot graphite rod with a very stiff action. The long rod enables you to pull the lure upward ten to twelve feet with one stroke. A graphite rod with a good backbone also enables you to feel even the lightest strike and set the hook hard on a deep-feeding striper.

When a fish is boated, it is wise not to waste time with the camera or reliving the exciting fight of the fish. Remember, you are jigging in schooling fish and usually when one fish is hooked it will excite the entire school. On numerous occasions, Steve Baker has brought a fish up to the boat only to see a dozen or more stripers following in hot pursuit. Get your spoon back down into the school as quickly as possible. Baker has seen times when a school of fish would move on, because they simply had no reason to stay in the particular area.

When searching for cold-weather stripers on any lake, the first place that Baker looks is in a main feeder creek branching off the river channel. If the water temperature is below fifty degrees, he looks for stripers suspended thirty to fifty feet deep. In most cases, they will be close to some type of structure, such as a point, ditch or old creek bed. Always be alert for huge clouds of shad that show up on your recorder. If you locate baitfish, the stripers will be close by.

Standing timber located in deep water near the river channel will also hold stripers and hybrids during the winter months. Jigging directly down into the trees will produce good strings of fish, but the limbs call for plenty of lures or a good plug knocker.

On overcast days, the fish will congregate around the outside perimeter of a tree line, which is much easier to fish. Bright clear days will push the stripers inside the timber and force them to hold tight in the limbs. It is wise to use at least twenty-pound-test line to turn a big striper away from a maze of hanging limbs. Even with the heavy line, it is sometimes impossible to keep a good fish from breaking you off.

Steve Baker has located big schools of winter stripers by noticing one single fish chase a shad to the surface. Young, small striper are very aggressive and will often break away from a deep school and chase baitfish completely to the surface. This aggressive behavior often gives away the presence of a large school of suspended stripers located in the general area. Anytime you see a surface-feeding fish, always graph the nearby area for what may turn out to be one of the best trips of your life.

Locating big schools of suspended fish can be a time consuming process. But once they are located, the cold, miserable rain and the biting, cold wind is forgotten.

SUMMER

Steve Baker likes to use a spoon during the late summer when the thermocline has been forced down to forty or fifty feet by high water temperatures. One of the big advantages of using a heavy spoon at that time of the year is that once you locate a school of stripers, you can get the lure down to them fast, before they move.

In the hot weather, Baker uses a one- to two-ounce Hopkins or Mann-O-Lure, the size varying with the depth of the fish. He prefers the narrow body of the aforementioned spoons when jigging real deep water, because the narrow-bodied spoons fall faster than a wider-bodied slab spoon.

Before leaving home, Steve Baker stretches out the monofilament line on his reels along his driveway and measures it with a tape measure. He then uses a waterproof marker to mark the line at the forty-, fifty-, sixty-, and seventy-foot mark. Each mark is made with a different colored marker. By marking the line, Baker can easily control the depth of his spoon.

When vertically jigging a spoon, you don't need to put a lure into the water until you see some fish on your flasher, graph recorder or video screen first. In the summer, Baker often spots the baitfish first in deep water. When he does, he slows down his boat to search for stripers in the surrounding vicinity.

In late summer it is not uncommon to see with the aid of a video screen, stripers stacked up ten feet high on the bottom in fifty to seventy feet of water. This situation usually occurs on the lower end of the lake, and the fish seem to congregate over gravel and sand bottoms where there are huge schools of baitfish.

"Sometimes, you will think your video screen is torn up, because the screen will be almost totally black from all the shad in the area," Steve Baker says.

When he spots the vast schools of shad in fifty to seventy feet of water, Baker diligently searches the area for a school of stripers. Usually, the screen, which has been a mass of black from all the baitfish, will lighten up, showing no fish activity at all. Then, you will spot a school of stripers.

"What happens is that schools of shad try to keep a distance between themselves and a school of feeding stripers. When a screen that was showing a lot of baitfish suddenly becomes clear, you may have found the gap or dividing line between the prey and the predator," Steve Baker explains.

Once he spots a school of stripers, Baker quickly pushes the free spool button on his reel and lets the lure fall straight down under the boat. Keep the rod parallel to the surface of the water and do not pull up on the line while the spoon is making its initial fall into the strike zone. If you jerk on the line, the spoon which is falling fairly straight to the bottom will respond to the motion by starting to flutter to the bottom, thereby slowing down the spoon's descent into fifty to seventy feet of water. "Don't move the jigging spoon until you get it to the depth where the fish are, because you don't want it fluttering down in twenty feet of water. You want to get it down to the stripers in fifty feet of water, before they move," says Steve Baker.

If the video screen shows a school of stripers suspended at fifty feet, Baker lets the spoon drop until the colored mark indicating fifty feet passes through the rod tip and into the water. He then engages the reel and jerks the rod to the twelve o'clock position with a seven and one-half-foot rod. He then lets the spoon flutter back down as he follows its descent with the rod tip. Once the rod tip reaches the nine o'clock position, he jerks the rod back to the twelve o'clock position and repeats the sequence.

A striper almost always hits a spoon on the fall, so if the line stops as the spoon is falling, set the hook, because a striper has inhaled the lure.

Baker has found that deep-water stripers will often hold onto a spoon for several seconds. Sometimes, they will even swim around with the spoon in their mouths. By watching your line, you can often detect a strike by noticing the line jump or move off to the side as a striper grabs the falling spoon.

Once you hook a striper in a deep-water school, it often results in several other fish becoming aggressive. Because of that fact, when one person in the boat hooks a striper, everybody else in the boat needs to keep his spoon in the water.

For jigging a spoon in fifty to seventy feet of water, Steve Baker uses fourteen-pound-test line, because it has less resistance or drag in the water than heavier line. The deeper you fish, the greater the drag created by heavier line which affects the falling action of even a two-ounce jigging spoon.

In the summer, the depth of the shad will vary greatly. You are likely to find schools of shad from the surface where the water temperature is in the nineties to the thermocline which may be seventy feet deep. But if you spot a school of stripers at forty feet on a given day, then it is a safe bet that every school of stripers that you find that day will be in forty feet of water.

Chapter 9
NIGHT FISHING

On many reservoirs around the country, especially the clearer, deeper lakes, fishing at night is a popular way of catching stripers. Once the sun goes down, stripers are not as wary, and, as a result, the fish are easier to trick into hitting an artificial lure. The dark of night, especially when the surface temperature is below seventy-five degrees, causes many stripers to move up from deep-water structure into shallower water near the banks as they prowl for shad or herring.

Night fishing for stripers is productive on a year-round basis, but the most popular periods seem to be late spring, early summer and late fall. Fishing during the above-mentioned seasons usually finds the temperature chilly at night, but not extremely uncomfortable.

EQUIPMENT

Most of the same equipment and tackle that you utilize during the day for striper fishing is also effective at night. There are a few items, however, that you will want to add to your inventory in order to make fishing after dark easier.

A black light is very helpful when fishing jigs and spoons as well as other types of falling lures. There are several brands of black lights on the market, but they all basically consist of a metal or plastic housing into which the black light snaps. The housing normally has two large suction cups underneath it for affixing the light to the gunwale of the boat. A long cord with two alligator clips runs out the back of the housing, which you clip onto a twelve-volt battery to power the light.

A black light that causes flourescent monofilament line to glow in the dark greatly increases your fishing abilities at night.

Some anglers cut off the clips and replace them with a special plug that fits into the cigarette lighter on their boats. Other anglers fit the cord with a regular plug and then wire an outlet into the side of the boat for plugging in the light, just like you do a lamp at home.

Both methods are safer than using the alligator clips, because a number of black lights using the clips have overheated during a night's fishing and caught the boat on fire. What often happens is that a fisherman will run the cord to the back of the boat, raise the lid where the batteries are stored, attach the clips to a battery and shut the lid back down on the cord. The cord then overheats where the lid is pinching it and starts a fire. To eliminate that problem if you choose to use the alligator clips, set an extra battery in the open floor of your boat and attach the clips to it.

Some of the better brands of black lights will have a fuse that fits into the handle of one of the alligator clips to prevent the cord from overheating and starting a fire.

What a black light does is to make fluorescent monofilament line glow in the dark. Fourteen-pound-test line looks like a piece of kite string under a black light. The advantage of the light for night fishing is obvious. Instead of peering into the darkness, wondering where your line is, you can see your line better than you can during the day.

A black light is really helpful when fishing a jig or spoon at night, because you are able to see your line twitch or jump sideways when a striper inhales the dropping lure. The black light also allows you to maintain better depth control over a sinking lure. Instead of wondering whether a jig is five feet deep or twenty feet deep, you can watch your line as soon as the lure hits the water and count the lure down as it falls in order to keep up with its depth.

For example, if you cast a jig toward a mud point, you should start counting with a cadence of one thousand one, one thousand two, one thousand three, and so on until the line goes slack which means the lure has touched bottom. Most lures sink at the rate of one foot per second, so if you have reached the count of one thousand fifteen when the lure hits bottom, the you know your jig is in fifteen feet of water.

Some anglers do not use a black light when fishing diving crankbaits and topwater lures. But even when using those lures, a black light will improve your fishing, because you can track the movement of the lure as it comes through the darkness by watching the glowing line. It also helps to prevent a fisherman from casting over the top of his partner's line.

In addition to a black light, many after-dark striper chasers employ a soft white light to help illuminate shoreline features. A helpful combination is to mount a white light on top of your black light. That way, you have the advantage of a glowing monofilament line while at the same time being able to make out prominent features along the bank in order to improve your casting accuracy.

When the moon is full and the sky is clear, you may not need a white light. But when it is pitch black in a favorite creek, you will be glad to have the aid of the little artificial light when you are trying to decide how far the bank is from the boat.

For selecting a lure from your tackle box, picking out a backlash or retying your line, you will need to carry a conventional light. A penlight that clips onto your belt or pocket is an ideal choice. The penlight produces a small, concentrated beam of light that does not "blind" your partner while you are changing lures. By choosing a light that clips onto your person, you will be able to find it when you need it, instead of fumbling around in the dark searching for it.

When running your boat at night, safety should be of paramount importance. At night, visibility is a major problem on a lake. If you are not careful, you will run aground or even worse into another boat.

Headlights that attach underneath the bow of the boat help improve your ability to navigate at night.

Fishermen who do a lot of night fishing often attach headlights underneath the bows of their boats to help in navigating. At least one manufacturer, and there are probably others, makes a headlight that has three powerful suction cups on it in order to temporarily attach the light to the hull of a boat. A set of headlights comes with an on/off switch that you lay in the floor and control with your feet, similar to a dimmer switch on a car.

With the switch, you can be running down the lake with just your running lights on and if you need help in determining how the shoreline turns or you spot something floating in the water, you just tap the switch with your foot and the headlights will light up the water in front of the boat without blinding you like a spotlight does, because the headlights are mounted underneath the bow.

SPRINGTIME: THE RIGHT TIME

Night fishing in the spring is very popular because at this time of year a lot of trophy stripers are in shallow water. With a surface temperature in the fifties and sixties, stripers are very comfortable in the shallows and they will be cruising the banks in search of forage.

You can catch stripers during the day, but the really big fish will often wait until after dark to move up on the banks and flats. The clearer the water, the more likely the big stripers will be feeding after the sun sets.

What many striper fishermen like to do in the spring is to start fishing a few hours before dark in order to take advantage of any late afternoon action, and if fishing is poor, they make plans to fish into the night. Such a schedule affords you maximum opportunity for hooking a giant striper.

When casting artificial lures, fishing after dark has a distinct advantage over daytime fishing. In the dark, a striper cannot scrutinize a lure as critically as it can during the daylight hours. As a result, it is easier to dupe a striper into believing a shad-shaped silhouette with two treble hooks dangling down from it is a real shad.

It is best to night fish a lake that is familiar to you, because after dark it is not easy to locate potential striper-holding structure. By knowing the location of several areas that will attract after-dark stripers, you can move from spot to spot until you find some actively feeding stripers. If you are fishing an unfamiliar lake, get out on the lake before dark and locate some likely-looking areas that you can find after dark.

In the spring, fish the points, shallow mud flats, sloping clay banks and islands in major feeder creeks. The majority of stripers will be between five and fifteen feet deep.

Keep an eye on your temperature gauge, and search for the warmest water in a creek. The difference of a few degrees will often cause a concentration of shad to prefer one area of a creek over another area. By locating shallow-water structure near deep water that has shad around it, you can bet some ravenous stripers will move up on the spot sooner or later.

Bucktail jigs and medium-running crankbaits are excellent choices for night fishing, because the lures can be easily fished in fifteen feet of water and less.

As the water temperature warms into the high sixties and low seventies, shad become even more concentrated along the banks as the baitfish spawn in shallow water. Striper fishing hits a frenzied pitch as the fish take advantage of the favorable water temperatures and huge schools of shad in shallow water. On some lakes, the action is referred to as "May Madness," because it usually occurs during the month of May in the central and southern United States.

When casting the banks in May, it will often sound like a boulder rolled into the water as a thirty-pound striper attacks a gizzard shad near the surface.

In the spring, Steve Baker will fish cut bait at night when a cold front has passed through and the accompanying high, blue skies have shut off the topwater action.

If the spring nights are still cool, which they usually are after the passage of a cold front, Baker will sometimes beach his boat on the bank and have his guide parties fish from the bank, so he can build a fire to help keep them warm.

"Some of my clients look at me a little funny at first, because it's sort of like catfishing," Steve Baker says. "We cast the cut bait out on the bottom and prop the rods up on the bank with forked sticks."

Their doubts about the effectiveness of the method soon disappear when a thirty-pound striper goes racing off with the dead shad.

"I've found that the best places to fish cut-bait at night in the spring are the same points, humps and sloping banks where you have been catching stripers on topwater lures before a front shuts off the fish," Steve Baker explains. "Apparently the stripers are still in the area, but they won't hit during the day because of the bright skies."

When using cut-bait, Baker threads a three-quarter to one-ounce egg-shaped sinker onto his line. Then he ties a barrel swivel to the end of the line. To the other end of the swivel, he ties a three- to four foot long leader. A 2/0 or 3/0 style 42 Eagle Claw hook is then tied to the end of the leader.

To bait up the hook, Steve Baker uses a three-quarter to one inch wide piece of shad, and he prefers to cut the strip from the area right behind the shad's head which is where the stomach cavity and most of the innards are located.

When using cut-bait, Baker always makes sure that he is fishing on a firm sandy or gravel bottom. "A striper is not like a catfish. You don't want your cut-bait buried in muck on the bottom," Steve Baker advises.

Baker's favorite places to use cut-bait at night are gently sloping points, bars and humps. He likes to have his cut-bait lying on a hard bottom in ten to twenty-five feet of water.

Leave the reel out of gear and the clicker on to alert you to a strike. When a striper takes the cut-bait, it will be able to take out line without feeling any resistance from the egg sinker which is lying on the bottom.

Let the striper run with the cut-bait for a few feet, then engage the reel and tighten up the line. When you have most of the slack out of the line, set the hook hard!

"The swivel acts as a stop to keep the egg sinker from sliding down the leader and burying the cut-bait on the bottom," Steve Baker says. "When a striper grabs the cut-bait, free line will thread through the sinker with very little resistance which prevents alerting the striper that what it has grabbed is booby-trapped."

Fishing cut-bait at night will produce stripers like this one especially when a cold front shuts off the daytime fishing.

LINE FROM REEL

CUT BAIT AND HOOK
3/4 to 1 oz. EGG SINKER
3 to 4 ft. LONG LEADER
BOTTOM
BARREL SWIVEL

BAKER'S SETUP FOR FISHING CUT BAIT

LATE FALL AND EARLY WINTER

Starting in October, a lot of striper fishermen like to fish shallow water at night for stripers. With the surface water temperature cooling off into the sixties, stripers that were confined to the thirty and forty-foot depths during the warmer-water months can now comfortably roam the shallows in search of shad.

In the cooler months, the major factor that will keep stripers in deeper water is bright sunlight, because they are very light sensitive. By fishing at night, you eliminate the problem of bright light, and you can usually find some stripers feeding in less than ten feet of water.

For striper fishermen who like to fish at night during the fall and winter, a crankbait fished in five to twelve feet of water across sand bars, mud flats and points is a very productive method for catching stripers.

Since you don't need to get maximum diving depth from a crankbait at night, switch to fourteen- or seventeen pound test line after dark to help minimize the chances of a forty-pound striper breaking off if it rips through shallow-water cover when you hook it.

A crankbait is an ideal lure for night fishing, because you can fish a lot of water with it fast and still get maximum striper-attracting action from the lure as it scurries through the shallows like a frightened shad or herring. A striper-size crankbait also creates an easy silhouette for a striper to see as it swims through the water at night.

A bucktail jig is also a good lure choice for night fishing. With a single hook that rides upright in the water, a jig does not hang up very often as you swim it through the water. When using a three-eighths to one-half ounce jig in water less than ten to twelve feet deep, you can swim the jig with a fairly fast retrieve and still keep it in the strike zone.

Depending on the mood of the fish, a plastic trailer added to the jig may increase its effectiveness. However, at times, stripers will hit a plain bucktail jig better.

Because they are often located in shallow water, stripers are usually easier to catch at night during the fall and winter than they are during the day. The biggest problem facing the night fisherman during the winter months is not finding stripers, but staying warm enough to continue fishing into the night.

Besides dressing in insulated clothing, avid night fishermen often place a catalytic heater in the floor of their boats to help warm up their hands and feet when the air temperature drops into the thirties. It can get bitterly cold on the water at 3:00 a.m. on a December night, so be prepared in order to avoid hypothermia.

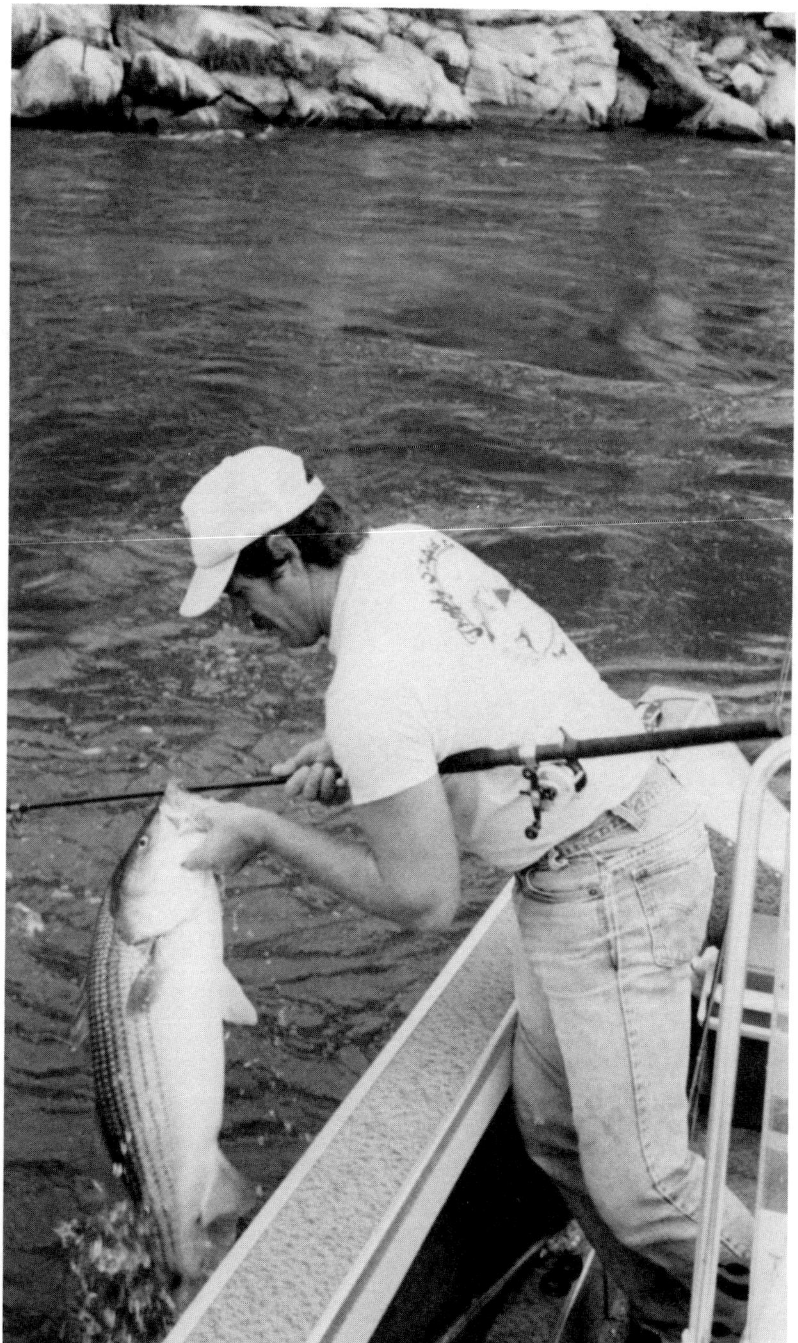

Chapter 10
RIVER FISHING

Fishing for striper and hybrids in a river is a lot different than fishing for them in a lake, because the environment of a river is very different from that of a manmade reservoir. As a result, stripers and hybrids adapt differently in a river than they do in a lake.

Stripers thrive in many rivers around the country, especially during the summer months, because the moving water stays cooler and is more oxygenated than a stillwater impoundment.

Shad and other baitfish are more concentrated in a river than in a lake, because there are fewer areas suitable for the baitfish to congregate. With the environment of a river forcing huge schools of shad into small areas, river stripers forage at optimum efficiency which results in many stripers attaining weights of over twenty pounds.

Many anglers may be surprised at the size of river stripers. While lots of huge deep reservoirs have yielded stripers in the thirty- to fifty pound class, most fishermen don't think of shallow rivers that are often less than a quarter of mile wide as big-fish waters. Oh sure, when conditions are right, you can catch limit after limit of stripers in the five- to fifteen pound range. But if you want to catch a trophy striper, you have to go to the lake. That's what most fishermen believe.

An angler who knows better, however, is Arthur Kelso, Jr., of Loudon, Tennessee. Kelso, a seventh grade science teacher, taxidermist and striper guide, began striper fishing in the mid-1970's. At that time there wasn't much information available about where and how to catch the

Arthur "Bear" Kelso (on right) and Big Bass Professor Doug Hannon pose with a 20-pound striper that Hannon caught while fishing a river with Kelso.

saltwater imports. So Kelso gathered tidbits of knowledge about the fish any way that he could.

One day as he was fishing for stripers in the tailwaters below East Tennessee's Fort Loudon Dam, Kelso watched as an electro-shocking boat manned by biologists from the Tennessee Wildlife Resources Agency worked the tailwaters in order to study the fish population. When the boat got close to where Kelso was fishing, he started asking the biologists questions about the habits of stripers.

The most important question that Arthur Kelso asked that day was "Why don't people catch bigger stripers in the tailwaters?" The reason for the question was that Kelso had been fishing tailwaters for several years at the time, and he had never caught a striper over twenty-five pounds from the river. He caught plenty of fish, but the majority of them were in the five- to ten pound category.

One of the biologists told him that because the water released below the dam was from near the bottom of the lake, that the tailwaters did not contain enough dissolved oxygen for larger stripers. The biologist told Kelso to go three to four miles below the dam, and he would find a suitable dissolved oxygen (d.o.) level for stripers weighing more than twenty pounds.

The reason for the improved d.o. is that as the water released from near the bottom of the lake moves downriver, it is exposed to the air on the surface where it picks up more oxygen. Since there is a very strong current and numerous variations in the depth and composition of a river, the water near the surface is constantly mixing with the water near the bottom as it tumbles downstream. This mixing results in oxygen-rich water from top to bottom.

While tailwaters are certainly oxygenated as evidenced by the vast numbers of fish found below most dams, the d.o. is not high enough to meet the demands of the really big stripers which require more oxygen to sustain themselves than smaller stripers and hybrids. It is the need for a higher d.o. level that causes trophy stripers to leave the easy pickings of the tailwaters for structure further downriver.

After talking with the biologists, Arthur Kelso told his fishing buddies about what he had learned. He suggested that they try fishing further downriver in order to find bigger stripers, but they weren't interested in leaving the easy fishing of the tailwaters.

So, one day, Kelso loaded his gear in his boat and set off drifting downriver by himself. He had fished about three hours and was about three miles below the dam when he heard a splash that could only be made by a surface-feeding striper. The sound had come from the opposite side of a mid-stream island. Kelso steered the boat across the river. As he came around the island, he saw a huge school of trophy stripers breaking on the surface.

Kelso dropped his live bait over the side of the boat and drifted downriver across the area. On twelve drifts, he hooked twelve stripers. Nine of the fish broke off, and he landed three that weighed over thirty pounds apiece.

"I knew then that I was through with tailrace fishing," Arthur Kelso says. "Let other fishermen crowd into a half mile stretch of tailrace with forty other boats in order to catch ten-pound stripers. Not me!"

Since his initial experience with river stripers, Kelso has spent several years developing a successful system for catching stripers in moving water. He has caught stripers from the river below several different dams with his methods, and has taught numerous other fishermen how to catch river stripers.

RIGGING UP FOR RIVER STRIPERS

Arthur Kelso uses live bait for the majority of his river fishing. When holding the rod as opposed to placing the rod in a rod holder, Kelso prefers a seven and one-half to eight-foot heavy-action rod. In fact, one of the rods that he uses is sold commercially as a muskie fishing rod.

"When I'm using a rod holder, I switch to a medium-heavy rod which has a softer tip action," Kelso says. "But when I'm holding the rod, which is most of the time, I want all the power that I can get out of a rod."

Kelso uses a big spinning reel spooled up with twenty-five to thirty-pound test line. In the rivers that he fishes there is quite a bit of color to the water, which makes it possible to use heavy line without spooking the fish.

"The places where I fish have plenty of rough cover and a powerful current. I need at least twenty-five pound test line to handle a thirty-pound and up striper," Arthur Kelso says.

When rigging up for live bait, Kelso threads a one-ounce egg sinker onto the end of his line. Then, about two or three inches from the end of the line, he crimps a small split shot onto the line. Next, he wets the line and slides the split shot up the line approximately eighteen to twenty-four inches.

"The reason I crimp the split shot on the end of the line

and slide it up the line is because where you crimp the split shot onto the line, you weaken the line," Arthur Kelso says.

Once the split shot is slid into place, Kelso clips off the end of the line where he crimped the split shot and ties on a 5/0 Eagle Claw hook that he has sharpened with a stone. The rigging is very basic, but effective. The small split shot keeps the egg sinker from sliding down onto the hook. Since the split shot can be slid up and down the line, Kelso can easily adjust the distance that he wants to keep the egg sinker above the hook. "In a river, you break off a lot. I use a split shot for the same purpose that many people use a barrel swivel. The advantage is a split shot costs less than a swivel," Arthur Kelso says.

Kelso doesn't vary the weight of his egg sinker. He always use a one-ounce weight. When fishing a river, Kelso doesn't make long casts into the current. Instead, he drifts downstream with his line vertically beside the boat.

"Because I drift downstream at the same rate of speed as the current with my line straight up and down beside the boat, it doesn't take a lot of lead to get a hook and line to the bottom, even in a strong current, Arthur Kelso says. "The reason that I need a one-ounce sinker is to get the size shad that I use down to the bottom and keep it from swimming back up. Since I always use approximately the same size shad, I always use the same amount of weight."

Kelso's favorite live bait is a five- to six-inch threadfin shad, but threadfins that big are hard to come by. So most of the time, he uses an eight- to ten-inch gizzard shad, which is easier to catch.

Most of the time Arthur Kelso catches his shad with a dip net in the water immediately below a dam. He believes that when a shad is stressed it emits a mucus or slime that is repugnant to game fish. Because of that belief, Kelso likes to dip up only three to six shad at a time. "Most people dip up too many shad at a time. They try to fill up their net," Kelso says. "When you do that, the shad get packed in on top of each other, and they secrete a slime that I believe repels stripers."

When dipping up bait in the tailwater, Kelso stands on

the bank and uses a soft, quarter-inch mesh net with a five-foot handle to which he has added a three-foot aluminum pipe. He reinforces the original handle by inserting a piece of broom handle in it, before he slides the extension pipe over the top of it and secures it with screws. "The extension pipe, which I buy at a hardware store, is made from heavy gauge aluminum. But the handle on most dip nets is not strong enough. So I like to strengthen it with a broom handle," Arthur Kelso explains.

He wears polarized sunglasses which makes it easier to see underneath the water. He also carries a plastic bucket to dump the shad into after he dip nets them.

Once he has several shad in the bucket, Kelso carries the bucket to his boat. Using a small, cloth net, he transfers the baitfish from the bucket to his bait tank. He makes it a point never to touch a shad with his hands until he puts it on the hook. "I don't cull shad out of my dip net. When I scoop up three or four shad, regardless of their size, I dump them into the bucket," Kelso says. "Then, later I dip them up out of the bucket to put them in the bait tank. When I do that, I toss the shad that are too small back into the water.

"It may take me three hours to get my bait, but I'll get the right-size bait, and the bait will be in good shape," Kelso adds.

Kelso hooks a shad by starting the point of the hook underneath a shad's chin in one of the creases and bringing the hook out near the corner of the eye.

When fishing for river stripers, you need to make sure your drag is adjusted properly. To land a thirty-pound fish in a strong current and relatively shallow water, a well-adjusted drag is the only way to keep from popping off more stripers than you land.

In order to properly adjust the drag, string your line through all the guides on the rod and either have someone hold the loose end of the line or tie it to something solid. Then, pull back on the line with a full bend in the rod. In this manner, the bend of the rod is factored into the drag setting.

Before leaving home, Kelso checks the drag on his reels by tying his line to a post or similar object and applying pressure with the rod. He also checks the drag every time he puts a bait over the side of the boat to make sure the drag hasn't locked up. On the water, he will just pull on the line in front of the reel to check the drag, because he knows he has properly adjusted the drag at home. When he drops a shad over the side, he just wants to make sure the drag is functioning properly. He also checks to make sure the line hasn't gotten wrapped around the tip of the rod.

WHERE TO CATCH RIVER STRIPERS

Arthur Kelso's favorite time to fish for river stripers is June through September. When the air temperature is in the nineties and everybody thinks all the stripers are in deep water, Kelso heads for shallow-water structure and cover in the river.

Because of the current, rivers maintain a more uniform temperature and oxygen content from top to bottom. As a result, there is no need for a striper to go deep in a river. Kelso has caught hundreds of river stripers in the twenty- to forty-pound range during the summer, and the average depth of the fish he catches is seven to nine feet.

If there is one word that summarizes the most important factor in river fishing, it is current. Current controls where the baitfish and stripers will be, and when they will get there. The majority of rivers with productive striper fishing are actually the headwaters of a manmade reservoir. On most major river systems in the country today, there are a series of dams that create a number of large impoundments. Where the water is released below the dam of one reservoir, it creates a tailrace area for a short distance. Then the water flow becomes more like a true river for a number of miles until the river environment is swallowed up by the next reservoir downstream.

How far downstream the river environment is maintained varies from lake to lake, but it is in the limited miles

Learning how the current affects river stripers and hybrids is essential to becoming a good river fisherman.

of fast-flowing river that Kelso concentrates his summertime striper fishing. The rivers aren't wide, often less than a quarter of a mile across, and the majority of the bottom is not deep, often averaging less than five feet. It is true river fishing, and that is what Kelso enjoys!

The pulse of the river is the dam above it which controls when and how much new water will move downstream. When the water is moving, stripers feed. When the water is still, you are wasting your time.

In a river, schools of feeding stripers will congregate around shallow structure and cover on the bottom which breaks the flow of the current. Kelso will not fish for river stripers around any type of structure or cover that is deeper than fifteen feet.

"When river stripers are hungry, they move into shallow water to feed. If you can find something that breaks up the current in less than fifteen feet of water, you will catch stripers," Kelso explains.

A variety of structure and cover will attract fast-water stripers. A ridge with a row of stumps situated along it; a rock pile; a pile of concrete dumped into the water from the construction of a bridge; bridge piers; an old ferry crossing that was inundated when the reservoir downstream backed up the waters of the river; a junk car or a tree washed up on a bar are all potential striper hangouts.

When fishing a river you need to remember that even though it is shallower, a river's topography is similar to a manmade reservoir. It has a deeper channel surrounded by shallower water. The bottom along the channel will have variations along it, such as where a ditch or secondary channel intersects the main channel or where a point or bar runs out from the bank. A river fisherman needs to use his eyes and depth finder to locate such places, because that is where the stripers will be.

HOW TO FIND STRIPER HANGOUTS

Finding a school of feeding stripers along a river is a lot easier than finding them in a lake, if you know what to look for.

Since you are looking for something in shallow water that breaks the current, the surface of the water is often more helpful than the most expensive video screen on the market. As water flows downriver, objects in the water divert the flow, because water is not as dense as wood or rocks. So water has to go around, over or under a denser object. If it is a bridge pier or island that diverts the flow, it is very obvious, because you will see the water flowing around the pier or island.

If it is an object below the surface, the diversion will not be as obvious, but it will be visible. When you have a change in the flow of the water, it is evident by a disturbance on the surface. The greater the change in the water's flow, the greater the disturbance. For example, a rock the size of a chair lying in six feet of water will obviously create a greater disturbance or boil on the surface than a rock the size of a basketball in the same depth of water.

What determines the amount of disturbance that a sub-surface object creates on top as water flows around it is the size of the object, the depth of the object and the speed of the current.

Since most productive structure and cover for river stripers is in less than ten feet of water, every object in the river that will attract a striper creates some type of tell-tale swirl or boil on top when the current is flowing. By being alert for changes on the water's surface, you will be able to locate stumps, rocks and other sub-surface cover and structure that stripers congregate around when feeding.

The area mentioned earlier where Kelso found his first school of heavyweight river stripers is a good example of sub-surface river structure and cover. Kelso initially discovered the spot because the stripers were fishing on the surface. As he fished through the area, however, he noticed several places where the water was swirling on top. When he dragged a big gizzard shad beside one of the swirls, a striper would streak off with the bait. Kelso knew there were several "somethings" scattered across the area, but he couldn't figure out what they were. As he studied his depth finder, he noted that the piles of "something" were situated on a flat that varied from five to nine feet deep. Approximately forty yards from the bank, the flat dropped out into the river channel which was thirty-five feet deep. The piles of "something" closest to the drop-off held the biggest stripers.

After finding the school of trophy stripers on the flat, Arthur Kelso began asking some of the old-timers around the river about the spot. He soon discovered that the flat had been the scene of a train wreck back in the early 1900's. The piles of "something" were rails that had been twisted and damaged beyond repair. The railroad had piled them up and left them near the wreck. There were even some pieces of train cars on the bottom that were damaged in the derailment. The former railroad bed and site of the wreck were covered with water when a dam was built across the river forty miles downstream. Kelso boated over five hundred stripers from the area in three years.

BRIDGE PIERS

Some of Arthur Kelso's most productive and dependable structure for river stripers are bridge piers. Railroad and highway bridges cross most major rivers numerous times. When they do, there are usually several concrete piers sitting in the water to support the bridge.

The bridges that Kelso has fished along the Tennessee River, regardless of whether they are interstate highway bridges, railroad bridges, or state highway bridges, are all constructed basically the same way. There is a concrete footer or pad on the bottom. Then the pier or concrete column holding up the bridge is set on the pad.

LOCATION OF STRIPERS AROUND PIER

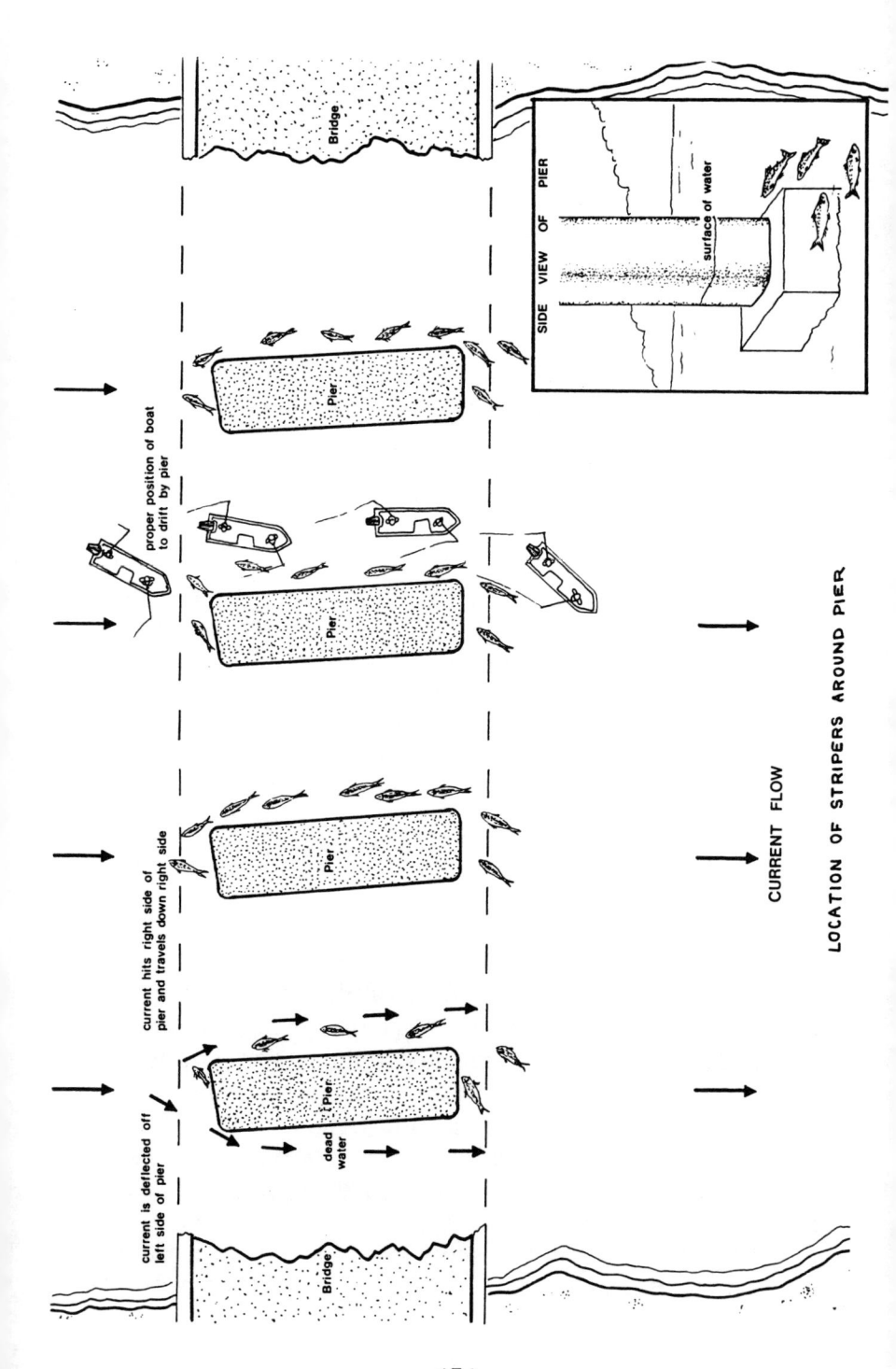

While it is not readily noticeable by looking at the piers, Kelso has discovered that on every bridge that he has ever fished the piers are set at a slight angle to the river's current or flow. Because of that engineering design, every bridge has a current side and a dead-water side.

Any pier situated in fifteen feet of water or less is a likely place to find a school of river stripers. "If you're real quiet, you can catch thirty pound stripers off piers in five feet of water," Kelso says. "On more than one occasion, we have hooked triples from a pier in five feet of water."

If a pier is sitting in water deeper than fifteen feet, Kelso won't fish it. According to him, it is too deep.

To fish a pier, Kelso first determines in which direction the pier is angled to the current. For example, assume that the up-river end of a pier is angled slightly to the left of the river's flow. In that case, the right side (facing upriver) of the pier will be the current side and the left side will be the dead-water side. When you fish that pier, you want your bait to drift down beside the current side of the pier.

The pad or footer on most piers is four to five feet high. Then the pier or column sits on the footer. So assuming that the water around a pier is eight feet deep, you would find four feet of water over the top of the footer and then a drop-off of four feet from the top of the footer to the river bottom.

"Sometimes, stripers will be situated over the top of the footer and next to the pier itself. Then, other times or on the next pier, the fish will be located on the bottom next to the footer," Kelso says.

To fish a pier, Kelso starts his drift about twenty yards or so above the upstream edge of the pier. He shuts off the outboard motor and uses an electric motor mounted on the bow of his boat to keep the bow of the boat pointed downstream as he drifts past a pier.

He lowers a shad over the side of the boat, and using a seven and one-half to eight-foot rod, keeps the bait in front of the bow of the boat, approximately two feet off the bottom.

With the aid of the electric motor, he controls the drift

of his boat so that the shad drifts across the upstream edge (or point) of the pier and then drifts down the current side of the pier before swinging across the downstream edge (or point) of the pier. After the boat drifts twenty-five to thirty feet past the pier, Kelso reels in the bait and motors back up above the pier to drift it again.

"You need to get the shad right against the pier, because a big striper is lazy, and it won't chase a baitfish far in the current," Arthur Kelso explains. "Sometimes the boat is so close to the pier that I have to reach out and hold it off the concrete."

When fishing a bridge pier, it is one rod per man, because you need to be holding the rod in order to properly maneuver a shad around the structure.

With two men in the boat, the man in back needs to place his shad on the opposite side of the boat. That way, as the man in front drifts his shad against the side of the pier and across the top of the footer, the man in back will be in perfect position to drift his shad over the outside of the footer. "Many times the man in front will hook a striper against the pier, and at the same time, the man in back will hook one off the side of the drop-off formed by the footer," Kelso says.

When fishing piers, you will soon learn that a school of stripers is either there or they're not. If you don't get a bite fairly quickly, you need to move to the next pier. "It normally takes about ten to twelve minutes to make a proper drift," Arthur Kelso says. "I'll make two or three drifts down a pier, and if the fish don't bite, I'm gone."

Kelso believes in keeping a lively shad on his hook. After two drifts he puts on a fresh shad. He may go through half a dozen big gizzard shad while fishing one bridge.

Contrary to what some fishermen believe, a pier doesn't hold just a lone striper. A pier attracts schools of stripers. Kelso can often catch six stripers off one pier before the school spooks.

"Schools of stripers are constantly moving as they hunt for food. Sometimes, I'll fish a pier and won't get a bite," Kelso says. "I'll leave the pier and fish the rest of the piers on the bridge. Then, I'll return to the pier where I started and a school of stripers will be all over it.

A trick that Kelso often uses when searching for trophy stripers around piers is to cruise the bridges at daylight looking for wet places or "splash marks" as he calls them upon the piers. The splash marks are made by a really big striper throwing water upon a pier as it chases shad.

"That's how I got started fishing piers for stripers," Kelso explains. "I spotted splash marks upon the pier of a railroad bridge, and they looked just like the marks that I had seen on the dam when stripers would chase shad against it. So, I dropped a shad around the pier, and I confirmed what I thought had made the marks--a striper over thirty pounds."

Now, Kelso uses splash marks to help him determine which piers to fish first, and where the striper is positioned on the pier.

When water conditions are right, stripers may feed around a certain pier every morning for a week. So, when you locate a productive pier, don't hesitate to return to it. Once you catch several stripers from around it, another school of stripers will move in to replace them.

ISLANDS

Islands are the source of some of the best structure and cover available in a river. When dams and locks are built along a river, the river's natural water level is raised, which inundates a lot of low-lying land. Natural islands in the river are reduced in size, and the submerged portions of an island often create prime habitat for heavyweight stripers.

Islands along a river are usually timbered. Willow, sycamore, birch and oak trees are found growing on most islands.

"Before the government closed the dams along the rivers, the trees along the edge of an island that was going to be flooded were cut down, which left a row of stumps around almost every island that has enough soil on it to support some trees," Arthur Kelso explained.

The head and tail of many islands will have a row of shallow-water stumps. In the early morning, Kelso fishes a topwater lure across the shallow points. He uses twenty- to thirty-pound test line and casts either a swimming-minnow type plug or a Creek Chub Darter across the stump rows.

"With the swimming minnow, I just slowly crank it across the top to create a "V"-shaped wake," Kelso says. "With the Darter, I pop it in the same place two or three times. If a striper doesn't hit it, I'll move it."

Topwater action on the river can account for some really big stripers. But once the sun pops up, you need to switch to shad.

Even though stripers are not considered a real cover-oriented fish like a black bass, Kelso has found that stripers in a river relate closely to stumps, rocks and other cover when feeding. He has caught hundreds of stripers over twenty pounds by drifting a shad over a stump or similar piece of cover.

"You can't fish a weighted shad around stumps in less than five feet of water without hanging up a lot, so that's why I fish the real shallow wood early in the morning with a topwater lure," Arthur Kelso says.

Sometimes, Kelso does anchor his boat at the head or tail of an island and use a balloon to float an unweighted shad through the shallow stumps. The technique has accounted for some huge stripers, but usually Kelso moves out into water that is in the five- to twelve-foot range and drifts a weighted shad across cover.

"I like to determine where the edge of the original island was before the dam raised the water, because that is usually where you will find some stumps," Kelso said. "I stand up in my boat and cruise around the entire island looking for a swirl or boil on the surface that indicates there is a stump or rock under the surface."

Once Kelso spies a promising piece of cover, he positions his boat upstream and lowers a shad directly underneath the boat to drift the baitfish across the cover.

Since the cover is in shallow water, he is very careful

LOCATION OF STRIPERS AROUND ISLAND

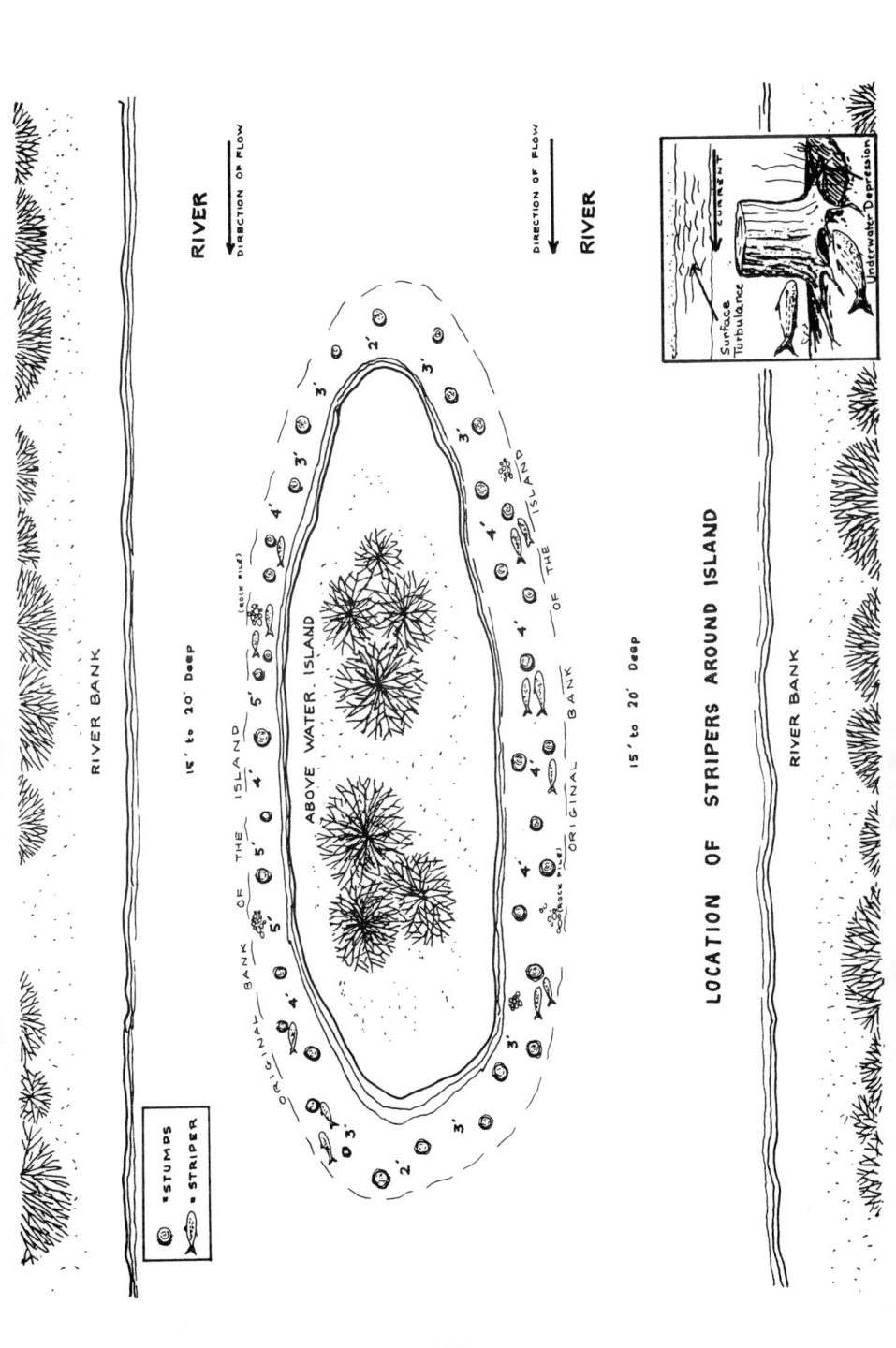

not to make any noise as he drifts over the cover. Kelso doesn't use his electric motor. He even turns off the pump to his bait tank in order to eliminate any noise that might alarm a striper.

With the bow of the boat headed directly downstream, Kelso keeps the rod in front of the boat as he drifts. It is very important that you keep the bait and line vertical in the water to eliminate hang-ups.

When the one-ounce egg sinker bumps the cover, you want to raise up on the rod and walk it over or around the debris. If a striper takes the bait, set the hook immediately.

"Some people won't believe it, but it is very important that the shad bumps the stump or other cover," Kelso explains. "One huge stump can hold a whole school of stripers"

As an example of how important it is to place the shad directly against the stump or rock, Kelso tells about a guide trip when he had two other fishermen with him. They made three drifts across an area that Kelso knew held a single, massive stump without a single strike. The clients were ready to move on, but Kelso wasn't satisfied because he hadn't felt his sinker touch the stump which was sitting in fifteen feet of water.

Kelso lined the boat back up again, and on the fourth drift, he felt the sinker tap against the mammoth stump. When it did, a twenty-five pounder inhaled the shad.

Kelso and his guide party caught three more stripers over twenty pounds off that one stump once they started bumping it with their sinker and shad. "Those stripers were schooled up over top of that stump, and they wouldn't move three feet either way to take a shad," Arthur Kelso explains.

When searching for likely striper hangouts, Arthur Kelso will start at least three miles below a dam. He locates the bank closest to the original river channel and slowly moves down the river looking for swirls on the surface and watching his depth finder for any changes in the underwater contour. Since Kelso fishes out of an eighteen-foot boat, he can safely stand up as he motors downriver, which improves his ability to spot faint changes on the water's surface.

If Kelso encounters an island that he has never fished before, he will idle around the entire island as he tries to follow the original edge of the island with his depth finder. He also scans the surface for swirls produced by submerged stumps and rocks.

When exploring a new section of river, Kelso will carry "marker buoys" with him. His "marker buoys" consist of plastic caps off aspirin bottles or quarter-size pieces of styrofoam. To the "buoy," Kelso ties a short length of monofilament line. Then he slides a slip sinker onto the line and ties a treble hook to the end.

If Kelso locates a shallow bar or ridge along the river that he is not familiar with, he drops a marker overboard. The current washes the marker over the shallower structure and the treble hook catches on the bottom and holds the marker in place.

A bottle cap or piece of weathered styrofoam goes unnoticed by other river fishermen, who are accustomed to seeing bits of debris floating in the water. Kelso may drop several markers to help outline the shape of a bar or ridge. As Kelso motors around the shallow structure studying it with his depth finder, the motor and other boat noises will usually spook the stripers from their shallow-water locations. So, after Kelso explores a newly found piece of structure or cover, he will sometimes leave the tiny markers in place until the next morning when he will return to actually fish the spot. The markers help him line up on the structure in order to get a proper drift.

"On a particularly long piece of structure, I sometimes leave the marker out for several days until I become familiar with the contour," Arthur Kelso says. "Nobody ever notices the scraps of styrofoam or bottle caps. And if they do, they just think somebody has set a trotline in the water."

WHEN TO CATCH RIVER STRIPERS

Arthur Kelso has found that the best time to catch river stripers is during the hottest months of the year, especially July and August. He likes to fish from daylight until about ten a.m. Then he returns to the river about four p.m. and fishes until dark, which is often as late as 9:30 p.m. during the summer.

"I'm sure that in a river as long as the current is moving that you could find feeding stripers all day long, but it gets too hot for me during the middle of the day," Arthur Kelso explains.

Current is crucial to successful striper fishing on a river. If there is no current, you are better off at home. Because of that fact, Kelso carefully monitors the generation schedule of the hydroelectric dam above the section of river that he plans to fish. If you intend to become a proficient river fisherman, you need to be able to interpret the information that the dam authorities provide. While the way that the generation schedule is explained may vary slightly from dam to dam, an example of how the Tennessee Valley Authority provides generation information will be helpful to river fishermen across the country as they attempt to understand the lingo used by dam authorities. On the Tennessee River where Kelso fishes, the generation schedule uses one a.m. as the starting point. For purposes of this example, assume that the dam in question has four turbines.

If Kelso calls the dam and is told, "Zero for two hours, one for four hours and two for fifteen hours," that translates into "there will be no generation for the first two hours (1 a.m. to 3 a.m.). At 3 a.m. one turbine will turn on for four hours (until 7 a.m.) then at 7 a.m., two turbines will turn on for fifteen hours.

Armed with that information, Arthur Kelso knows that at 7 a.m. there will be plenty of current moving down the river as the second turbine is turned on, and it will cause stripers to school up around shallow structure and cover to feed.

The biggest disadvantage that most fishermen have when it comes to river fishing is the fact that most dams don't generate electricity on weekends because the factories are shut down. If the dams don't generate electricity, there isn't any current and river stripers simply do not feed very well.

Because of that fact, you need to take advantage of the extra hours of daylight available during the summer months and head to the river during the week after work. Kelso says that from 7:30 p.m. until dark is the very best time for catching river stripers. He also believes that stripers probably feed right on into the night, a belief supported by the fact that a former world record striper which weighed fifty-nine pounds, twelve ounces, was caught from the Colorado River at 2 a.m. on a topwater lure.

"I think you can catch stripers at night on a river if the current is running," Arthur Kelso says. "But by sundown, my arms are usually too sore to stay at it!

Giant stripers can be taken around warm water discharges during the coldest months of the year.

Chapter 11
WARM-WATER DISCHARGES

Steve Baker's radio alarm went off at 3:45 on a Tuesday morning in mid-January. As he lay in bed trying to convince himself to get up, Baker heard the weather report on the radio. The present temperature hovered at 22 degrees below zero, and in the last four days, the temperature had never risen above twenty degrees. The last thought in most people's minds would have been fishing. But if more fishermen knew what Baker knew, there would have been more alarms going off.

The bitterly cold weather had brought millions of shad to the warm-water discharge area below a local steam plant. The stripers had followed in hot pursuit. Steve Baker had made good catches of stripers every day for the past three days with several fish over twenty-five pounds.

As Baker left his home on Norris Lake, he was thinking about how to keep his cold-weather striper hang-out a secret. He didn't have much to worry about. There was hardly a car on the freeway at 4:00 a.m.

Arriving at the steam plant's parking area, Baker could see that he wasn't the only striper-fishing addict out in the sub-zero temperatures. There were three more cars parked in the lot. As he walked down the riprap to the discharge area, Baker could hear the big rods whipping lures into the freezing darkness. Before he reached the water's edge, Baker heard an explosive strike and a faint voice yelling, "Fish on." With all this commotion, Steve Baker almost broke his neck hustling down the rocks to get in on the short feeding spree the stripers had been making in the early morning hours for the past few days.

The discharge area below the steam plant looks as

though it was engineered and built for attracting stripers. A narrow canal carries the water from the plant into a small bay which connects with the main lake. The water in the canal and confined bay is always eighteen to twenty degrees warmer than the lake. Thus, the discharge area creates a sanctuary for shad to escape the near freezing waters of the lake.

Steve Baker nervously tied on a large chrome-colored swimming minnow and strained his eyes to see into the darkness. He heard another striper explode on one of the other fishermen's lures. He cast his lure slightly up current so his retrieve would end up almost straight in front of him.

Baker had made ten or twelve casts when what he thought was a bragging-size striper nearly tore the rod out of his hands. After a brief foot race up and down the bank, he slid the net under an eighteen-pound, three-ounce hybrid. The large female measured nearly thirty-one inches long and looked almost as big in girth as she was in length. It was, and still is, the heaviest hybrid that Steve Baker has caught to date.

After a trip to his truck to put the taxidermist-bound hybrid in the cooler, Baker was back casting his lure into the pre-dawn darkness. He landed a small hybrid and three stripers in the fifteen-pound class before daylight. One of the old regulars at the discharge area caught a thirty-four pound striper just at daybreak, and everybody that Baker talked to that morning had caught some good-sized fish. The morning's fishing below the steam plant had been about average for the middle of January.

There are numerous plants around the country that heat water to produce steam which in turn is used to turn turbines that create electricity. The used steam is then converted back to water by piping it into condensers which use water pumped from the lake or river to cool down the steam in order to condense it back to water. The condensed water, which has been treated to eliminate corrosive minerals, is then recycled by heating it again to produce more steam. The water in the condensers used to cool the steam is then discharged into the lake which creates a warm-water discharge.

By law in most states, a plant cannot discharge cooling water back into a lake that is more than eighteen to twenty degrees warmer than the lake. So the actual water temperature at a discharge area varies during the year. For example, if the water temperature in the lake or river is forty-five degrees in January, then the cooling water being discharged from a steam plant cannot be warmer than sixty-five degrees. The purpose of the law is to prevent utility companies from overheating the lake.

During the winter, the artificially heated water attracts millions of shad into the area of the discharge. Usually, the shad migration begins in late December to mid-January depending on the weather. As the surface temperature of the lake falls down into the mid- to low forties, large numbers of shad seek refuge in the warmer discharge water.

Stripers and hybrids do not mind the cold water in the lake, but they cannot pass up the abundant forage around a warm-water discharge during the winter months. So large schools of stripers and hybrids gather in discharge areas to feed on the easy prey.

The productive water around a discharge is limited. The exact area which holds fish depends on the volume of warm water discharged and the configuration of the route along which the water is funneled back into the lake. Because of this, fishing from the bank is often more effective than fishing from a boat. In fact, at some warm-water discharges, there is an informal sportsmen's agreement that you do not take a boat up into the canal where the warm water is released, because boats moving in and out of the canal will spook stripers and hybrids.

The physical layout of many steam plant discharges is similar. The water from the plant is released into a short man-made canal or ditch which is often less than thirty to forty yards wide. Since the water is released into such a constricted area, a strong current with eddies and boils is created as the water moves down the canal.

As the water moves out of the canal, it usually empties into a wider bay or slough before flowing into the main lake. You can usually catch stripers and hybrids from the area of the discharge itself to where the warmer water mixes with the colder water of the main lake.

Discharge areas often receive a lot of fishing pressure, because they offer some the most productive wintertime striper fishing available. The intense fishing pressure in such a constricted area often results in the real heavyweight stripers feeding at night. Steve Baker has found that he catches ninety percent of his stripers between two a.m. and seven a.m. It gets plenty cold at that time of the morning in January and February. But to catch stripers in the thirty- and forty-pound class, you need to fish at night.

When fishing discharges, Baker uses both artificial lures and live bait. For fishing live bait, he rigs up two different ways. To fish a shad on the bottom, Baker uses an egg-shaped sinker weighing between one-half to one and one-half ounces, the size varying with the speed of the current. He threads the egg sinker on his line and cuts off a two-foot long leader. He then ties a barrel swivel to the end of his line and ties the leader to the other end of the swivel. A hook is then attached to the end of the leader.

The reason for this rigging is to keep the sinker from sliding down on the hook. With the swivel acting as a stop, a shad can swim a couple of feet above the bottom on the short leader. When a striper hits the shad, the egg sinker remains on the bottom as the line passes freely through the sinker so that the fish doesn't feel the weight.

The shad that Steve Baker prefers in a warm-water discharge situation is a six- to twelve-inch long river herring which is often called a hickory shad. Most of the shad in a discharge area are gizzard shad. Because of such an abundance of gizzard shad, a striper will hit the less prevalent river herring before it will take a gizzard shad.

River herring are not as easy to catch for bait as gizzard shad, because they are very fast. Unlike gizzard shad which can be caught in great numbers with a net, herring often dart out from under a falling net before it can capture them.

Since herring, which are carnivorous, feed on small threadfin shad that gather around a warm-water discharge, Steve Baker takes advantage of this habit to catch his bait. He uses a spinning rod and reel spooled with six-pound-test line to cast tiny crappie flies or jigs into the discharge area. He uses two flies at a time on his line, about a foot apart, and then clips a float about two to three feet above the top fly.

To catch a herring, Baker casts the rig into the water and uses a jerk-and-pause retrieve to entice a herring into hitting. Sometimes he catches two herring at a time. "Most of the herring that you catch will be too big, often twelve to fifteen inches long, but you just keep fishing until you catch the right size bait," Steve Baker says. "Catching the bait can be a lot of fun. A river herring jumps like a miniature tarpon."

Since he can catch his bait in the same area where he is fishing, Baker only catches a few herring at a time. Once he catches enough herring to bait up the number of rods he intends to use, Baker hooks them onto twenty- to thirty-pound-test line and casts them out on the bottom. Since the area around a discharge is usually rocky, Baker sticks the butt of his rod into a rock crevice to keep a striper from pulling the rod into the water. The reel is left out of gear with the clicker on to alert Baker to a strike. Since he is usually fishing in the dark, the sound from the clicker as a striper takes off with the herring is the best way to detect a strike. When fishing on the bottom, Baker will fish three to four rods at a time.

For fishing a discharge area, Steve Baker uses a seven and one-half to eight-foot heavy-action rod with a stiff tip. When fishing from the bank, you need plenty of power to land a forty-pound striper. Some anglers even use a nine- to ten-foot surf rod.

Besides the bottom rig, Baker also uses a slip float set-up to suspend a river herring off the bottom. The set-up consists of either an elongated styrofoam float or a round two-inch cork both of which have a hole through the center of them so that the line can easily slide through it.

A commercial bobber stopper, which looks similar to the spring out of a ball point pen, is placed onto the line or you can simply tie a piece of rubber band or a strand of living rubber from a jig onto the line to stop the line from passing through the slip float when the herring reaches a certain depth.

When fishing a float, Steve Baker uses both unweighted and weighted lines, depending on the circumstances. When using a weighted line, he pegs a three-quarter to one-ounce egg sinker with the aid of a toothpick a couple of feet above the hook. There is no need to use a sliding egg sinker, because the weight is not lying on the bottom. So when a striper takes the herring, the fish will be towing the sinker with it regardless of whether it is sliding on the line or pegged tight.

The water around most warm-water discharges is normally ten to twenty feet deep. Steve Baker will adjust the strand of rubber or bobber stopper affixed to his line so that it is six to ten feet above the hook. He then reels his line up so that the sliding float is butted up to the pegged egg sinker (assuming he is using a weighted line) and two feet of line with the hooked river herring is dangling from the rod tip.

When he casts the rig into the water, the line slips easily through the float until the strand of rubber spools off the reel and catches when it tries to pass through the hole in the float. The herring is then suspended six to ten feet below the water where it can swim around in the current. One of the biggest advantages of a slip float set-up is that you don't hang up as often as you do with a bottom rig.

Because of the current, Steve Baker normally uses one rod at a time when fishing with a float. When you cast out the float, the current will carry the float downstream, unlike the bottom rig which sinks to the bottom and stays in one place. If you place out a number of rods with floats on them, the current will wash the floats together and tangle the lines.

If stripers are feeding on top, which is easy to determine even in the dark because you will hear the explosive sound that a striper makes when it attacks a shad near the surface, Steve Baker fishes a swimming-minnow type lure or a Tennessee Popper. Depending on the layout of the discharge area, some fishermen even wade out into the water to cast a topwater lure across likely looking eddy areas.

"I like to keep a rod rigged up with a topwater lure so that if I see a striper explode on top or a shad jumping out of the water while I'm fishing live bait, I can quickly pick up the rod and work the lure across the surface," Steve Baker says.

Crankbaits cast along the rocky banks in the discharge area also account for some hefty stripers. Cast a crankbait upstream at a forty-five degree angle and bring it back with the flow of the current.

A bucktail jig with a plastic trailer fished in the same manner is also a favorite lure for casting in a warm-water discharge.

The colder and more miserable the weather in January and February, the better the striper fishing gets around the steam plants. Steve Baker's favorite time to fish is the fourth or fifth day into a severe cold front which has plunged the temperature into the single digits.

To fish comfortably, as well as safely, under such adverse weather conditions, it is imperative that you dress properly in order to withstand the low temperatures. One trick that Baker employs to keep his hands from freezing when casting artificial lures is to put on a pair of thin rubber gloves that women often wear when washing dishes. Then he puts a pair of cloth work gloves over the top of the rubber gloves.

"When cranking a lure back, the reel is constantly spraying water on your hands and a pair of cloth gloves quickly become soaked and your hands get numb," Baker says. "With the rubber gloves underneath the cloth gloves, you keep your hands dry."

As the water temperature nudges toward the fifty-degree mark in early spring, the vast concentrations of shad that have infiltrated a warm-water discharge in December begin to move back into the lake, and the majority of stripers and hybrids leave the discharge area along with the baitfish.

Chapter 12
FISHING WITH DOWNRIGGERS

For years, fishing with downriggers has been a very effective method for catching freshwater fish such as salmon and lake trout that frequently school in deep water. With the introduction of stripers into fresh water, it was not long before innovative anglers were using downriggers to catch stripers from deep water.

While downriggers are still not a common sight, even on some of the very best striper lakes in the country, more and more anglers are discovering the effectiveness of downriggers for striper fishing. An angler who has been experimenting for the past several years with downriggers to catch stripers is Charlie Guffey, a science teacher and fishing guide from Somerset, Kentucky. Guffey was one of the first fishermen to start fishing with downriggers on Lake Cumberland, which is only a few miles from his home.

Guffey started with one downrigger. He now has half a dozen, and after over seven years of experimenting with downrigging for stripers, Guffey is convinced that downriggers should be an important part of every striper fisherman's tackle.

WHAT IS DOWNRIGGING?

A lot of freshwater fishermen have never seen a downrigger. This is because until the introduction of stripers in so many lakes around the country, there were only a few lakes with the kind of deep-water species of fish that made downrigging worthwhile.

There are many different brands of downriggers, but the basic unit and its components are the same. The downrigger sits on a base which is securely anchored onto the gunwale of the boat, usually on or near the stern. On the base is mounted a wheel or spool which is equipped with a hundred yards of heavy, woven wire cable. The spool will either have a hand crank or an electric motor for lowering and raising the cable.

The cable leaves the spool and is threaded through a pulley which is mounted on the end of a metal arm called a boom, which resembles a short rod. The arm extends out over the side of the boat and with the cable hanging down from the end of the boom, you attach the downrigger weight, often called a cannonball, to the end of the cable.

Downrigger weights come in all sizes, shapes and colors. Some of the more popular shaped weights resemble a cannonball, banana, fish or aspirin. Most of the weights have a fin on them to make the weights track true in the water.

The weights are usually sized in one-pound increments with weights available from one pound up to twenty pounds. For most striper fishing, weights in the six to ten-pound range are usually the most effective.

On most weights there is a place to clip a line release mechanism. There are different types of line release mechanisms, but the one that Charlie Guffey prefers is a clothespin-type release. When you push down on the release, it opens like a clothespin. Inside the jaws of the clothespin is a lining of rubber on both sides to help minimize line abrasion. You place the monofilament line from your rod inside the jaws. When you release the clip, a spring clamps the jaws shut and holds your line firmly in place.

The line release mechanism is attached to the downrigger weight by a short length of cable so that the monofilament line held by the clothespin-type release will be pulled down by the weight as it is lowered on the cable.

Instead of the clothespin-type release, some companies market a similar type release, but instead of a spring to snap the jaws shut, there is a knob on the side that you screw in and out to open and shut the jaws which hold your line.

Some line releases such as the Free 'n' Easy Release made by Big Jon involve wrapping the monofilament line around a metal post that snaps into a plastic holder which is threaded onto the wire cable above the downrigger weight. When a fish hits, the impact of the strike snaps the metal post open and the monofilament line slides free from the post. Guffey doesn't like that type of release because it involves wrapping your line around the post which he believes may weaken the line.

Another line release device consists of running your monofilament line through a plastic O-ring. The O-ring has a pin attached to it which fits into the slot of a metal or plastic sleeve which is affixed to the downrigger cable right above the weight. When a fish strikes the lure, the pin attached to the O-ring pops out and the line is free. On paper, it looks like a good idea, but Charlie Guffey has found that the drag on the monofilament line created by the water as you troll will cause the line to slip through the O-ring and pull the lure up closer to the weight than you want it.

The only way that he has found to prevent this problem is to wrap the monofilament line around the O-ring a few times, before clipping it into the pin. Again, Guffey prefers not to have to wrap his line.

On most downriggers there will be a gauge to measure the amount of cable that you lower into the water. The gauge is usually mounted on the side of the spool. Some of the less expensive downriggers do not have a gauge, and you have to measure the depth by counting the revolutions of the spool as you lower the cable and weight. On most downriggers one revolution will equal one to two feet depending on the diameter of the spool.

A rod holder, which is usually nothing more than a hollow piece of plastic pipe which you slide a rod into, is normally attached behind the spool.

If the downrigger is powered by an electric motor, the

motor will be mounted on the side and an on/off switch beside it. A short length of cord and a two prong plug-in will be attached to the motor. In order to power the motor, you need to either wire a plug-in switch in your boat or clip off the plug and attach alligator clips to the cord. With the clips, you just run the cord directly to the posts of a twelve-volt battery.

HOW TO FISH A DOWNRIGGER

To properly put a downrigger down, you need to put the boat's motor in gear and be moving slowly forward in a straight line. Cast your lure directly behind the boat. The length of the cast depends on the amount of line that you want to troll between the downrigger weight and the lure. If you want to troll more line than you can cast out, simply let out more line as you move forward.

"I like to troll my lure at least seventy-five to one hundred feet behind the weight, which is a fairly long cast behind the boat," Charlie Guffey said.

The amount of line that Guffey fishes between the downrigger weight and the lure is more than most downrigger companies recommend as well as more line than most downrigger fishermen on the Great Lakes fish when trolling for trout and salmon. Guffey, however, has experimented with various lengths of line between the weight and the lure, and he has found that he catches more stripers when he increases the distance from the weight to the lure to a length of seventy-five to one hundred feet. He believes the reason for this is that stripers in clear water are very wary, even in deep water.

"If I'm trolling for white bass or crappie, I can move the lure closer to the weight, and it doesn't seem to matter." Charlie Guffey says.

Once you have the desired amount of line out, attach the monofilament line hanging from the end of your rod to the downrigger weight by whatever line release mechanism that you choose to use. As mentioned earlier, some line release mechanisms are threaded onto the wire cable itself right above the downrigger weight. So if you choose

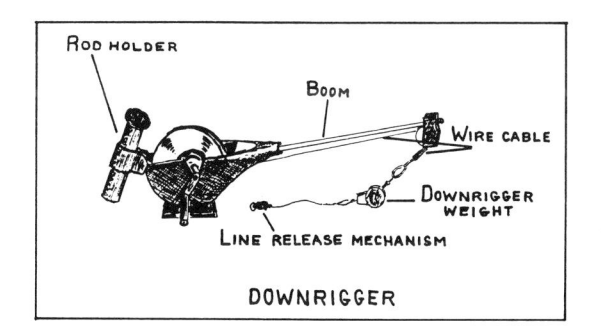

HOW A DOWNRIGGER WORKS

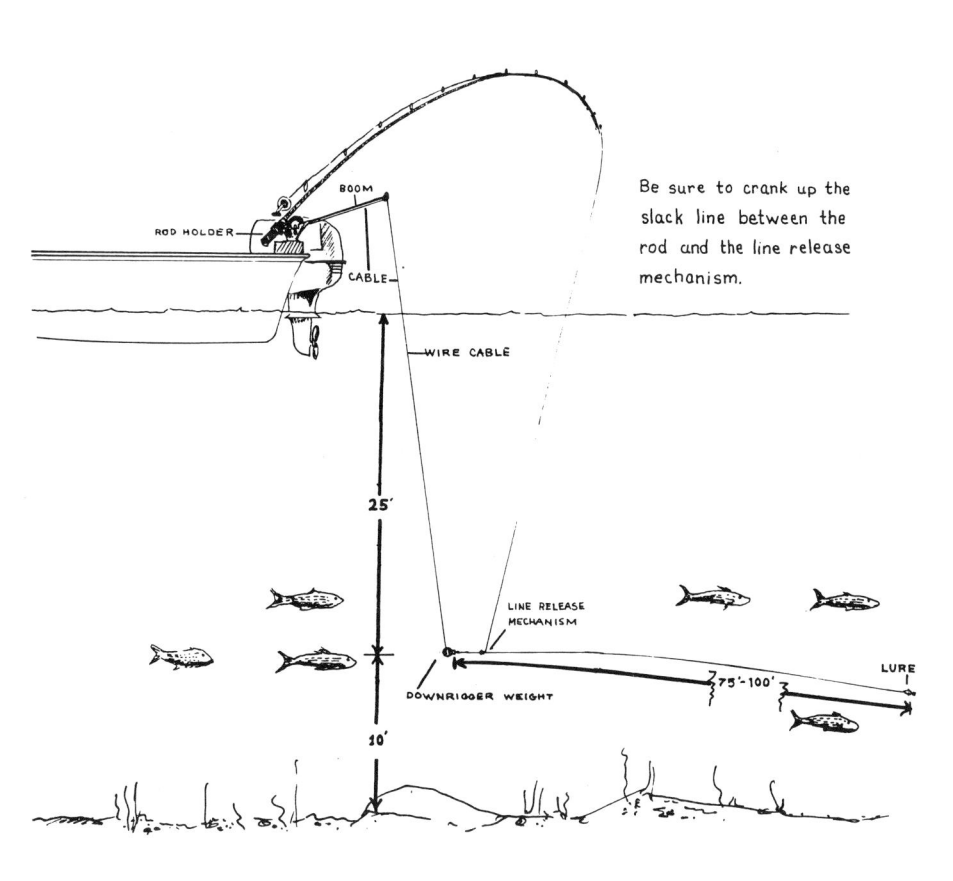

DOWNRIGGER — Rod Holder, Boom, Wire Cable, Downrigger Weight, Line Release Mechanism

Be sure to crank up the slack line between the rod and the line release mechanism.

to use that type of release, then you wouldn't attach the line to the weight, but above it.

Guffey, who uses a clothespin type release exclusively, puts his line as far back in the jaws between the rubber pads as the line will go. You vary the amount of force that it takes to pop the line free from the clip by the distance inside the jaws that you clamp it. If the line is clamped near the mouth, then the line will pop loose easier than if it is near the back of the clothespin clip.

"The reason that I like to place the line near the back of the clothespin is that I have found if you don't keep enough tension on the line, then the line will slip forward through the clothespin. The lure will then be pulled up closer to the downrigger weight than you want it." Charlie Guffey says.

By positioning the line near the back of the clip, a striper will usually set the hook as it pops the line free. Guffey doesn't even worry about setting the hook. "Sometimes a four- or five-pound striper won't pop the line free when it first hits the lure," Guffey says. "But I want a striper to pull hard before the line pops loose, because when the line first pops free, it creates a lot of slack line for a few seconds and if you don't have the fish hooked well, it may get off."

Once you attach your line to the line release, which is attached to the weight or cable above the weight, you then lower the weight, which is on the end of the wire cable down into the water. Your reel should still be out of gear, because you need to let out line as the weight sinks or you'll break your line or, worse, your rod. Charlie Guffey's reels have a clicker on them, and he just flips the clicker on as he lowers the weight to keep his reel from backlashing.

If you have a manual downrigger, you back crank the handle to lower the weight while you watch the depth gauge. If you have an electrically powered downrigger, you simply have to flip the switch to the down position and the motor slowly lowers the weight.

"I have used both manual and electric powered downriggers and besides eliminating the strained muscles, electric-powered downriggers have an added advantage.

When a fish hits, you can grab the rod with one hand and with the other hand hit the up button on the motor, and it will quickly get the cable and weight out of the water before the striper tangles up in it," Charlie Guffey says.

An electric-powered downrigger is really appreciated when you troll through a school of stripers and three rods hook-up at the same time. Without an electric motor, it would be almost impossible to hand crank three cables up before one of the stripers tangles up.

As the weight on the cable is lowered down into the water, the fin built onto the weight will catch in the water and the weight will run straight in the water instead of spinning. That is why you need to have the motor in gear and the boat moving slowly forward in the water when you lower the cable. If you don't, the weight, regardless of its shape, will start spinning on the braided cable as it sinks and the motion will wrap the cable around the line.

Watch the depth gauge as you lower the cable and when it indicates that you have reached the desired depth, stop the spool. At that point, engage the reel to prevent any more line from feeding out and crank up the slack between the tip of the rod and the line release mechanism. Charlie Guffey winds up the line until the reel, which is set on a medium drag, slips. The rod tip will be bent down in the same shape as if you had a fish hooked.

Guffey believes that a common mistake beginners make is not eliminating the slack line between the rod and the line release mechanism, which means putting pressure on the rod to pull the slack out. If you don't eliminate the slack or bow between the rod tip and the line release, then when a fish hits, it may not be able to pop the line loose from the mechanism. Instead, all that will happen is that the fish will pull the slack line or bow in front of the downrigger weight through the line release and you will not solidly hook the fish.

Once he tightens down on the rod and line, Guffey places the rod in an adjustable rod holder mounted on the back of the downrigger base. He prefers to set the rod holder at a sixty-degree angle.

The rods that Guffey uses are seven and one-half, eight, or nine-foot fiberglass rods with a stiff backbone and a slow tip. The rods all have long straight handles so that they will fit into the tube-like holders that come with most downriggers. For fishermen just getting into downrigging, Guffey recommends using low-priced fiberglass flippin' sticks. "When trolling, you don't need the sensitivity of graphite or boron," he says.

The rods are equipped with baitcasting reels. You can use spinning rods with downriggers, but their biggest disadvantage is that it isn't easy to spool line off a spinning reel as you lower the weight into the water with the line attached to it.

Putting a lure down on a downrigger sounds more complicated than it really is. With electric-powered downriggers, Charlie Guffey can put three downriggers in the water and be working on a fourth downrigger in less than three minutes. When putting out downriggers by himself, Charlie Guffey has a cord that he attaches to his steering wheel and the console to keep the boat running straight until all the lines are down.

On Guffey's boat, there are four downriggers mounted across the stern. The two inside downriggers are mounted on a solid base and are pointed directly behind the boat. The two outside downriggers have an adjustable swivel base and when they are in use, Guffey swings them out over the side of the boat with the rods positioned perpendicular to the boat as he trolls.

When using downriggers, Charlie Guffey usually trolls one and one-half to two miles per hour. He monitors his speed by the speedometer built into his graph recorder. "I've noticed that some lakes seem to have a favorite speed at which just about everybody trolls," Charlie Guffey laughs. "I don't know why."

The one and one-half to two miles per hour range seems to work well for Guffey and that is why he normally stays within that range. When trolling a crankbait with a long lip, Guffey will lower the lure into the water on a short line behind the downrigger weight and watch the lure as it runs behind the downrigger weight near the boat. He can then note his boat speed and decide at what speed a certain crankbait performs best. Then, when he is running the lure seventy-five to one hundred feet behind the boat, he will keep his speed in the range where the lure runs best.

THE VARIABLES

Charlie Guffey recommends a seven- to eight-pound weight as a good all-around size to start downrigging for stripers. He uses a variety of different shaped weighs, including some homemade weights, but his favorite is an aspirin, or as he calls it, a "bean-shaped" weight with a fin on the back of it.

Guffey recommends that you stay with the same size weight until you learn how that weight performs as you troll it at a variety of different depths with a number of different types of lures. Once you know how that weight reacts, then you can experiment with another size weight if you choose.

The advantage of a seven- to eight-pound weight is that it generally performs well with a variety of different types of striper lures when trolling at different speeds in water from ten feet to sixty feet deep.

"A one-pound weight will quickly sink to the bottom in a hundred feet of water if the boat is just sitting still," Charlie Guffey explains. "The reason for different size weights is that as you increase your forward boat speed, the drag or resistance created by the water as you troll will push a cable with a three-pound weight further toward the surface than an eight-pound weight under the same circumstances."

The deeper you run the lure, the more resistance, because there is more cable in the water to create drag. So, when choosing the proper size weight, you need to consider the speed you want to troll and the depth you are going to set the lure.

The length of line that you run between the line release mechanism and the lure also affects the depth of your lure.

For example, as mentioned earlier, if you cast out one hundred feet of line behind the boat before you attach the line to the line release mechanism, then when you lower the weight into the water the lure will have one hundred feet of line between it and the weight. If your lure is a bucktail jig, then the jig will sink a little deeper than the actual downrigger weight itself. The additional depth that it sinks will, of course, depend on the weight of the jig and the rate of speed that you troll.

Regardless of the weight of the jig and rate of speed at which you troll, you can increase or decrease the additional depth that the jig sinks by shortening or lengthening the amount of line that you troll behind the downrigging weight.

The same principle holds true for a crankbait. A crankbait with a diving bill will run deeper than the downrigger weight, because it is designed to dig into the water and dive. The depth that the crankbait dives will depend on the length of line that you have for it to dive on. (Just like when trolling without a downrigger, a crankbait will dive deeper if you put out more line.) The length of the crankbait's bill also determines how much additional depth that it will obtain.

When trolling a crankbait with a downrigger, consider the level where you have lowered the downrigger weight as the surface for purposes of calculating the depth that the crankbait will dive. If the crankbait is designed to dive six to ten feet deep when you crank it back from the surface, then the crankbait will dive six to ten feet below the level where you sunk it with the downrigger.

THE LURES

Charlie Guffey's favorite lure for downrigging is a bucktail jig. He uses four different sizes: one-fourth, one-half, five-eighths, and three-fourths ounce. The size that he chooses depends on how deep he wants to troll. Normally when trolling a jig, Guffey runs the lure behind the downrigger weight approximately one hundred to one hundred-twenty-five feet.

He likes to use a jig with a longer bucktail dressing in the summer, and a short bucktail in the fall.

Guffey uses a white bucktail the majority of the time, because he has found that stripers usually prefer a white jig over other colors. He does, however, vary the color of the jig head. From his fishing experiences, Guffey has discovered that whether or not the jig head is red, pink, green or white makes the difference sometimes between catching stripers or not.

"If I put four downriggers out, I may put four white bucktail jigs on them, but the color of the jig heads will vary," Guffey says. "Then, if I start catching most of my fish on a white jig with a green head, I will put green-headed jigs on all the rods."

Charlie Guffey often dresses up a jig with a plastic grub or worm. The trailer adds more action as well as size to a jig. His favorite colors for a trailer are chartreuse, white, red and yellow.

Another lure that Guffey catches a lot of stripers on when downrigging is a jig with a small spinner mounted underneath the jig head. Guffey makes his own, but the lure is sold commercially under several brand names including Roadrunners, Stump Jumpers and Pony Heads. Guffey uses the one-half, five-eighths, and three-fourths ounce sizes when trolling, and the lures that he makes have an extra-strong hook in them.

He uses the same kind and colors of trailers on the Roadrunner type jig as he does on a regular jig.

Charlie Guffey trolls jigs the majority of the time, because they are inexpensive, don't hang up a readily as many other types of lures and once you hook a striper on the single hook of a jig, fewer fish get off as compared to a treble-hook lure.

When stripers aren't interested in jigs, Guffey will troll the same swimming-minnow type lures that he used for topwater fishing in the spring or crankbaits with short-to-medium-length bills which dive six to eight feet. With a swimming-minnow type lure, you don't have to be concerned too much with the additional depth that it dives, because it only dives one to three feet deep. But when trolling a deeper-diving crankbait, you need to compensate for the additional depth that the lure dives below the downrigger weight when deciding how deep to set the weight.

TROLLING TECHNIQUES

Trolling with downriggers is a method that produces stripers on a year-round basis, but it seems to be the most productive during the late summer and early fall when the warm water temperatures of July and August have driven stripers into deeper water. Guffey often finds the top of the thermocline in thirty-five to thirty-eight feet of water by late summer, and stripers will situate themselves near the top of the temperature change. When fishing during that time period, Guffey will adjust the depth of the downrigger weight to keep his lure at or above the depth where he sees stripers on his depth finder.

If he is trolling a downrigger and the thermocline, for example, is thirty to forty feet deep, Charlie Guffey will make a trolling pass as close to the bank as he can and still keep his boat over thirty to forty feet of water. The lure will be traveling near the underwater contours of the bottom which are situated in the cooler water of the thermocline.

If that trolling pass is unsuccessful, he will move off shore approximately one hundred to two hundred yards and make another trolling pass in deeper water as he looks for schools of suspended shad. If that pass is still unsuccessful, Guffey moves another one hundred to two hundred yards off shore and makes a final pass before moving on.

"On Lake Cumberland, which is a mountain lake, there is plenty of deep water near the banks, so I can start trolling underwater contours near shore and still be in water deep enough to attract stripers in the summer. If you are trolling a flatter, shallower lake, you may need to start trolling near the old submerged river channel which may be a mile out in the lake," Charlie Guffey says.

The reason that Guffey starts near the bank and works

his way progressively further from the shoreline is that on a mountain lake he has found that shad often make a horizontal migration instead of a vertical migration. For instance, if he locates huge schools of shad in thirty feet of water over a sunken bar that runs out from the bank for a hundred yards, and he catches several stripers from the place, Guffey may go back the next day and not get a bite. His video screen may show that there aren't any shad near the bar.

Why the baitfish decide to move, especially when weather conditions remain stable, is something that Guffey is not sure of, but he thinks that it may be caused by the free-floating plankton, that shad feed on, drifting away from an area. When the above described situation occurs, Guffey moves his boat a hundred yards or so offshore from the bar and starts trolling while searching for suspended baitfish. Instead of the shad moving deeper or shallower over structure situated in the thermocline, schools of shad remain at the same depth as the day before, but the fish situate further from shore and suspend over deeper water. Of course, the stripers follow them, and the fish that you caught trolling over the bar yesterday can be caught trolling over schools of suspended shad today.

"The vast majority of stripers that I catch while trolling with downriggers, I never see. I just spot schools of baitfish suspended over deep water and when I troll through them, a striper will hit," Charlie Guffey says. "I have noticed that the tighter that the baitfish are schooled up, the better the fishing."

On some days, even on some of the nation's best striper lakes, you won't spot anything, including baitfish, on your depth finder or video screen. As Charlie Guffey says, "It looks like the whole lake is sterile." When that happens, you can bet that the fishing is going to be extra tough.

In that situation, Guffey puts a banana-shaped weight on the end of the cable because it hangs up less and lowers the weight to the bottom. He trolls the contours along the bottom that are located in the thermocline band in order to catch stripers holding tight to the bottom. The technique has paid off several times for Guffey in striper tournaments when the fish seem to disappear from an area.

"You'll hang up the weight when you troll it near the bottom, because there will be humps and bars that jut up from the bottom, and the weight will snag on them occasionally," Guffey says. "But when fishing is tough, dragging a downrigger near the bottom will catch inactive stripers."

In the fall and early winter, Charlie Guffey likes to troll in major feeder creeks. He will motor up a creek until he notices a change in the tint of the water. When he sees that, he puts the downriggers down and starts trolling up the creek, because he has found that when the water clarity decreases, then it won't be long until he starts seeing schools of shad on his video screen.

In a creek that is four hundred to five hundred yards wide, he will troll a zig-zag pattern back and forth across the creek to cover as much water as possible. If he locates several schools of baitfish concentrated in an area, Guffey will troll in a wide circle through the schools of baitfish numerous times as he tries to elicit a strike from any stripers tracking the schools. When he is trolling circles through baitfish in a relatively small area, Guffey will shorten the length of line between the weight and the lure down to fifty to sixty feet on each rod in order to keep the lures from getting tangled during the close turns.

Even when stripers are in ten to fifteen feet of water, where a lure trolled on a flat (unweighted) line could reach the fish, Guffey still often prefers to use a downrigger. The reason is that he can drop a lure down at fifteen feet using a down-rigger and put less line out to get it down. Because of that fact, he can make tighter turns as he trolls a particular piece of structure without the lines tangling or running off course.

"When trolling in less than fifteen feet of water, you need to troll a long line and run an irregular route to reduce the number of stripers that you spook," Charlie Guffey says.

When the water cools in late fall and early winter, there are often numerous schools of stripers at a variety of different depths because the water temperature is suitable for the fish from top to bottom. If the water is clear, which it usually is in most striper lakes, Charlie Guffey says down riggers are still important, because you can troll your lures deeper.

"In clear water, you often have to catch your stripers deep even when there are fish in shallower water," Charlie Guffey says. "The reason is that you will often spook the stripers in shallow water as you troll over them, so you are better off to concentrate on the slightly deeper fish."

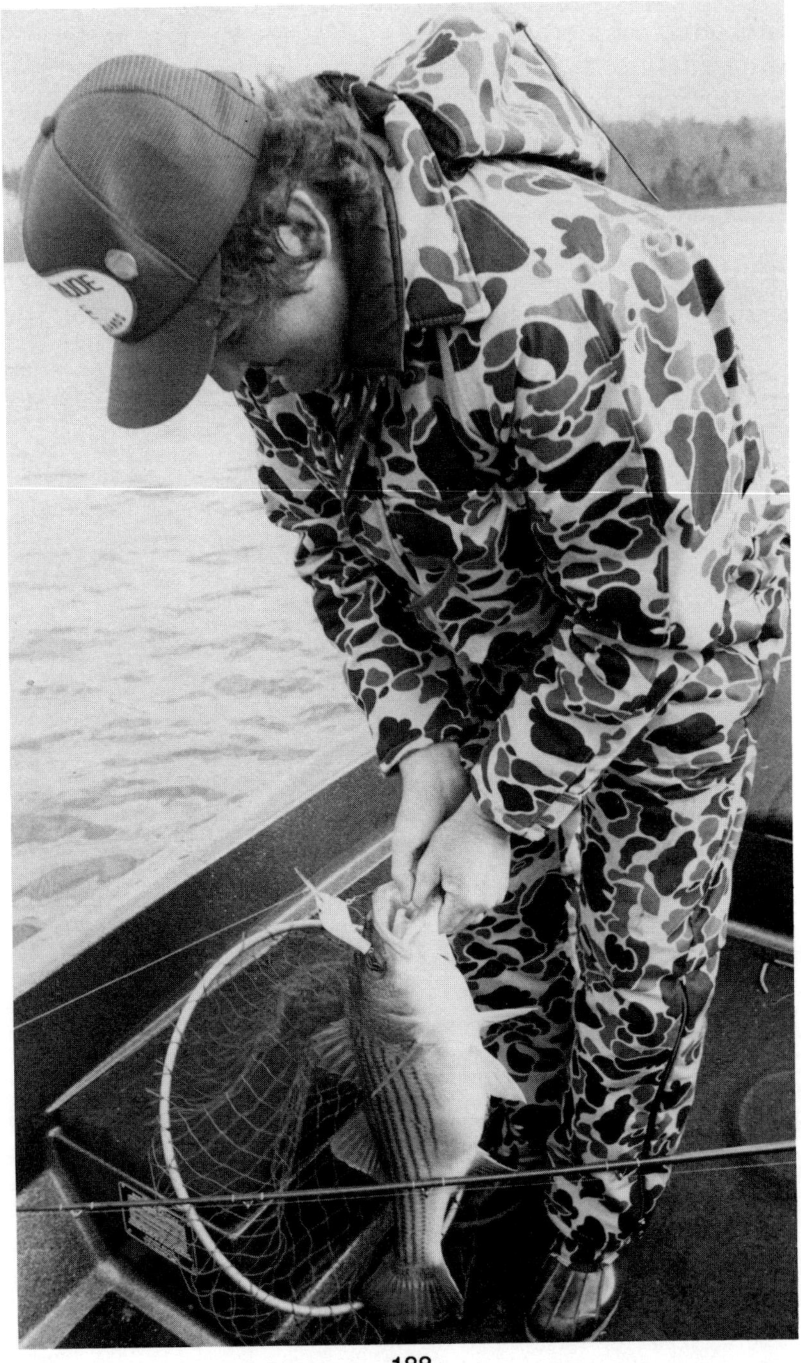

Chapter 13
CULINARY SKILLS

Since stripers have only been introduced to freshwater in most areas of the country during the past fifteen to twenty years, many experienced anglers, who traditionally have caught bass, bluegills, crappies and catfish, are unaware that a striper makes excellent table fare. In fact, some fishermen, who have accidentally caught a striper while fishing for other species, have cooked the striper and ended up believing that it is not a good tasting fish. This misconception is usually the result of the fisherman cleaning and cooking the fillets of a twenty-pound striper in the same manner that he cleans and cooks the fillets of a crappie or bass.

A striper or hybrid can be filleted in the same manner that you fillet any other fish. But after you remove the fillets, it is imperative that you trim away all the dark red meat. There are usually several streaks of dark meat running through the lighter-colored fillet of a striper.

Do not be conservative when trimming up a fillet. It is better to end up with several smaller pieces of fish that taste delicious than to have a huge fillet that tastes strong and fishy, because you were too frugal to cut out all of the dark meat.

After you remove the dark meat from the fillets, you should soak them overnight in a solution of water and lemon juice. Use a plastic bowl and cover it with an airtight lid or plastic wrap to keep out the air. After a night of soaking, the fillets will be as "white as chalk" to quote Robbie Bell of Monticello, Kentucky, who in 1986 held the Kentucky State record with a fifty-eight-pound striper. His record held up for only a year.

Once the fillets have been properly cleaned, the best

time to cook them is right away. Fish never taste better than when fresh from the water.

If you have had a particularly successful striper fishing trip and find yourself staring at fifteen pounds of striper fillets, you will probably want to freeze some of the fillets to cook later. The best way to protect the taste of fillets is to submerge them in water and freeze the fillets in the water. Plastic zip-loc freezer bags or plastic containers with snap-on lids, both, make freezing fillets in water an easy task.

Whether you are preparing fresh or frozen striper or hybrid fillets, there are a variety of ways to cook the fish in order to enjoy some of the best tasting fish now swimming in freshwater. Try the following recipes in order to avoid "burning" your family and friends out on fish.

RECIPES

The following dip was created by Jim Wilson, who is a co-owner of Lakeview Dock on Norris Lake. Living on one of the top striper lakes in the country, Jim quickly learned several ways to enjoy the delicious taste of striper fillets. He has been known to smoke several pounds of fillets before Christmas in order to prepare a number of helpings of his smoked rockfish (as a striper is called in East Tennessee) dip. He then puts the great tasting dip in small crocks and gives them to close friends for Christmas gifts.

SMOKED ROCKFISH DIP

1-1/2 cups of smoked rockfish fillets, flaked
6 ounces cream cheese
1 clove garlic, finely minced
3 tablespoons minced onions
1/4 teaspoon salt
2 tablespoons Worchestershire sauce
1 tablespoon lemon juice

Mash smoked fish with cheese and mix in seasonings. Chill for several hours to give flavors time to blend. Use as a dip for crackers, potato chips or corn chips. Makes about 2-1/4 cups.

Here is another unique Jim Wilson recipe that is simple to make, but will have your neighbors raving when they sample it. It makes a great party dish.

SMOKED ROCKFISH MOUSSE

1 envelope unflavored gelatin
1 cup milk
16 ounces of smoked rockfish fillets, flaked
1 cup sour cream
1/3 cup Dijon mustard
1 envelope Italian salad dressing mix
2 tablespoons dillweed (preferably fresh)
2 tablespoons lemon juice

Combine gelatin and milk in small saucepan. Cook and stir over low heat until gelatin is dissolved. Place remaining ingredients in food processor and process until smooth. With processor running, pour in gelatin mixture. Pour into 3-cup mold or bowl. Chill until firm, serve with cucumber slices or crackers if desired. Makes 3 cups.

One last Jim Wilson recipe that everyone will love, especially the kids.

PAN-FRIED ROCKFISH

Cut fillets horizontally into strips 2 to 3 inches wide. Combine 2 cups buttermilk, one beaten egg, and 2 teaspoons soy sauce in a bowl large enough to contain fillets. Soak fillets approximately 30 minutes. Combine 2 parts cracker meal, one part corn meal, seasoned salt and pepper in a plastic bag. Shake fillets to coat and pan fry in modest amount of hot oil. Turn once, until golden brown—enjoy.

For anglers watching their cholesterol intake and/or calories, try the following alternative to fried fish and taters.

NEW ORLEANS STRIPER BAKE

2 pounds striper fillets or steaks
1/2 teaspoon salt or salt substitute
dash pepper
2 cups cooked rice
2 tablespoons grated onion
1/2 teaspoon curry powder
6 lemon slices
1/4 cup margarine
Chopped parsley, as desired

Cut fillets or steaks into serving-size portions and place in a well greased baking dish, about 10 by 14 inches in size. Sprinkle fish with salt and pepper. Combine rice, onion, and curry powder and spread mixture over fish. Top with lemon slice and dot with margarine. Cover dish and place in a moderate oven, about 350° F., for 25 to 35 minutes, or until fish flakes easily when fork tested. Remove the baking dish cover for the last few minutes of cooking to allow for a light browning of fish. Sprinkle with chopped parsley and serve. Serves 6.

Cajun cooking has become very popular around the country as city folks have discovered what Louisiana coon asses have known for over a hundred years—Cajun cooking is good! The following recipe was supplied by Eason Mitchell. The fishermen around Louisiana's Toledo Bend Reservoir have hauled a lot of stripers out of that lake and used Cajun cookin' know-how to prepare many memorable fish fries.

CAJUN STRIPER

Striper fillets for 8
16 ounces crabmeat
2 bunches green onions
1/2 cup fresh mushrooms
2 cups milk
1 egg
bread crumbs
flour
margarine
Cajun seasoning

First, prepare the fish by soaking the fillets in the egg and milk. Sprinkle lightly with flour, roll in bread crumbs and fry until golden brown. Saute´ chopped onions in margarine (tops and all) until translucent. Add sliced mushrooms and once the mushrooms are done, add crabmeat. Season the topping with Cajun Seasoning. The trick to the right amount of seasoning is to add seasoning until the crabmeat topping is properly salted

For striper chasers out in Texas and Oklahoma who love good barbecue, try this recipe and you will quit barbecuing cows.

BARBECUED FISH FILLETS

2 pounds fish fillets, fresh or frozen
1/4 cup chopped onion
2 tablespoons chopped green pepper
1 garlic clove, finely chopped
2 tablespoons melted butter or cooking oil
1 (8 ounce) can tomato sauce
2 tablespoons lemon juice
1 tablespoon worchestershire sauce
1 tablespoon sugar
2 teaspoons salt
1/4 teaspoon pepper

Cook the onion, green pepper, and garlic in butter or cooking oil until tender. Add the remaining ingredients and simmer for 5 minutes, stirring occasionally. Let the mixture cool. Cut the fish into serving portions and place the pieces in a single layer in a shallow baking dish. Pour the sauce mixture over the fish and let it stand for 30 minutes, turning the fish once. Remove the fish and reserve the sauce for basting.

Place the fish in a well-greased, hinged, wire grill, or grills. Place the fish about 4 inches from moderately hot coals and cook for 5 to 8 minutes. Baste with sauce. Then turn and cook the other side for 5 to 8 minutes, or until the fish flakes easily when fork tested. 6 servings

Striper and hybrid fishermen spend a lot of time on the lakes and rivers during extremely cold weather. Some of the heaviest stripers are caught when the weather is at its worst. To warm up after a day or night of fishing during the late fall, winter and early spring, fix the following stew which takes less than an hour to prepare.

STRIPER FISHERMAN'S STEW

2 pounds fish fillets
1-1/2 cups sliced celery
1/2 cup chopped onion
1 garlic clove, minced
1/4 cup butter or margarine
1 (28 oz.) can tomatoes
1 (8 oz.) can tomato sauce
2 teaspoons salt
dash of sugar
1/2 teaspoon paprika
1/2 teaspoon chili powder
1/4 teaspoon pepper
1 (7 oz.) package spaghetti, uncooked
2 cups boiling water
1/4 cup grated parmesan cheese

Cut fillets into 1-inch chunks. Cook celery, onion, and garlic in butter or margarine in large, heavy pan until tender. Add tomatoes, tomato sauce and seasonings. Bring to a simmer. Cover and cook slowly for 15 to 20 minutes. Add uncooked spaghetti and boiling water. Mix and cover pan. Cook slowly about 10 minutes or until spaghetti is almost tender. Add fish, cover and cook slowly for another 10 minutes, or until fish flakes easily when fork tested. Serve hot with cheese sprinkled over the top. Serves 6.

When you want to prepare an extra special dinner for guests, try this recipe. Once you put it in the oven, you can sit down and visit with your company until dinner is ready.

BAKED ROCKFISH WITH SPINACH
1 rockfish 3 to 4 pounds, dressed
2-1/2 teaspoons salt
1-1/2 cups celery, thinly sliced
1/4 cup green onions, sliced
1/2 cup butter or margarine, melted
4 cups soft bread cubes
4 cups spinach leaves, washed
1 tablespoon lemon juice
1/4 teaspoon pepper

Clean, wash, and dry fish. Sprinkle inside and outside with one and a half teaspoons of salt. Cook celery and green onions in 6 tablespoons of butter or margarine until celery is tender. Stir in bread cubes and spinach leaves. Cook and stir until spinach is tender. Add lemon juice, remaining 1 teaspoon of salt and pepper, toss lightly. Stuff fish loosely and close opening with small skewers. Place fish in a well-greased baking pan. Brush with remaining butter or margarine. Bake in a moderate oven, 350° F. for 40 to 60 minutes, or until fish flakes easily when tested with a fork. Serves 6 to 8.

Try this recipe when the green peppers ripen in your garden.

GREEN PEPPERS STUFFED WITH FISH

2 pounds fish fillets
6 large green peppers
3 tablespoons chopped onion
1/4 cup chopped celery
6 tablespoons diced bacon
1/4 cup chili sauce
1 teaspoon salt
dash pepper
2 tablespoons butter or margarine
1/2 cup dry bread crumbs

Skin fish fillets and cut into 1/2 inch pieces. Cut a thin slice from the top of each green pepper and remove the seeds. Simmer peppers in boiling salted water for 10 to 12 minutes, or until almost tender. Drain. Fry bacon until crisp, then add onions, celery, chili sauce, seasonings, and fish. Simmer about 10 minutes or until fish flakes easily when fork tested. Fill peppers with fish mixture. Combine butter and crumbs and sprinkle over top of peppers. Place stuffed peppers in a well-greased baking pan and bake in a moderate oven, at 350° for 20 to 25 minutes. Garnish and serve hot. Serves 6.

For striper and hybrid anglers who love fish anytime, the following recipe from overseas will surely be a favorite. The recipe is great to fix after you conclude your early morning topwater fishing, which as most striper fishermen know usually lasts from daylight to about 9 a.m.

SCOTTISH FRIED BREAKFAST FISH

4 striper fillets   2 ounces bacon grease
1/2 pint milk   Salt as desired
1 cup coarse oatmeal   Pepper as desired

Salt and pepper the fillets the night before and refrigerate them. In the morning, dip the fish in milk, then roll them in the oatmeal.

Fry the fish in bacon grease for four or five minutes on each side until they are brown and the flesh flakes easily. Drain on paper towels. Serve the fish hot with a little butter on the side, sliced lemon and poached eggs. Serves 2.

POOR MAN'S SHRIMP

A very simple but tasty way to prepare striper is to cut a fillet into smaller strips about the size of a bluegill fillet. Add a little salt to a pan of water and bring it to a boil. Drop the strips of fish into the boiling water and cook them for two to three minutes. The strips of fish will quickly curl up and turn whiter in the boiling water. It does not take long to cook the mini-fillets. So be sure and get them out before the fish overcooks and gets tough.

When you remove the fillets from the water, immediately dunk the fish in a bowl of ice water which you have prepared beforehand. The cold water will chill the strips of fish so that the meat stays firm.

Leave a fillet in the ice water for only a few minutes so that it does not get water soaked. As soon as a strip cools, remove it from the water and pat it dry with a paper towel.

Roll each of the small strips of fish up and stick a toothpick through it. The fish is now ready to be dipped into some shrimp sauce and enjoyed.

The first time that I ever had striper prepared this way was at the home of Danny Bell, the owner of Bell's Marina, one of the most well known full-service marinas on Santee Cooper. Bell was entertaining a group of outdoor writers, and the trays of boiled striper fillets quickly disappeared.

If you really want to impress your company, try the following recipe, which is in a similar vein to the above recipe, but is a whole lot more involved. Just be sure you enjoy the company, because after you feed them this they may not go home.

FISH ROLL-UPS IN SHRIMP SAUCE

2 pounds fish fillets
1/2 cup celery, thinly sliced
2 tablespoons green onions, sliced
1/3 cup butter or margarine
2 cups soft bread crumbs
1/4 teaspoon tarragon leaves
1-1/4 teaspoon salt
1/8 teaspoon white pepper
1/4 cup dry white wine
2 tablespoons flour
1 cup "half and half" (milk and cream)
1 egg yolk, beaten
1 cup cooked shrimp
1 teaspoon lemon juice

Saute´ celery and onion in 2 tablespoons butter or margarine until tender, but not browned. Stir in bread crumbs, tarragon leaves, 1/4 teaspoon salt, and pepper. Divide fillets into serving portions and sprinkle fillets with 3/4 teaspoon of salt. Cover each fillet with an equal amount of bread mixture. Then roll fillets and secure with wooden toothpicks or metal skewers.

Place rolled fillets in a shallow baking dish and drizzle with wine and 2 tablespoons of melted butter or margarine. Bake in a moderate oven at 350° F. for about 25 minutes, or until the fish flakes easily when fork tested. Baste with pan juices several times during cooking. Pour shrimp sauce over roll-ups and serve.

SHRIMP SAUCE

Melt remaining butter or margarine in small saucepan; blend in flour and remaining 1/4 teaspoon of salt. Stir in cream-milk mixture (or fresh milk); cook, stirring constantly, until thick and smooth. Fold a small amount of hot mixture into egg yolk, then stir egg yolk mixture into remaining sauce. Add shrimp, lemon juice, and pan juices to sauce, blending carefully. Heat to serving temperature before pouring over fish.

Chapter 14
STRIPER SAVVY

As a striper guide for the past seventeen years and editor of *Trophy Striped Bass* magazine, Steve Baker has been asked a lot of questions concerning striper and hybrid fishing. Many of the questions he has taken the time to write down, so that other anglers could also learn from the answers. Following are some of the questions and answers that have proven to be beneficial to many anglers around the country.

Q. What size cast net is best for catching live bait?

A. That is a complicated question. Live bait is captured dozens of different ways across the country. Water depth, water clarity and the size of the bait are three major factors in choosing a net size to fit your needs. Common sense will tell you that the bigger the net, the more bait you will catch, but only if you are able to open the net to its full capacity. When shad or herring are in deep water, try an eight-foot Betts Super Pro cast net which has extra weights and a three-quarter-inch mesh size. Because of its ability to sink fast, the net is ideal for catching bait in clear, deep water. When catching shad or herring in swift water below a powerhouse, I prefer a lighter-weight six- or seven-foot net with a three-eighths- or one-half-inch mesh size. A heavy net will get you in serious trouble in swift water. The shallow water and unpredictable currents can hang a fast-sinking net on the bottom and possibly pull you overboard into the fast water. Always be sure and keep a knife handy to cut the draw rope from your wrist.

To catch trophy stripers on a consistent basis, an angler must be versatile in his fishing approach.

Q. What is the best method for taking a trophy-size striper in the fall months?

A. Many heavy-weight stripers and hybrids are taken in the cool months of fall and early winter using several different methods. Surface-feeding fish can be taken on minnow type lures. A bucktail jig fished underneath surface-feeding stripers will sometimes catch the bigger and slightly lazier fish that wait for an easy meal. Live bait fished on a free line forty to fifty yards behind the boat is deadly on shallow-feeding fish as the water cools off. This can be an exciting style of fishing as the bigger stripers will often chase the bait to the surface before inhaling the bait with an explosive strike similar to topwater lure action. Down-rigging will also produce nice fish in the fall. In most cases, experimenting with different sizes and colors of lures is necessary.

Q. Which style and size hook works better for stripers when live bait fishing?

A. There are several good brands of hooks on the market. Eagle Claw has a new hook with an extra bend to one side that will improve the percentage of hook-ups drastically. The hook is labelled a style 42 and is available in two choices. The Lazer Sharp 42 is a smaller diameter hook and has been honed to a fine edge for maximum sharpness. The regular style 42 is a heavier diameter hook and is a better choice when the big stripers are on the warpath. The most important factor is hook size. Always match your hook size to the size bait you intend to use. I have found that bait from two to four inches long will require a 1/0 or a 2/0 hook. For bait in the four to seven-inch size range, use a 3/0 hook and bait seven inches or longer requires a 4/0 hook.

Q. Under normal conditions, how long does it take a striper to reach a trophy size, let's say thirty pounds?

A. A striper will usually grow at an average of two and one-half to four pounds per year under normal conditions. Their growth rate depends on the quality of the water and the abundance of baitfish. I disagree with the theory that stripers eat their weight in baitfish every day. Ninety percent of the time when I have taken a trophy-size fish and examined the stomach contents, I have found only one very large shad or nothing. Stripers will grow a little faster in the areas below powerhouses where bait is extremely plentiful. Most of these fish will have short and extremely healthy bodies due to the heavy feeding and fast growth rate. The growth rate will vary in almost every lake. I caught a forty-two pound striper on Norris Lake in Tennessee that a biologist aged at sixteen years old. However, while on a trip to Lake Seminole in Georgia, a biologist that I know checked a forty-four pound striper caught in that lake and found it to be only seven years old.

Q. What period during the fall months are topwater lures effective for hybrids and stripers?

A. Topwater action in the fall will usually pick up when the surface temperature drops below sixty degrees. The time this occurs will vary in different parts of the country due to different weather patterns. In most cases, November and December will be perfect months for topwater action. Always watch for any sea gull activity to help locate a school of surface feeding stripers. Be very observant of any surface activity. Many times, I have noticed one small minnow racing across the surface in a frantic manner and have cast a topwater lure to that area and have gotten an instant strike from a feeding striper.

Q. When fishing live bait, is there any way to keep the hook from turning and foul hooking the bait in the head?

A. That is a problem that every live-bait fisherman

faces. As a shad or herring is swimming along on the end of your line, the hook will sometimes turn sideways and slightly penetrate the bait's head. If a hybrid or striper strikes the bait, the hook will simply bury up in the bait and not the mouth of the striper or hybrid. I have experimented with several ways to prevent this. A way to help, but not completely solve the matter, is to pinch off a small section of plastic worm and slide it onto the hook. Then hook the bait through both lips and slide another piece of worm past the barb and snug against the baitfish to prevent the bait from working up and down on the shank of the hook. I have also cut one-fourth inch circles out of a plastic milk carton then went through the same procedure. This works better, but the plastic must be cut off the hook every time a new bait is used.

Q. What time of the year is the most productive for catching a trophy size striper?

A. There are two periods of the year that consistently produce the biggest stripers. The last two weeks of March through the entire month of April is the first period. The last two weeks of June through the entire month of July being the second period. The early spring months find the big females heavy with roe and the male fish carrying an additional ten percent of body weight due to heavy sperm sacks. In the early summer months of June and July, the bigger fish will have replaced the weight that they lost from the false spawning activities of spring by extra heavy feeding activities. This can be an excellent time to put a trophy on your wall.

Q. What types of structure are the most productive for larger trophy-size stripers during the early spring months?

A. One of the most important factors that influences productive areas in the spring is the number of fishermen on the lake. Stripers are very wary, especially when feeding shallow in the early spring. The type of structure that comes to mind first, especially when casting topwater lures, is deep points running directly into the river channel. These areas are often productive, but unfortunately a good looking point is often fished numerous times by different anglers in the course of one morning or afternoon. When this occurs, stripers will often shy away from these particular areas because of continuous disturbance. I seem to catch most of my larger fish on areas overlooked by other anglers. Underwater humps that are twenty feet deep or less on top and are near deep water will consistently produce larger fish. Rough, rocky or stumpy bottom cover on the humps will give baitfish a hiding place. The baitfish in turn attract stripers. Secondary points located in large feeder creeks are often good because they don't receive a lot of disturbance. Any secondary point can hold stripers as long as the point leads into deeper water. Both live bait and topwater lures are productive on the points.

Q. What is your favorite bait in the month of April?

A. Topwater baits would have a slight edge over other lures in the month of April. The secret to the success of a good topwater man is not only the color of the lure that he fishes and the types of topwater lures that he uses, but also his ability to read the changing weather patterns to take advantage of the feeding frenzies triggered by incoming weather fronts.

Q. What sections of the lake are stripers holding in April and early May?

A. I have found in the months of April and May that stripers of all sizes will be scattered over the entire lake. The mouths of feeder creeks are excellent areas to concentrate your casting. Shallow humps and sand bars in the main body of the lake are also good. This is a time of year when stripers are probably the easiest to locate. I have caught a limit of good fish one morning in the upper reaches of the headwaters, and turned around the next day and caught a limit within sight of the dam on the lower end of the lake.

Q. Do all stripers make a migratory spawning run up the headwaters of the lake during the spring?

A. Many stripers will travel up the narrow river area of a reservoir, mainly because of current and an abundance of baitfish. Even though many fish will be taken from the river area, a couple of important factors are often overlooked by most anglers. Stripers in one sense are like the whitetail deer, during the rutting season, not all does are in heat at the same time. When the spawning season begins in the spring, all the stripers will not venture up the river at the same time. This information can be used to an angler's benefit. The headwater areas often draw a lot of boat traffic and competition that leaves the mid-section of the lake less crowded, but sometimes full of feeding stripers. The headwater areas are better during the week because of less boat traffic. I have found the mid-section of a lake will produce fish throughout the entire spring as stripers work their way up and down the lake. Almost all reservoirs contains several long, winding feeder creeks. The creeks warm faster than the main lake which draws an abundance of baitfish into the creeks. Many creeks will have a slight current that attracts stripers with spawning on their minds. Only about a half dozen lakes in the country support natural striper reproduction, but the natural instincts of these fish push them toward river and creek areas in the spring.

Q. What type of weather do you prefer for a spring striper outing?

A. During the spring months, the weather plays a more important role than at any other time of the year. The rise and fall of the barometer is a big factor in how successful a day will be when chasing stripers. You should keep a close watch on the weather, whether it be from the TV or radio, and listen for a report of an incoming front. The best fishing is when a period of mild, stable weather is interrupted by a falling barometer, incoming clouds, winds and rain. This may sound like a miserable time to be on the water, but these fronts can trigger stripers into a feeding spree like you have never seen. The timing is critical. It is a must to make the most of the changing weather, which is usually twelve to twenty-four hours before the arrival of the front. As the front passes, there will be falling temperatures and bright blue skies, which are a total disaster for striper fishing in the months of April and May.

Q. How is live bait fishing in April and May?

A. Live bait can be an excellent choice during the spring months. Due to the cold water temperature, most stripers are holding relatively shallow this time of year, usually less than twenty feet, unless a cold front has just passed through. Graphing fish in shallow water with the big engine running can be a fruitless task even for an experienced fisherman. The engine noise will frighten the fish away from the path you are graphing. The best way to fish live bait this time of year is simply trial and error. If you have a good place in mind, fish it before you idle around trying to locate the fish on your graph. I always prefer to fish a free line, which is simply a baitfish with no weight added, which I trail approximately forty to sixty yards behind the boat. The baitfish swims naturally and is great for attracting shallow-holding stripers. I've caught many fish over forty pounds with this method in the spring months.

Q. What type of live bait is best in the spring?

A. I prefer shad over any other type of live bait. On rare occasions, bluegills will outfish shad. But nine times out of ten, shad will not only catch more stripers, but also the largest stripers. I always try to follow a rule that I made for myself many years ago. When fishing live bait, always fish a bait that is natural to that particular lake. If shad are present in your lake, try your best to catch your shad there, instead of transporting shad from areas where baitfish are much easier to obtain, such as below dams. A slight change in body shape or maybe a barely noticeable difference in color can make the difference between a trophy striper taking a shad or swimming on by it.

Q. What size line do you prefer when fishing topwater lures in the spring months?

A. I almost always use twenty-five pound test line. This might seem too heavy for some anglers, but in the spring months I hook a lot of big fish in shallow water around points and underwater humps. Most of these areas will have either rocks or stumps nearby for a big striper to run into. Even though not aerobatic like a largemouth, a striper when hooked in shallow water will run for cover in a desperate attempt to free itself. With the heavy line, you can simply steer the fish away from the cover that it is headed toward. The heavier line also will not abrade as quickly as smaller line when it comes into contact with the rough contours of the bottom. If you will stop and think, when topwater fishing the majority of the line does not touch the water. So, just as long as it does not affect your casting, the heavier the line the better.

Q. Is there any simple solution to dealing with stained water after spring rains?

A. Stained or muddy water in spring months is a common problem on many lakes around the nation. Stained water is particularly tough on topwater fish, because stripers depend primarily on their sight to hone in on a potential meal. The first alternative is to move to another section of the lake where the water is still clear. Stained water that moves in often forces stripers to clearer-water areas. Stained water usually flows from the headwaters down. So the lower end of the lake usually remains clear for a day or so after a heavy rain. By the time the stained water reaches the lower end much of the silt will have settled to the bottom, often keeping the water at a fishable color. If the entire lake is stained, cut bait fished in the same areas that produced fish before the rains is often the ticket. I have caught stripers on bone-colored topwater baits in stained water. Baits with a built-in rattle chamber can also be a plus. I've had better luck working a lure much slower in the stained water, allowing a striper to home in on the bait much easier.

Q. What do you think of striper tournaments?

A. I think striper tournaments are good in several ways. First of all, tournaments are a good way to broaden your knowledge of striper fishing by fishing different lakes and learning different methods used on those lakes. Tournaments are also useful to the game and fish departments, because they can actually see how the striper fishery in a particular lake is progressing by the amount of fish caught in a tournament. Biologists can obtain scale samples to determine the growth rate of the fish, plus other vital information to help preserve our growing striper population for years to come. Stripers are rapidly growing into one of America's top freshwater gamefish. It's time this exciting gamefish started getting the recognition that it deserves.

Q. How effective is cut bait in early spring?

A. The early spring months can be one of the most productive periods of the season for cut bait when using the proper methods. The first warm, spring rains will raise the surface temperature to a more desirable range, causing stripers to become very active and begin their rounds in search of food. One trick I use that seems to make a definite difference is to keep the bait alive and fresh until it is ready for the chopping block. The fresh blood of a shad or herring will draw feeding stripers like a magnet. I like shallow, sandy or gravel bottoms in the spring months, especially if the water has a little color. I seldom fish depths over twenty-five feet in the spring. Long, sloping points and flats near deep water are key areas to look for when using cut bait.

Q. Do you think different color lures make a difference in striper fishing?

A. Yes. Stripers are sometimes very wary, especially in clear water. In my seventeen years as a professional guide, I have seen color make the difference between a good day and an unsuccessful one. When guiding, I almost always have two customers in the boat, plus myself. At the beginning of each morning when using topwater lures, I rig each man's rod with the same lure, but in a different color. It often happens that a certain colored lure will out produce the other colors on a given day. When I see that pattern develop, I will change each man's lure to that color for the remainder of the day. Several factors will determine the best color for a particular day. Cloud cover, water clarity, and drastic temperature changes call for changing color patterns.

Q. In the early spring months, I continuously get numerous runs, but can't seem to put the fish in the boat. What am I doing wrong?

A. This is a problem that happens to every fisherman during the spring months. With the constant weather changes during the spring, stripers sometimes can't make up their minds whether to feed or not. What happens when fishing live bait is that a striper will grab the bait just behind the head and have the clicker singing on your reel. Many times, they will hold the bait for several seconds after you have set the hook, only to turn it loose. In reality, the striper never had the hook in its mouth. I have sometimes changed to a very small bait and turned the situation around. I have also tried adding a trailer hook in the bait's tail, but this seems to restrict a baitfish's natural movement and draws less attention. When using artificial lures in the spring, keep the hooks as sharp as possible. Think back on the times when you have hooked a striper in the head or tail in the spring months on artificial lures.

Q. What is the best method for producing a trophy-size striper in the spring?

A. I have two methods that I use when I am after a wall-hanging fish in the spring. An extremely large shad fished on a free line at least fifty yards behind the boat would be my number one choice for a big fish. When I say a big shad, I mean one at least twelve inches long. I have used bait up to fifteen inches long on certain occasions. When fishing very shallow water, a balloon works very well when tied six to ten feet above the shad. My second choice would be a swimming-minnow type topwater lure. I personally fish several different styles of topwater lures, but a swimming minnow will produce the bigger fish on most days. Always keep your eyes open for any surface activity from a very large fish. I have seen schools of big shad literally flip up on the bank in a desperate attempt to escape a big striper.

Q. What is the best way to keep shad alive?

A. My bait tank is forty gallons, and you will need to vary the amount of chemicals for more or less water. First of all, don't pour the chemicals into the tank directly. Mix all salt and chemicals up thoroughly in a clean bucket before pouring into holding tanks. For forty gallons, I use two pounds of rock salt, which is half a box. My chemicals come in two liter coke bottles, so I add three caps of Bait Saver and two caps of Foam Kill. More Foam Kill may be needed later.

Q. On certain days a striper will only boil at a topwater lure without being very aggressive. Is there a method to coax the fish into striking the bait?

A. I have found that by changing to a popper bait or a stick bait, you can sometimes entice a striper into taking the lure. I like to draw the fish's attention with a swimming-minnow type lure and then do a change-up and throw the popper or stick bait at it. If this doesn't work, try a white bucktail jig with a plastic twister-tail worm. A big shad on a free line will also catch stripers when the fish won't take an artificial lure.

Q. What is the best way to deal with a late spring cold front that always seems to turn feeding stripers off?

A. Cold fronts in late April or early May seem to occur every time you get on a good school of fish. If the fish were schooling on the surface and feeding on topwater lures, it seems all activity comes to a halt with a northwest wind. I have found that when fish have been feeding shallow on topwater lures or on free lines with live bait, the cold front will move the fish into deeper water during the daylight hours. Fish that were located on shallow structure in feeder creeks will move to deeper water areas, such as the bend of the old creek channel or a creek ledge. Weighted, live-bait rigs fished twenty-five to thirty feet deep will often produce. I have found that stripers will return to shallow water structure after dark for some reason. I like to fish the same shallow-water areas that were productive before the front, but get up on the banks and fish cut bait on shallow points and bars near deeper water. Stripers will hit the cut bait with a lot of aggressiveness and will literally yank the rods in the lake if they are not secured. Shallow-running crankbaits such as the Baby Mac will often produce when cast against the banks at night during a cold front. As soon as you begin to see surface activity again, your old methods will become productive again.

Q. How far away should I shut off my engine when approaching a school of surface-feeding stripers or hybrids?

A. When a big school of feeding stripers is sighted, it is hard not to run the boat up on the fish. However, a striper is one of the spookiest fish I have ever dealt with. Engine noise and boat wake will almost always put the fish down and sometimes drive them completely out of an area. A good rule of thumb I use is to never wash any waves into the feeding fish. It is hard to slowly idle toward a flock of screaming sea gulls when the water is flying four feet in the air as a school of big stripers attack baitfish, but it makes the difference in "catching 'em" and "not catching 'em."

Q. What are some good tips when searching for productive underwater structure during the summer months?

A. When looking over a contour map or simply riding around a particular lake graphing and searching for potential spots where stripers may hang out, remember one factor: stripers are an open-water fish. The only time they move up on most underwater structure is during a feeding period. The structure must be in an area that will attract baitfish. Before I begin searching for an area that supports baitfish and stripers, I check for a thermocline. In July and August, this underwater comfort zone will run around twenty-five to thirty feet deep. I always concentrate my efforts on structure where the high spots run at these depths. Stripers won't venture too far away from their deep, open-water homes in the hot summer months. I have found most productive types of structure will always be close to very deep water. My favorite types of structure are underwater high spots near the old river channel or the ledges on the old river channel itself. The sheer wall ledges on the outside bend of a river channel with a very rough bottom seem to produce better than a sandy or gravel bottom.

Q. Which type of live bait seems to produce trophy-size fish in the summer months?

A. I prefer large gizzard shad that are caught from the lake you are fishing. Some people think all gizzard shad are the same, but they are not. The native gizzards which come out of very clear water will have a golden tint to their color. Because they don't have to swim against any swift currents, the shad caught out of a lake will often have a chunkier body than shad taken in tailraces. Lake shad may be very difficult to catch, though, in the hot summer months on lakes where clear water is predominant. A large, heavy, cast net with one-half to three-fourths-inch mesh will better your chances of catching them.

Q. What are a few simple pointers for keeping shad alive in the hot summer periods?

A. Most striper anglers have found that shad and herring are terribly hard to keep alive. The most important factor in maintaining shad is water temperature. As the summer air temperatures warm the surface temperature, using water directly from the lake becomes a problem. In July and August, I like to maintain a sixty- to seventy-degree water temperature in my shad tank. Well or spring water can be a lifesaver, because it usually has a constant fifty-six-degree temperature. A good, insulated, shad tank is a must in maintaining a controlled water temperature. A round tank is preferred if you are carrying a big number of baits or if you are making an all-day trip. Don't overcrowd your tank. A thirty-gallon tank will hold four dozen six- to eight-inch shad with no problem. Ice can be added to cool the water in your tank, but remember to add a little extra Bait Saver to the water to kill the chlorine. A cup of rock salt and a tablespoon each of Bait Saver and Foam Kill should put you in business.

Q. Why do the game and fish agencies shy away from stocking stripers in shallow, flat lakes?

A. In most cases, shallow lakes across the country have stained or dingy water. The discolored water warms fast in the spring and maintains a high water temperature throughout the entire year. The oxygen level will usually become very low in the hot summer months, doubling the problems facing a striper. A striper cannot tolerate these problems, and in many cases will literally starve to death because the fish does not have the energy to feed. The hybrid, on the other hand, has inherited a few of a white bass' characteristics. Their bodies can tolerate much warmer water temperature and lower oxygen levels. Most fishermen don't understand why their lake doesn't receive the striper stockings that they would like, but it has been proven in several studies that stripers are fighting an uphill battle in a shallow, flat lake.

Q. What type of rod works best when live bait fishing in the summer?

A. I have experimented with different live-bait rods over the past several years. Most fishermen fail to observe the finicky feeding moods of the stripers and hybrids. On some days, a line tied to a broom handle would work perfectly when a big striper is inhaling a bait with vicious aggressiveness. On other days, the slightest resistance from a rod will send a striper in the opposite direction. In the past few years, I have gone to a medium-action rod with a good backbone and a soft tip. I always use a seven and one-half foot rod with live bait and also when casting artificials. I have found that by using a good, heavy-duty rod holder and locking the reel in gear, set with a medium drag and the clicker on to act only as an alarm, my percentage of hook-ups has increased dramatically. I never touch the rod until the second or third guide goes into the water. In most cases, the fish has already set the hook itself. A stiff, heavy-action rod will always be my first choice when casting topwater lures and jigs.

Q. I've heard loons (a diving water bird) can be very beneficial in locating a school of stripers. What do you think about this?

A. A loon is a large, dark-colored water bird that resembles a duck. The loon feeds primarily on fish and can often be seen around large schools of shad diving under the water looking for an easy meal. Remember, schools of baitfish are the first priority when searching for a school of feeding stripers. Once you have located an area where schools of shad are congregated, the stripers won't be far away. A loon can be heard from a great distance because of its loud, lonely call. Once you have spotted a loon, stay back a good distance and observe its movements. If it is diving under the water, watch to see if it comes up with a shad in its mouth. If the bird has found the baitfish, turn on your graph and comb the area for feeding stripers. Last year in early summer, I saw two loons diving and coming up each time with small threadfin shad in their mouths. As I approached the birds, the stripers erupted in a feeding frenzy. It didn't faze the birds one bit. They kept right on feeding along with the stripers.

Q. Shad seem to be impossible to keep alive in the hot weather of August, September, and October. What are some tips to prevent my live bait from dying?

A. The most predominant killer of live bait is an uncontrolled water temperature. As the air temperature climbs to the nineties, a suitable water temperature in bait tanks becomes harder to maintain. The first factor is to start out with a good insulated tank with at least two inches of insulation on top, bottom and sides. If the surface temperature on a lake is in the high eighties or low nineties, the bait should be tempered slowly to the cool water that is necessary to keep them alive for a long period. Both shad and herring will go into shock and die if they are subjected to a fifteen or twenty degree temperature change, whether it is from warm water to cold water or vice versa.

Slowly lower the water temperature in your tank by adding ice to the water. Be sure to add a little extra Bait Saver to kill the chlorine in the city water. The perfect water temperature in your tank is around sixty degrees. If the water temperature goes above seventy degrees, the shad will get the red nose and begin to die. One word of precaution: when you put on a fresh bait, get it down into the deep, cool water as soon as possible. A few seconds in the hot surface water will kill even the toughest shad or herring.

Q. What particular method seems to be the most productive when the fish are deep in late summer?

A. Downrigging is one of the most productive methods of catching both stripers and hybrids when they are deep in late summer. Stripers are on a constant move while on feeding sprees. I have found that once you locate a school of feeding stripers that the fish will stay in one spot for only a short period. I have often found a huge school of fish on my X-16 graph only to have the entire school move before I could get one bait down to them. When using downriggers, you are constantly on the move. When you pass through a school of feeding fish, you will sometimes get hook-ups on every rod. As the roaming stripers continue on their way, you are already in pursuit of another school. Downriggers also keep your lures in the water while searching for a school of feeding fish. A myriad of lures are effective on downriggers. Crankbaits, bucktails and even live bait can be used in conjunction with a downrigger to produce healthy stringers of fish. Vertical jigging is another method that works well. I pre-mark my line at one-foot intervals with a permanent magic marker so I can quickly get my lure to the fish before they move by counting off the marks in order to place my lure at the depth where the stripers are. A jigging spoon worked with a quick, upward rod motion which allows the lure to fall directly under the boat will entice stripers into taking the spoon.

Q. Do you think the same lures or live bait that work on stripers will produce hybrids equally as well?

A. In most cases, yes. You must remember one important factor: a striper is usually larger than a hybrid in body size. In addition, the hybrid's mouth is very small compared to a striper's. If I am fishing a lake that is primarily stocked with hybrids, I tend to use smaller artificial lures and smaller live bait. There are, of course, exceptions to the rule, such as when you catch a seven-pound hybrid on an eleven-inch gizzard shad. But hybrids usually prefer a scaled-down size of the same lures and live bait that catch stripers.

Q. When I locate a school of stripers in the late summer, they will hold in the area for only a short period of time. What causes these fish to move so rapidly?

A. This is a common problem that occurs on many lakes around the country. It seems to me the fish are on a constant move in search of baitfish. With the hot surface water, the thermocline is usually fifty to sixty feet deep. Most of the stripers and baitfish will hold at these depths. I have watched schools of baitfish and stripers that were located on deep underwater structure on several occasions at this time of year, and the baitfish seem to move first. Common sense will tell you that baitfish are not going to follow stripers. When the baitfish move, the stripers will move also. You can go after these fish in two ways. You can simply pick a good spot and wait for the traveling stripers and baitfish to come to you. This is a gamble, but sometimes it pays off. Or you can idle slowly, looking for schools of baitfish or stripers on the chart recorder or video. When you locate the school, get the baits down as fast as possible and hang on.

Q. What style of boat works best when fishing swift water below a powerhouse?

A. I prefer a light boat with a flat bottom. There is a reason for using this type of boat. When drifting the fast water, I run all the way up to the discharge. As soon as you shut off the engine and begin your drift, the boat needs to travel as slowly as possible. Using a boat with a deep V bottom causes the boat speed to pick up rapidly as the rush of water pushes directly against the section of the boat that is protruding down under the water. With a light, flat-bottom type boat, the boat sits flatter on the water with less drag on the bottom. The fast water will actually run under the boat, and the boat will not reach the same speed as the water for several hundred yards. This is important because many stripers are caught just below the discharge area. A long, wide boat is also safer in the treacherous water below a discharge area. A sixteen- or eighteen-foot jon boat with an eighty-four-inch beam is an excellent boat to use below a dam.

Q. Does current have an effect on stripers in the hot summer months?

A. In a lake or reservoir that is a major source of hydroelectric power, stripers and hybrids tend to feed after the generators are turned on at the dam which pulls water down through the lake. On many lakes, the generators will not be turned on until late in the morning. Even though on most lakes the early-morning feeding period is over, the moving water will trigger the fish into another feeding spree. The moving water will pull baitfish toward shallow structure near deep water, such as underwater humps, and stripers will be close by. A few fish can be caught early in the morning before the moving current is started, but the major feeding period will not begin until the generators are started at the dam. To keep from wasting time, it is a good idea to call the day before to get a generation schedule, that way you can be sitting on your favorite hole when the water begins to move. Many lakes are not major power sources, because their small dams have only one or two generators. There is little or no current to affect the fish, so the early morning and late afternoon feeding periods are the best.

Q. Live bait is always extremely hard to find in "dog day" type weather. Where do the baitfish go then and how can a person catch them?

A. As the water surface temperature continues to rise in the hot summer months, shad and blue-back herring will simply go deeper as they seek cooler water. Most people see a large cloud of baitfish on their graph and feel confident they can catch them. In most cases, the clouds are only small threadfins, two or three inches long, which will pass through the net as it goes down. The best way to catch bait is at night under a light. This is a hard, time-consuming process, but sometimes it is the only way to catch bait. I have found that the boat must be anchored in deep water to be effective. The areas around bridges are often key areas. A large net with a long rope is a must, because baitfish, especially blue-back herring, may be fifty to seventy feet deep. If you know where an old spring is located, the cool water will draw shad like a magnet. Be sure to make the first throw with the net a good one, because the bait will usually spook. The cool water traveling through the generators below a dam will also attract baitfish in large numbers. I have found that the mid-day period is usually best around the fast water. I watch the birds below a dam, because you will usually find baitfish where they are congregating. Both cast nets and wire dip nets can be used in the fast-water areas.

Q. What amp battery charger works best on a marine battery?

A. I prefer a six-amp trickle charger rather than a ten-amp manual charger. A ten-amp charger will charge batteries faster, but will also boil the water and acid from a battery faster. The trick to a long-lasting battery is to keep the water at the maximum level and maintain a constant hot charge. By using a slow six-amp charger you can leave the batteries on charge constantly when you are not fishing without any damage to your batteries. I always make it my first chore to hook up the chargers after I come in from a fishing trip, no matter how long before going again. A slow, steady charge will give you a longer-lasting charge.

Q. What seems to be the general depth where stripers feed in June and July?

A. One of the most important factors of summertime striper fishing is the thermocline. The thermocline is an underwater area where the deep cooler water off the bottom meets the warm water coming from the surface. In most cases, this area is the comfort zone for all gamefish. In the summer months, the water temperature in the thermocline is sixty-seven to seventy-two degrees. Not only is that a comfort zone for gamefish, but it is also more tolerable for all species of shad. The thermocline will appear on a good quality chart recorder as a distinctively cloudy area on your screen. The thermocline depth will vary as the surface temperature continues to warm and forces the thermocline deeper. The depth you find the thermocline is usually the depth the stripers will hold in. In June and July, the thermocline will usually be at twenty-four to thirty feet depending on the weather.

Q. What areas of the lake are stripers using in June and July?

A. By early June, most stripers are settling into deep water areas to spend the hot summer months. The mid-section of the lake seems to have a slight edge over the remainder of the lake. The stripers traveling down the lake from the spring spawning activities will usually seek out the first open water that has deep-water access. Any type of open-water structure with deep water nearby will attract large schools of stripers. Underwater humps located near a river channel are good places to crank up the old chart recorder. Some of the deeper points that lead directly into the channel will hold fish consistently, both during the early morning and late afternoon. Although sometimes hard to locate, don't overlook the suspended fish hanging over the deep water. If you fail to locate many stripers around the underwater structure, spend some time searching areas close by over the deeper water.

Q. How productive is night fishing in June and July?

A. Nighttime striper fishing in the warmer, summer months can be very productive for several reasons. First of all, as we all know, especially on weekends, the lakes become very congested in the daylight hours. Stripers are not only sensitive to light, but also seek deep-water refuge from the noisy traffic above. Nighttime angling will usually remedy the hectic boat traffic and naturally the bright summer sun. Sometimes, stripers will not feed immediately after dark. But if you will hang in there and keep plugging, you will find stripers on a feeding spree at some time during the night.

Q. What size live bait works better in the warmer, summer months?

A. As a rule of thumb, stripers have a tendency to feed on the size shad that are most available at that time of year. In most cases, by June and July, the larger shad become more plentiful. One big factor plays an important role in the size shad an angler uses in the warm summer months. If you are primarily interested in trophy-size stripers, the large seven- to twelve-inch shad will usually do the job. If quantity is what you are after, the three- to six-inch size is a sure ticket.

Q. What are your thoughts on line sizes for stripers in the summer?

A. With lack of rain in the summer months, the water in most reservoirs becomes very clear even in the flat lakes in the Southwest. Stripers become very wary in the clear water, especially the older trophy-size fish which we all are in hopes of catching. The new small-diameter lines are naturally less visible in clear water which improves your chances of outsmarting old linesides. In the summer months, I use as light a test line as I can get away with under the conditions. Twelve- and fourteen-pound test line is a happy median. The smaller line sizes also enable both artificial lures and live bait to be worked with a more natural action. I have landed hundreds of stripers over thirty pounds on twelve- and fourteen-pound test line.

Chapter 15
MORE STRIPER SAVVY

Q. When fishing live bait, do you think engaging reels in gear before placing them in rod holders, will produce more hook-ups than using a disengaged reel with just the clicker on?

A. It all depends on the time of year that you are live-bait fishing. Overall, if you put your reels in gear and use a medium drag with the clicker on to act as an alarm, you will hook more fish. I have found that an added advantage is using a soft tip rod. The soft tip will offer little resistance to a striper or hybrid during the first few seconds after they have taken the bait. By the time the fish feels the pressure of the rod, the point of the hook has already penetrated the flesh around the mouth area. In some cases, like during the winter months, a striper will not be quite as aggressive as in the summer. If you fail to get hook-ups and continue to get runs, leave the reel out of gear with just the clicker on.

Q. There always seems to be a dull period between spring topwater action and prime live-bait fishing. What methods will produce fish in this period?

A. After the water temperature warms above seventy degrees, topwater action will slowly die off. For a short period, stripers won't venture far away from the areas which held them during the spring months. The fish may even stay on the same exact points, but suspend near the edge of deep water. In late May and early June, I use a one-half-ounce bucktail jig rigged with a six-inch curly-tail grub. White on white seems to be the best color combination. The trick when fishing a jig is not to fish very deep. Use a long, sweeping motion of the rod to swim the lure ten to twelve feet deep. I usually cast the jig on the same points that are productive topwater areas. Be prepared for the strike to come as the lure is on the fall, and don't expect an arm-wrenching hit. The use of a sensitive graphite rod will help in detecting a strike from a striper, because a striper can inhale a jig and blow it back out before you can blink your eyes.

Q. Do you feel that a circular bait tank is a necessity in keeping shad alive?

A. In all reality, the need for a circular tank is true only if you overload your tank with more bait than it is capable of handling. It is true that shad swim in a circular motion when feeding on bottom algae. But I don't think with all the salt and chemicals added to the water, shad are going to settle down to their natural habits in a tank. Shad will, however, bunch up in the corners of a square tank when too many shad are put into the tank. I have used virtually everything from styrofoam coolers to a wire fish basket as a bait tank. Round tanks are better, but it is not necessary to go out and spend a lot of money on a circular tank. The only catch is that a square tank will not hold as many shad as a circular tank for lengthy periods of time.

Q. In the spring, we locate big schools of surface-feeding stripers, but seem to have a tough time coaxing the fish into striking our lures. What are we doing wrong?

A. The most common mistake a fisherman makes when casting to a school of surface-feeding stripers is not matching the size of the lure to the size baitfish that the stripers are feeding on. In most cases, finicky stripers will be feeding on small threadfin shad that are one-and-one-half to three inches long. The first topwater lure that usually comes to the mind of striper fishermen is a swimming minnow. This lure, along with almost all topwater striper lures, is approximately seven inches long, which obviously doesn't resemble a small threadfin. I have found a bucktail jig or a Tony Accetta Pet Spoon worked behind a popping cork will do a good job when small baitfish are on the menu. Sometimes, casting a jigging spoon past the school and working it below the surface-feeding stripers will produce larger fish.

Q. What is the thermocline?

A. The thermocline, in simple words, is an area below the surface that usually represents a comfort zone for both baitfish and gamefish. The thermocline will vary in depth with seasonal weather changes. The thermocline represents an area where the warmer surface temperatures meet the cooler water coming off the bottom. This area not only contains comfortable water temperatures, but also a more enriched oxygen level. The thermocline appears on a chart recorder as a faint gray area. Starting in the spring, the thermocline will be nonexistent because the water temperature from top to bottom will run approximately the same. When this is the case, stripers can be caught at almost any depth. As the warmer weather progresses, the thermocline will begin moving downward. In June and July, the thermocline in most lakes will run twenty-four to thirty feet deep. The temperature change can be used to a fisherman's advantage, because almost all baitfish and stripers will hold in the thermocline. This is only a fisherman's definition of the thermocline. A trained biologist could go into more detail.

Q. When fishing a new lake, what are some tips for quickly locating both hybrids and stripers?

A. First of all, a well pre-planned trip will always turn out to be a more successful venture. Write the Corps of

Engineers or TVA for any topographical maps that they have on your chosen lake. Study a map and look for areas such as humps, ditches, river beds or creek channels located near deep water. Do a little homework and find one of the better fishermen on the lake. In some cases, he may not be a guide. Most anglers will share information as long as you don't ask for information about the location of personal hotspots. The main questions should be the best times of year to fish the lake and information about obtaining live bait. You should be able to put your own fishing experience to work and figure out areas to scout for stripers. When you choose a marina to fish out of, I have found it pays to listen more than you talk. The tales of your thirty pounders on the wall will usually be a turn-off to anyone who might be of help. After a few friendly questions, a generally productive area can be pinpointed. With a couple of rolls of graph paper and a little gas, you should be in business.

Q. What other types of live bait, other than shad or herring, are effective on stripers?

A. There is a small fish called a warmouth that is in the bluegill family. The warmouth is much tougher than the bluegill, however. A bream or bluegill will usually die in water over thirty feet deep. A warmouth can tolerate greater depths plus bounce back after a vicious bone-crushing strike to continue its erratic effort to escape, which usually only infuriates a striper into coming back for the kill. In the cool fall and winter months, commercial shiners work well. Live eels (which are often hard to come by) will work very well, even though they may not be native to your lake. Eels may be frozen and shipped from coastal areas. Creek chubs will often work very well, especially in deep mountain lakes. Native sucker minnows caught in traps around fast flowing creeks are also good. One live bait that most fishermen never dreamed of is the freshwater drum. A six- to eight-inch drum is one of the most deadly striper baits, especially for a big fish.

Q. What artificial lures would you recommend for nighttime plugging for stripers in the early summer months?

A. The Baby Mac made by Storm Lures is a very productive lure in the summer. The Baby Mac will run five or six feet deep on a steady retrieve. The strawberry color seems to produce best anytime of the year. A white bucktail jig with a white plastic trailer has produced good strings of fish for me at night in late May and June. A couple of factors need to be taken into consideration when making your lure selection. The most important is the size of baitfish that the stripers are feeding on. Match your lure size as closely as possible to the baitfish. Stripers are sensitive to water temperature and sunlight. If the shallow-water temperatures do not exceed seventy degrees, stripers will feed relatively shallow in the dark hours. Experiment with different speed retrieves to discover the magic depth.

Q. How productive is striper or hybrid fishing in January and February?

A. January and February, even though regarded as the coldest months of the year, can be an excellent time for both stripers and hybrids. Early January will find stripers in the larger bodies of water chasing shad on the surface. Seagulls are helpful at this time of year. Locate the gulls and usually the stripers will be nearby. As a general rule, stripers can be found in January suspended between twenty-five and forty feet over deep water. Both live and artificial bait can be productive. By late January and February, fishing in large open bodies of water can be tough. Concentrate your efforts on warmer water around major springs and creeks. Sometimes, because of clear shallow water around springs and feeder creeks, night fishing can be more productive. Don't forget about warm-water discharges at steam plants. The warm water can be a wintertime paradise for both hybrids and stripers.

Q. What types of artificial baits are good in January and February?

A. It all depends on at what depth the stripers are feeding. If they are suspended over deep water, vertical jigging is sometimes the answer. A spoon or a bucktail jig with a six-inch twister grub for a trailer can be effective. If the fish are back in the feeder creeks or springs, casting a bucktail jig is a good plan. If the fish are suspended in creeks, you should use a counting table of one second equals one foot. Let your jig sink to a desired depth by counting it down. This is the table that I use for a one-half ounce jig. Heavier jigs will naturally sink faster. Sometimes in the cold winter months, stripers will move into areas of fast moving water caused by heavy generation at the power plants. A Storm Baby Mac works extremely well when worked around rockpiles and underwater cover that provide the fish an ambush spot.

Q. Where can live bait be caught during the winter?

A. When the surface temperature drops below forty-five degrees, live bait gets harder to come by. The first place to look in a lake is around the larger springs. The warmer water will sometimes draw thousands of shad seeking refuge from freezing water. In some lakes, especially the shallower lakes, shad can be caught below the dams around swift water. The only problem with this is that with the high power demand in the cold weather, the water becomes so swift shad simply can't stay in these areas. If you're fortunate enough to live around a steam plant, you won't have any trouble obtaining all the bait you need. Shad will travel for miles to spend the winter months around these warm waters.

Q. How do you rig for live bait in the winter?

A. I use a one and one-half ounce weight with a swivel on each end to keep the bait from twisting my line. I usually tie a seven-foot leader to the swivel so the shad's natural movements won't be restricted. I fish the rig at exactly the depth I am seeing the fish on my chart recorder or video screen. A trailing line with no weight is generally useless in the winter.

Q. Each winter, the stripers on my lake will surface lazily both early in the morning and late afternoon, but I just can't seem to coax the fish into striking a lure or live bait. What is the problem?

A. This is a common problem that many fishermen face after the water cools down in the winter months. It is a biological fact that stripers feed on smaller baitfish as the water cools down. The body chemistry of a striper slows down, which calls for less food in cold water. After the water temperature drops below the mid-forties, stripers feed on smaller shad and become less aggressive. Remember, the important factor is to match your artificial lure or live bait to the size baitfish that the stripers are feeding on. In January and February, small bucktails without a trailer can be the ticket. Small crankbaits such as the Baby Mac can also be good. If you are a live bait person, small shiners can be deadly in cold water. Fished on light line with a light hook, which enables the smaller bait to swim more naturally, two- and three-inch long shiners will often produce trophy-size fish.

Q. Should I take special precautions with my outboard engine in the winter?

A. Freezing temperatures can be a nightmare on outboards. As we all know, water will expand when it is frozen. The number one precaution to take is to make sure that you have no water in the gear housings of your lower unit. If your boat is left outside in the bitter cold, water will freeze and in most cases crack the gear case housing. After a winter fishing trip, always trim your motor down and allow all water to drain from the water jackets. If it is very cold, I briefly crank my motor when it is out of the water to blow all the water from the cooling system.

Q. Is there any way to prevent a steering cable from freezing up in the cold winter months?

A. Steering cables are enclosed in a protective housing to prevent moisture from entering the moving parts. The trouble is that the maintenance-free cable attracts moisture which sets up rust which will corrode the cable. In the cold winter months, the moisture freezes when trailering the boat on the road. The ice formed locks up the steering completely and can cause serious problems when you try to turn the steering wheel to break it loose. Only a few brands of cables come with grease fittings to lubricate and push out the moisture. If you have a system that has no grease fittings, and you do a lot of trailering, try wrapping the cable with foam pipe insulation. It is easy to install and will deflect the wind as you drive down the highway. If your cable has been frozen and is corroded, it is a good idea to replace it as soon as possible.

Q. What type of clothing should be worn in January and February?

A. Winter fishing can be an enjoyable time if you dress properly. We all know that once you get cold, you stay cold. I've found dressing in layers of clothing is better than a bulky type of winter wear. Insulated underwear comes in all styles. There are many opinions on different brands. The insulated coveralls have come a long way in the last few years. With the use of the new insulating materials in jumpsuits, even the coldest North wind can't get to your body. Felt-lined boots are a welcome product to keep your feet comfortable. There is no need for three or four layers of socks when wearing these boots. Body heat escapes through the top of your head. Be sure and wear some type of toboggan or insulated hat to retain the needed heat. One precaution that I must mention is that with all the clothing needed to keep warm on the lake in the winter months you become a walking disaster if you fall in the water. When all your clothes become wet, your swimming movements are almost zero. So be sure and wear your life-jacket at all times.

Q. What size fish can be caught in January and February?

A. I've caught several trophy-size stripers and hybrids in the winter months. I feel using the proper techniques and fishing the right places at the right time will produce the same size fish that you can catch during the spring and summer. In my opinion, some lakes are better in the winter due to the lack of boat traffic.

Q. What types of weather patterns are better for January and February fishing?

A. First of all there is usually one temperature in January and February--cold. I have had continuous good luck fishing two to four days before a bad cold front. As the cold front approaches, the northwest winds will always become more intense. The wind makes boat control almost impossible, and it can produce quite a chill to your body. With the passing front come blue-bird skies and a higher barometer. This for me seems to be the toughest time to fish. In January and February, always watch for several days in a row in which there are above-normal temperatures. This type of weather, added to an overcast sky or a slow, all-day drizzle, can set stripers into a feeding frenzy.

Q. Do stripers and hybrids congregate around standing timber in the winter months?

A. Remember one important factor: stripers are a deep-water fish. In most cases, stripers will hold and congregate around completely submerged standing timber, which may have twenty-five to forty feet of water over it. Certain water conditions will determine where the stripers hold around timber. An overcast day with mild weather will move the stripers to the outside of the treeline, preferable near the river channel. A bright sunny day or when an unstable weather front is approaching will move the striper deeper toward the center of the timber. Fishing live bait or downrigging can both be effective around standing timber.

Q. Are shad and blue-back herring easier to keep alive in the winter months?

A. Both shad and blue-back herring, as we all know, are very fragile. Water temperature is the biggest problem in keeping live bait fresh for a long period of time. Naturally in the cold winter months, the cooler water temperatures needed in holding tanks are much easier to maintain. I have found both shad and blue back herring become difficult to keep alive under high humidity situations in the summer months. Along with the cooler air temperatures of winter, comes low humidity in most cases. Both these factors will make keeping live bait a much easier chore in the winter. Bait Saver, Foam Kill and rock salt are still necessary ingredients to your water. But with the lower water temperature, your bait-tank water will not have to be changed as often.

Q. What would be a good striper boat on a large open water lake?

A. When choosing a striper boat for a large open-water lake, remember a sudden thunder storm and high winds can turn a big-water lake into a dangerous sea with deep swells that a small shallow boat simply can't handle. The first factor when choosing a boat for big lakes is a deep, high-sided boat, which should be at least eighteen feet in length. Starcraft makes an excellent high-sided, completely v-bottom boat that can handle even the roughest water. The Falcon line of striper boats built in Texas has built a large high-sided boat to deal with the big water on Lake Texoma. The heavy fiberglass hull and v-bottom will challenge the rough water anywhere in the nation. The Bullet Boat Company in Tennessee has just introduced a new twenty-one foot boat built on a bass boat pattern that should be a dream come true for many striper anglers who like this design.

Q. What time periods during the day do stripers and hybrids feed best in January and February?

A. I have found in the cold-winter months that both stripers and hybrids will feed during the midday periods, like from eleven a.m. to two p.m., just as well as the fish feed in the early morning. There is something about cold water that alters normal feeding patterns. Personally, after the sun goes over the horizon in the afternoon, I think the action will not be as good as at midday. In some rare cases, night fishing will be productive. The areas around warm-water steam plants will usually be more productive at night. I think this can be attributed to the shallow, narrow canals where the stripers become spooky in the daylight hours. On Lake Lanier in Georgia, all local striper anglers look forward to the cold January and February weather. In the past several years, many trophy size fish have been taken on topwater lures at night.

Q. In all honesty, at what cold winter temperatures do you think it is safe to be out on the lake?

A. The most dangerous factor about the cold-winter weather is not necessarily the cold temperatures, but the strong gusting winds that seem to always blow on big, open-water lakes. A fifteen-mile-per-hour wind coupled with a thirty-five degree air temperature can make life miserable out on the lake. Even the finest goose down clothing can't keep the wind from finally penetrating to your body and eventually sending you to the warm fireplace at home. I have found that with no wind and the proper dress, temperatures down in the teens are bearable for a lengthy period. But with gusting winds and temperatures below freezing, your body can tolerate these conditions for only a short period.

Q. Where do stripers go during the bright sunlight hours when they seem to vanish from the entire lake?

A. We all have experienced days when stripers are on every point that you look at daybreak only to see them vanish with the bright midday sun. It not only seems they have left their feeding areas, but that they have left the entire lake. Stripers and hybrids are the most sensitive freshwater gamefish as regards sunlight. When the bright morning sun reaches a direct penetrating angle in the clear water, stripers will retreat to open water and greater depths. Locating a tight school of stripers or hybrids in open water can be like looking for a needle in a haystack. In between feeding periods, they may go down sixty or seventy feet, suspending around no structure at all. When looking for suspended stripers, you may pass a school by only a few feet in open water and never graph a single fish. One problem that arises when you finally do locate a big school of fish is that the stripers have moved away from their feeding areas and are stubborn about striking any lure or live bait. In a sense, they are like you and me waiting for the afternoon meal.

Q. What types of lakes are better for winter striper fishing?

A. Deep, clear, mountain lakes are usually better producers during the cold winter months. Shallow, flat lakes will cool off faster in the early fall and will continue to cool rapidly in colder weather which often causes an uncomfortable temperature for feeding stripers. Deep lakes with a lot of water between sixty and a hundred feet will offer stripers a more tolerable water temperature range during even the coldest winter months. A mountain lake usually has long feeder creeks that are fed by warm spring water which draws shad like magnets. When the shad hold around the slightly warmer water temperatures, the stripers will not be far away. The shallow flat lakes will generally have a tremendous shad kill during the dead of winter due to the cold water temperature. I have seen this have an effect on the entire fishery for the coming year. Mountain lakes are also easier to fish during windy conditions. The back sides of high ridges and hills can cut the wind down to a minimum.

Q. How would an angler cope with a winter cold front on a shallow striper lake?

A. Severe cold fronts can seem like a bad dream when you are on a good school of fish. Unlike the day before the front passes, when the fish seem to be on every hole in the lake, the bright bluebird skies of a passing cold front change the feeding patterns of stripers and sometimes seem to cause them to vanish from the entire lake. With the cool surface temperatures, most stripers will feed in shallow water on a mild winter day. As the bright, clear skies move in, the fish will move toward the open part of the lake and suspend over deep water. This movement is brought on by the high pressure system and the bright sunlight following a front. Unlike a black bass, however, a striper will often continue to feed. Weighted live-bait rigs or jigging spoons fished deep are the best ways to catch cold-front stripers. Night fishing is often good as the bright sunlight is eliminated and the fish move back into shallow water. Often, the biggest problem for a fisherman is the wind. Daytime fishing on the open water is rough, but the winds will often die down at night and make boat control much easier.

Q. Can night fishing be very productive for stripers in the cold winter months?

A. Night fishing can be extremely productive during the cold weather. Use common sense about the cold winter winds and temperatures and pick mild, calm nights. Night fishing is good as the water cools and stripers move in to the shallow water to feed. Stripers' sensitivity to sunlight means night fishing is often more productive on deep, clear mountain lakes. Several methods will produce heavy strings of fish. The minnow-swimming surface baits worked slowly across points and underwater humps can cause heart failure as a big striper explodes on it during a calm, dark night. The Baby Mac worked across shallow, clean, gravel bars has produced many linesides in the trophy size range. Bucktail jigs, worked with a medium steady retrieve along the same areas as the Baby Mac, will catch fish on a consistent basis. Live bait fished on a free line can also be good when fish are in shallow water. I prefer dark nights over a full moon night even though it might be difficult to see. The fish just seem to feed better on a dark night. Most fishermen don't realize how shallow a striper will feed at night. I have caught several big stripers in water less than three feet deep at night and many thrash the surface like a big black bass. The water in many lakes becomes very clear in the winter months, especially if the rainfall level is below normal. Sometimes, night fishing is the only alternative, if you want to catch fish.

Q. Is vertical jigging effective for cold water stripers or hybrids?

A. Vertical jigging can be one of the most productive methods for taking stripers during cold-weather periods. In cold water, schools of both stripers and hybrids will often hold in one area for several days. These fish may be suspended as deep as sixty or seventy feet, and even though not in a wild feeding mood, the fish can still be coaxed into taking a dying shad imitation. My theory is that the stripers are feeding primarily on small threadfin shad during the winter. The cold water will take its toll on thousands of threadfins. A spoon, such as a Hopkins or a Mann-O-Lure, imitates a dying threadfin which becomes an easy meal for a striper that is not willing to chase a bigger gizzard shad that is in good condition. Remember to be alert and keep contact with your bait as it falls through the school of stripers. A strike, due to the extreme water depth and the fish simply inhaling the spoon, will be only a slight tap.

Q. Are stripers as conscious of different color lures as a black bass?

A. This is one problem that stripers and hybrids anglers overlook. Fishing as many as two hundred days a year, I have noticed lure color does make a difference. Water clarity, sunlight and different types of forage fish will call for different color lures. I have found on bright, sunny mornings that a metallic chrome lure will work very well. On an overcast or rainy day, a dark-colored bait such as a grey-and-black pattern will out-fish lighter colored baits. When choosing a color pattern, use common sense. If stripers are feeding mostly on bream, don't tie on a shad-colored bait. I know of one rare instance in which stripers were feeding on crayfish. Light-colored lures, such as a bone color, will produce more strikes in stained water. A metallic color works well in clear water.

Q. It seems that black bass anglers and striper anglers are constantly battling among themselves. Do the stripers honestly pose any problems to black bass?

A. This is a controversy that has been going on for years, and I suspect that it will continue forever, despite numerous studies by fisheries biologists. It has been proven, in studies from almost every state, that both stripers and hybrids feed almost exclusively on shad and other baitfish. In fact, shad diet figures have been as high as ninety-five percent. I have personally dressed hundreds of stripers for myself and guide parties over the years, and I can honestly say that I have never found a bass in the stomach of a striper or hybrid. Occasionally, I will find a small bream and, on rare occasions, a small walleye in their stomachs. Stripers below the tailraces will eat small, freshwater drum which are considered rough fish. Having two young sons, I enjoy catching bass and crappies just as well as anyone. When I go out and come home empty handed, the first thing I do is hunt for an excuse. I think this is what many bass fishermen are doing, and the striper is an easy target. Stripers and hybrids have been introduced in several lakes that had an abundance of overgrown shad that were unsuitable as black bass forage. In almost every case, a few years after striper and hybrids were stocked, the quality of bass fishing improved. Fisheries biologists are well-educated people with a concern for all species of fish and the best interests of fishermen at heart. We need to let them do their jobs and continue to improve the quality of fishing in our reservoirs.

Q. What is the best advice for a striper angler who is thinking about becoming a professional guide?

A. One of the first thoughts that most would-be guides think of is the importance of establishing a reputation for catching more fish than their competitors. Speaking with many years of experience in this business, I think having an open mind and learning to deal with people in a friendly manner will gain you a better reputation than just catching more fish than any other guide. Most clients that hire your services know nothing about fishing. It is often hard to overlook some of the simple mistakes they make in the course of a day's fishing. The day will go by much faster and repeat business will keep you booked months in advance, if you can make a quick friend with a complete stranger and make your client feel at ease while in your boat. Never give a customer less than one hundred percent throughout the day. Most clients will recognize your hard efforts, even if you run into a bad day and no fish are caught. As far as fishing goes, it pays to be versatile and learn everything you possibly can about any method that will produce fish for your customers. If you limit yourself to one style of fishing, the word will get out and you will limit your number of clients.

Q. In the early fall, stripers seem to be easier to locate even though they may be thirty or forty feet deep. The trouble is staying with a moving school of feeding fish. What method seems to work most effectively?

A. This is a pattern that occurs on many good lakes in the early fall and will not change until the water cools way down. I have never come up with an answer as to why the fish move so quickly. I have set up on a school of several hundred fish, and in five minutes they will vanish. The only remedy I have come up with is to be fast and precise. There are two ways to approach these moving fish. Either sit on a proven productive spot and wait for the fish to pass by, which I feel is a big gamble, or move with the fish and establish a pattern that proves to be consistent. I like to choose a particular area and quickly idle along as I graph for a school of fish. When the fish are below thirty feet deep they are not quite as spooky. Also, watch the surface. Even though most of the fish are deep, many times, one or two stripers will chase a school of shad to the surface, which gives away the presence of the entire school. After I have located the fish, the trick is to get the baits down as quickly as possible. Jigging spoons such as the Mann-O-Lure, Bagley's Salty Dog and Bomber Slab are excellent lures when the fish are deep. These heavy spoons fall rapidly and resemble small threadfin shad. Live bait is also good, but it takes time to rig up four or five rods and drop them thirty or forty feet down. Downrigging is another method that is very consistent. When you don't know exactly where the fish are, the use of downriggers enables you to fish while searching for a school of feeding stripers. Bucktail jigs and small crankbaits trolled four to six feet above the stripers will often produce hook-ups on every rod. One advantage, during this sometimes frustrating period, is that while it may be a long wait between strikes, once you hit pay dirt, the action is fast and furious.

Q. Can spinning tackle be used effectively for live bait fishing?

A. Spinning tackle can be just as effective as baitcasting equipment if you choose the proper equipment. First a seven-to-eight-foot long rod with a good backbone and a medium tip action works best. I don't like long surf-casting rods because they are heavy and built especially for long casts. A variety of spinning reels will work as long as they hold at least two hundred yards of fourteen-pound-test line. Again, I wouldn't choose a large surf-casting reel because of the weight. A heavy-duty drag is a must when fighting a striper, which is easily capable of breaking your line if the drag is not set properly. When live-bait fishing, some anglers set the drag resistance to almost zero. When a fish takes the bait and the line is being pulled from the reel, they simply put their hand on top of the spool to stop the line from spooling off. Then they set the hook. After this, they turn the drag indicator to the desired tension. Shimano has a new reel on the market called the Bait Runner. This is the only spinning reel with a mechanical device that acts as a clicker just as on a baitcasting reel. More detailed information can be obtained on the Bait Runner by writing to: Shimano, One Shimano Drive, Irvine, CA 92718.

Q. How do electrical storms affect stripers when they are feeding in deep water?

A. Electrical storms almost always have a devastating effect on stripers, even though the fish may be deep. Most electrical storms bring a very erratic barometric change.

The barometer will often go up and down in a short period which shuts off any feeding activity that was occurring. Stripers seem to vanish when a storm is in progress. I believe that in most cases, the fish simply head for deeper water and suspend until the weather stabilizes. On the other hand, just before a storm arrives, fish go into a feeding frenzy, because they sense that bad weather is approaching and feeding activity may be shut off for a while. Be cautious of electrical storms, and remember that lightning and rough water are very dangerous.

Q. Do you think a tandem-wheel trailer is best for a heavy striper rig?

A. Tandem-wheel trailers work better than single-axle trailers for several reasons. The tandem trailer will support the extra weight that most properly rigged striper boats bear. If you are a live-bait fisherman, remember that water weighs over eight pounds per gallon. With a thirty- to fifty-gallon bait tank, this could easily account for as much as three hundred fifty pounds. Tandem-wheel trailers may be a little more difficult to turn in a tight area, but the difference is like night and day when towing on the interstates. Single-axle trailers have a tendency to swerve back and forth when additional weight is added to the boat. I have pulled both styles and have learned that the tandem trailer pulls with more ease and safety. A good idea is to add surge brakes to the tandem trailer, because when you are slowing down or stopping, the boat and trailer push your vehicle, which can become very dangerous.

Q. Do you think video sounders have any advantages over a chart recorder?

A. The video sounder and paper chart recorder both have certain advantages. Having used both types of machines over the years, I think a good quality video screen will reveal more information, such as the feeding activity of a striper. When a school of fish is located, but the fish simply make what we term a "straight line" across the screen that particular school is not feeding. Actively feeding stripers can be located with a video screen by looking for erratic swimming motion of a fish when it is feeding. The video screen uses no paper and can be operated throughout the day without the added cost of paper. The price of videos has dropped in the past few years with no decrease in quality. Both machines can be purchased with wide-angle transducers to display more of the bottom at one time. The chart recorder, on the other hand, will produce a permanent record of a lake's contours that can be used at a later date. The chart recorder will draw bottom features with more detail than the video. With the proper adjustment, I have actually seen a chart recorder draw a line of stumps with such detail that I could tell at what angle the trees were cut.

Q. What size stripers seems to be best for the supper table?

A. I have taken all size stripers from lakes across the country, and I can't say a fillet from a four pounder is any better eating than a fillet from a twenty-five pounder. The trick to tasty striper is proper care and preparation of the fillet rather than the size of the fish. Keep the fish fresh by putting them on ice until time for cleaning. Make sure all of the red meat is removed and I promise you that you can't tell the difference in a small or large fish.

Q. My cast net seems to deteriorate after only one year of use. It becomes stiff and hard to throw. What can I do to prevent this expensive deterioration?

A. Remember a cast net is made of monofilament just like the line on your reel. If a cast net is exposed to continuous sunlight and weather, it will become stiff and hard to throw. After you use a net, the worst thing you can do is to toss it back in the bucket and put it in the back of the boat. If at all possible, put the net in a bucket with a solution of dish-washing liquid. Wash the mud and shad slime from the entire net and rinse completely. The soapy solution will soften the monofilament. Hang the net up or spread it out to insure that it dries thoroughly. Then, fold the net up and store in a dry, dark area until its next use. Mud and slime are the most damaging to the monofilament and will ruin a net in a short time. A good quality net is very expensive, but proper care should make it last a couple of years.

Using quality live bait can give you a distinct advantage over other weekend fishermen.

Chapter 16
WEEKEND FISHING

Steve Baker can remember just a few years ago when lakes were not so crowded on weekends, and stripers were easier to catch. Those days are only memories now. But, by using some common sense and a few basic guidelines, you can ignore the annoying crowds and catch more fish than ever.

LEARN THEIR HABITS

The striper is a temperamental fish. Anytime you are on the lake, remember a few important facts. Both stripers and hybrids will not tolerate excessive disturbance or noise, whether from a water skier or from an inconsiderate fisherman slamming a live-well lid shut. Both fish are also very light conscious and feed best during low light hours or at night. Another important thing to keep in mind is water temperature. Stripers prefer a sixty- to seventy-degree water temperature and will travel great distances in search of this comfort zone. Keep these facts in mind when deciding when and where to fish.

BE A LEADER

The most important attitude that you can develop when fishing on weekends is to become a leader and not a follower. It is easier to follow the crowd to the favorite hot spot or ask the marina operator where all the fish have been caught than it is to start off "cold turkey." However, if any angler will stop and think for a moment, he will realize that finding the fish is half the fun. Pulling into a congregation of boats and catching a few fish is not as gratifying as finding a school of fish on your own. None of us has to catch fish to feed our families through the winter. If we figured the cost of a season's trips divided by the pounds of fish caught, we could buy T-bones for every meal.

So remember, it's supposed to be fun! And, again, you will never become a better striper fisherman by following the crowds. The best striper anglers on most lakes are not the fishermen who have the money to buy the biggest boat or the nicest rod, but the individuals who are willing to drive a little farther, get on the water a little earlier, develop confidence that they can find their own fish and understand how to cash in on such things as weather, boat traffic and changing conditions to turn a mediocre day into a great day.

When choosing a body of water where you will spend the weekend chasing stripers and hybrids, it often pays to concentrate your efforts on a lake that hasn't been bombarded with fishermen and skiers. It always pays to make friends with a local fisheries biologist or creel clerk and ask questions on stocking programs and other information about a potentially good lake. The game and fish agencies are very helpful with such information, but they don't like to publicize certain lakes until the fishery becomes stable and can support fishing pressure. These lakes may not exist in your area, but it may surprise you what an extra hour's drive will offer. Many of these lakes may not be developed and may have little or no access.

If you are lucky and can find a lake off the beaten path, you will have no one to blame but yourself if you don't catch fish. Again, it helps to make friends with the game and fish people. Prove to the local agencies that you are willing to work with them and provide information that could only be collected by a fisherman who has been on the water for many, many hours.

LEARN THE LAKE

If you must fish a lake that is well known and receives a great deal of fishing pressure, there are several ways to use the crowds to your favor. After you have decided where to spend your time, learn as much as you can about the lake. It does not pay to skip around to a different lake every weekend. Find a lake that has been producing fish consistently and buy good topographical maps of the entire lake. Learn the important deep-water areas, such as old creek beds, river channels and underwater high spots near deep water. Learn the areas where stripers and hybrids migrate as the seasons change.

After you have a general idea of the lake's terrain, find out what type of structure and in what part of the lake most of the fish have been caught. Use this information to establish a pattern and look for areas on the map similar to those where the crowds have been gathering to catch stripers. When you locate an area holding a school of fish, more than likely, it will be a few days before the crowd moves in on your honey hole. This is going to happen, so don't get frustrated. Simply move on and find another area.

Once you learn how to establish a pattern, you will locate a number of hot spots. The crowds will usually not cover all of your productive areas. Avoid the crowded spots as much as possible. Many times, Steve Baker has watched the crowds gather in an area and spook the fish to another piece of structure where he just happened to be sitting all by himself.

USE QUALITY BAIT

During the live-bait season, the quality of bait you have will make the difference between a good day and a bad day. If you can't avoid the crowds, the quality, size and liveliness of your bait will make a difference in catching fish when no one else can get a strike.

One time, Steve Baker's wife had booked a guide trip for

him at the last moment for a Saturday. He knew the weekend crowds had already discovered where he was fishing and to make matters even worse, he didn't have any bait.

Baker went to the dock the next morning and dropped a big cast net under the lights on his boat stall, which was fifty feet deep. He couldn't have been any luckier, because he caught four dozen big gizzard shad on the first drop.

As Steve Baker rounded the bend in the lake near one of his best places, he could see he would have a hard time finding a spot to fish because of all the boats. He started to move down the lake, but his instincts told him to stop. As Baker eased up to the crowded river ledge, which must have held fifteen boats in a one hundred yard stretch, he noticed most of the fishermen were fishing with shad that they had bought at the marina which were in terrible shape.

The first big shad Baker let down never made it to the bottom. A twenty-nine pounder globbed it down. Naturally, the boats moved in closer and closer until some of the boats were within a rod's length of Baker's boat.

He caught and released nine fish over twenty pounds apiece in forty-five minutes. The other boats didn't get a strike. Baker wasn't using any hidden secrets. His shad were just fresh and lively instead of half dead. This gave him the edge that was needed to catch stripers from a crowded area on a weekend.

So remember, always keep your bait as fresh as possible and notice the small things such as the size bait the fish are feeding on. It often makes the difference between catching stripers and striking out.

FISH IN THE DARK

Night fishing is one of the better ways to avoid the crowds. Only a small percentage of anglers like to night fish, and the skiers will definitely be gone. Night fishing is especially productive if your lake is clear. Remember, stripers are very light sensitive and will not feed very well in the daytime.

If you choose to night fish, you need to start at dusk. Steve Baker has gone out three hours before dark several times intending to fish all night, but got so disgusted from the boat traffic that he simply couldn't keep his confidence up until dark.

Live bait, downrigging, crankbaits and bucktails will all produce fish after dark. If a lake has a lot of traffic, the fish will feed primarily at night because of all the disturbance created by pleasure boats and fishermen. You can definitely use this to your favor, if you are willing to adjust your sleeping habits a little.

START EARLY

If night fishing is not your game, make it a point to be the first boat on a particular spot early in the morning. Very few weekend anglers will get up at four in the morning to go fishing. Steve Baker has seen stripers feed madly just at dawn for only an hour or so. By the time the crowds are on their way to the lake, he has his limit and is headed home to catch up on his sleep.

To insure you get the most out of these short feeding periods, keep your equipment in good shape. If you have only one day a week to fish and the fish are feeding for only a short period, you don't need to sit on your favorite hole and spool up a couple of reels with new line that you bought on your way home from work on Friday or fumble through your tackle box searching for a lure you left on the work bench in the garage.

If you are a live-bait fisherman and buy bait, have your bait reserved before the day of your fishing trip. If at all possible, catch it or buy it the night before so you don't have to listen to "Sorry, sold out," or learn too late that your favorite baitfish spot has dried up and bait is impossible to catch. Take care of these chores the day before and be ready to go on Saturday morning.

Fishing a lake during the winter draw-down is an excellent time to catch a trophy striper.

Chapter 17
SPECIAL TECHNIQUES FOR TROPHY STRIPERS

BALLOON FISHING

Steve Baker had located a small school of stripers on a short sloping sand bar that runs directly into the old river channel. There seemed to be only a few stripers feeding on the sand bar, but they were all exceptionally large fish. Baker spotted one of the largest fish feeding on a big gizzard shad as he made his way upriver one morning. As he circled around to take a second look, one of the big stripers chased a shad completely up on the bank. The sand bar was an area that he had overlooked all spring for some unknown reason, even though he had traveled by this particular area daily for almost two months on his way upriver to a series of shallow-water flats that were holding schools of small stripers.

Baker grabbed a rod with a swimming minnow plug tied on it and cast across the sand bar. He was too late, the fish had moved.

Baker rigged up a half-ounce white bucktail jig that hardly ever lets him down. He fired a cast toward the bar and retrieved the jig in a way that had paid off so many times in the past, but still nothing happened, not even a tap.

That night, while working in his office on a stack of papers, Steve Baker couldn't get his mind off that school of stripers. He enjoys the challenge of coaxing a wise old fish into striking, and he wasn't going to give up easily. As he sat looking out his window which overlooks the lake, he remembered a trick that a friend in Oklahoma had shown him a couple of years before. It was a simple rig that involved tying a hook to your line with no weight. Then, you attach a small balloon above the bait hook, before hooking on a shad.

Baker decided to give the balloon rig a try the next morning on his newly discovered honey hole. Live bait is usually very hard to catch before daybreak, but he had one area in the back of a major feeder creek where he knew he could catch at least three or four big gizzard shad. As he eased back into the feeder creek, Baker saw a big shad flip on the surface near an underwater spring. He made a throw over the spring with a cast net and caught two shad that were fourteen to fifteen inches long. Not knowing what else he would catch, Baker dropped the two shad in his bait tank. As it worked out, he didn't catch another shad even though he threw at least fifty more times.

So, Steve Baker went traveling ten or twelve miles up the river with two shad. As he approached the sand bar, the sky was just turning gray as daylight approached. The direction of the wind was perfect as it blew directly across the bar.

Baker anchored about eighty yards upwind so that the breeze would carry the balloon-rigged shad across the sand bar. As he was tying the balloon about ten feet above the hook, Baker worried because he hadn't seen any surface activity.

When he dropped the shad and balloon into the water, the rig worked perfectly. The balloon sat high in the water, and the breeze carried it toward the bar where he hoped the stripers were holding. It didn't take long for the balloon to drift over top of the bar which was in about twenty feet of water.

Steve Baker decided, that with only two shad, he would experiment with them one at a time. The breeze pushed the balloon across the point and the shad was calmly swimming eight feet below it.

No more than ten minutes had passed when he noticed the shad becoming very nervous. All of a sudden the big shad came to the surface and started swimming frantically toward the bank. The balloon offered little resistance as the shad towed it to the shallows. Suddenly, a huge swirl appeared directly behind the shad. Baker could feel his heart pounding faster and faster as he watched the action.

The shad went down to try and escape the big striper, but the balloon stopped him from going very deep. The shad continued toward the bank, dragging the balloon behind it. The shad came back to the surface only six to eight feet from the bank. Baker noticed the dorsal fin of a huge striper following directly behind it. He figured by this time that the trophy striper was simply toying with the frightened shad. If the striper had been serious about feeding, the shad would have been gone long before now.

The balloon kept the baitfish over the bar, which seemed to irritate the striper rather than tempt its hunger. The shad came back to the surface again, and the water exploded with the shad flying two feet in the air.

As Baker watched, the big striper slashed at the shad with its tail rather than its head. The balloon continued to hold the shad over the huge striper's territory. Finally, the water exploded again, and the clicker on the reel screamed as the striper headed toward deep water. The line was sliding through the knot on the balloon as it danced around on the surface. Baker set the hook and after a twenty-minute tug-of-war with the heavyweight striper, he eased the fish alongside his boat.

After the striper put on such a spectacular show, Baker decided to release the fish for someone else's enjoyment. He pulled the beautiful silver fish, which would have weighed at least forty-five pounds, beside the boat and freed the hook from its upper jaw.

Since that morning, the balloon rig has lured up hundreds of stubborn stripers for Steve Baker. A balloon rig can be used in a number of different circumstances to tempt finicky stripers with live bait. During the summer months, as the water temperatures rise and drive stripers to their deep-water hide-outs, a balloon can be rigged twenty to forty feet above the bait and fished over the deep drop-offs and ledges.

A balloon can also be used in the fast water below a

tailrace where you can pull it behind the boat with an electric motor or use it while anchoring and allowing the wind to position your baits.

When rigging up a balloon rig, use as light a line as possible. When most anglers think of doing battle with a twenty- to forty-pound fish, heavy line is always their first choice. Baker has found, however, that twelve- to fourteen-pound test line will give you a better drift with a balloon, because the lighter line adds little resistance to a bait's natural movements.

Baker prefers to use a balloon in a bright color for easy visibility, and he blows it up to about the size of a softball. He then attaches the balloon to the line with a simple overhand knot. Do not cinch the knot down too tight, because you want it loose enough so that the line can slide through the knot when a striper pulls on it. In some cases, Steve Baker has seen a striper release the bait if the knot is too tight and the balloon is pulled underwater as the fish makes its run.

You simply slide the balloon up or down the line to control the depth that you are fishing. The majority of the time, Baker sets the balloon ten to fifteen feet above the hook. When rigging up a balloon, he will often have someone stand in the back of the boat and hold the hook while he walks to the front of the boat with the reel in free spool. After he has walked off ten to fifteen feet of line, Baker ties on a balloon while the other person holds the line tight.

After the balloon is tied on, Steve Baker hooks a chunky gizzard shad on and lowers the balloon rig with the slack line over the side of the boat. He doesn't try to cast the rig, but instead lets the wind maneuver the bait into place.

The advantage that a balloon has over a cork float or a free line is important at times. A cork offers more resistance than a balloon as a shad tows it across the surface. With less resistance, a baitfish stays alive and friskier longer.

A balloon sits higher on the water than a cork, so the wind can easily maneuver the rig around. In fact, a balloon acts sort of like a sail. It will catch the slightest amount of wind and pull the shad through the water.

When using a free line, a baitfish will often swim down below the stripers in an attempt to escape. In most cases, a striper won't travel downward after live bait or an artificial lure. A properly adjusted balloon prevents a baitfish from swimming below the feeding fish.

Steve Baker has used a balloon rig to catch both stripers and hybrids under varying conditions. The most popular use is anchoring and drifting a shad over shallower structure as mentioned in the beginning of this chapter. The wind is used to work the shad over a larger area than you could fish with a simple free line. When anchoring, you can float several balloon rigs at a time.

Balloon rigs can also be pulled sixty to seventy yards behind the boat with an electric motor which can be deadly on stripers throughout the entire year. When pulling more than one balloon at a time, it is best to stagger the distances that you trail the balloons to prevent tangling the lines.

Baker has used balloons in fast water below dams to avoid the continuous task of re-tying hooks and sinkers that get broken off while fishing straight down under the boat. A balloon also works well in eddy water areas below a dam where big stripers sometimes hang out.

Baker has caught several trophy-size fish several miles below a tailrace using balloons. Big stripers seem to congregate around shallow, underwater sand bars located near the edge of the old river bed. As the fast-moving current washes over the sand bar, it will usually form an eddy where the end of the sand bar drops into the river. Steve Baker likes to anchor the boat on the upriver end of the sand bar and stagger two or three balloons at various distances along the edge of the underwater bar. The current is used to carry the balloons downriver. If a slight breeze is blowing across the river, the balloons work even better as the baits drift down and across the sand bar.

You need patience when fishing sand bars in the river. If you do get a strike right off the bat, don't run to the next potential hot spot. If water is being released from the dam, stripers will travel up and down the river all day long searching for food. Baker likes to wait at least an hour or so before moving on to another spot.

For striper fishermen who don't own a boat, a balloon can be used from the bank to get live bait out farther into the lake. When stripers make their spawning run up a river which is very narrow and shallow, Baker likes to fish from the bank using a balloon rig.

In a narrow river, boat traffic will spook stripers in the shallow water, so bank fishing is the most effective way to get a bait in front of a fish. Baker casts balloons out into the center of the river and lets the current do the work. He adjusts the balloon so that his bait is a few feet off the bottom to keep the shad from hanging up in rocks and stumps.

The balloon rig may seem a little silly to some fishermen. Some fishermen would be ashamed to be seen dragging a couple of pink balloons behind their boats. But when a thirty-pound striper chases your shad to the surface and the water explodes four feet into the air, you will be as hooked on balloons as the fish.

FISH CRAPPIE MINNOWS FOR COLD-WATER STRIPERS

In cold water, for purposes of discussion anything below fifty degrees, a striper's metabolism slows down and a fish does not need to eat as much as it did in warmer water to sustain itself.

As a result of this reduction in their appetites, stripers feed more on small baitfish, often less than an inch long, than they do on larger baitfish such as a six-inch gizzard shad. During the winter, Steve Baker has cleaned lots of stripers between twenty-five and thirty-five pounds, and he has found their stomachs full of threadfin shad approximately three-quarters of an inch long. Of all the stripers over twenty-five pounds that he has cleaned during the winter, he has not found one that had a big gizzard shad in its stomach.

As a result of his studies of the diet of cold-water stripers, Baker has started using small minnows normally used for crappie fishing to coax trophy-size stripers into biting during the cold-water period.

Baker prefers to use small commercially-raised minnows because they are more durable than small threadfins. "You can use tiny threadfins that are in the lake, but they are hard to keep alive," he says.

When fishing small minnows, Baker rigs up a seven-and-one-half foot rod and a baitcasting reel with fourteen-pound test line. He has tried using lighter line with the tiny minnows, but he broke his line too often when a big striper would hit.

To fish the minnows, Baker uses a style 84 Eagle Claw hook in the number 1 size. The hook is a heavy steel model which will not straighten out like a small, wire hook that fishermen normally use when casting small minnows. "The hook is real important. Don't use a wire crappie hook or a striper will straighten out the hook on the first run," Steve Baker advises.

Above the hook approximately two feet, Baker crimps on a number six split shot which is about the size of a pencil eraser. Fifteen feet above the hook, he attaches a clip-on float about the diameter of a quarter. He then hooks the minnow crossways through the nostrils.

Since there is fifteen feet of line below the float, Baker does not attempt to cast the set-up. Instead, he simply drops the minnow and float over the side of his boat and moves the boat forward with his electric motor until the float is forty to fifty yards behind the boat.

He then engages the reel, which is set with a medium drag, and places the rod into a holder. Baker has tried fishing the tiny minnows with just his clicker set, so that a striper can take some line before he sets the hook which is the way that he fishes a free-line with a gizzard shad on it. But in the cold water, Baker found that many of the stripers would go streaking off with a minnow for several yards and when he would engage the reel to set the hook, the fish would drop the bait. "When I would set the hook, nothing. I would reel in the minnow and it wouldn't even be scarred up," Baker says. "Can you imagine a thirty-pound striper carrying a crappie minnow for twenty yards and not leaving a mark on it?"

By locking the reel in gear with a medium drag, Baker hooks more cold-water stripers on the tiny minnows than he does with the reel disengaged and the clicker on. With the reel in gear, Baker waits until the rod tip goes into the water or until he can't wait any longer before he sets the hook.

When fishing crappie minnows, Baker observes his rod tip to make sure the bait is still lively. "In the cold water, minnows hold up real well. You can often leave one minnow on for thirty minutes or more. I watch the rod tip, and if the minnow is still lively, it will just barely cause the tip to quiver," Steve Baker says.

The tiny minnow and float are drifted over points, islands and flats in less than twenty feet of water, which is where plenty of cold-water stripers feed on the smallest of threadfin shad.

"You can still catch some big stripers during the winter months on six- and eight-inch gizzard shad, but you will catch more stripers, including plenty of fish over twenty pounds, on the crappie minnows," Steve Baker says.

TO CATCH A TROPHY STRIPER, CHOOSE THE RIGHT TOPWATER LURE

One of the best ways to catch a trophy striper is with a topwater lure. Unfortunately, the majority of striper fishermen do not catch as many stripers on topwater lures as they could, because they do not know when to fish which type of topwater lure.

Steve Baker likes to use three types of topwater lures. As a general rule, he uses a swimming-minnow lure when the surface of the water has a ripple on it. When the winds are calm and the surface of the water is slick, he prefers a stick bait. If the winds are up and the water is choppy, Baker switches to a popper. Some mornings, he may use all three types of lures as the conditions dictate.

"One of the major mistakes many fishermen, who are trying to become proficient topwater anglers, make is to tie on one type of surface lure and throw it all morning long," Steve Baker says.

If you are willing to experiment, Baker believes that the stripers will show you which type of lure they prefer at a given time and place. If you start out with a certain type of topwater lure and a striper swirls on it or swipes at it without taking the lure, then that will probably continue to happen all morning long with that type of lure unless the conditions change. Instead of cursing the stripers as they half-heartedly follow the lure, you need to switch to another type of lure that will trigger a more aggressive reaction from the fish.

"When a striper swirls or smacks at a topwater lure, if that fish is going to take the lure, then it will hit the lure solidly within the first five to ten feet from where you first see it swirl or wake on the lure," Steve Baker believes.

Because of that belief, when a striper boils on a topwater lure, but does not solidly strike the lure within ten to twelve feet of where it first takes a swipe at it, Baker will quickly reel the lure back to the boat. The reason for this is that he does not want to continue to have the indifferent fish following lazily behind the lure. If the fish does that, the only thing Baker will accomplish is to lead it into deeper water and away from the shallower point or bar where it is conditioned to feed. The striper may even follow the lure all the way to the boat where the sight of the boat will spook it.

Once Baker gets his rapidly-reeled topwater lure back to the boat, he has another type of topwater lure tied on another rod. He quickly casts it back to where the fish missed the previous lure. Many times, the striper, which was not really interested in the first lure, will immediately attack the new lure.

"It may be that the new lure has the type of action that it takes to trigger a strike from that particular striper," Steve Baker says. "And sometimes, I think the striper knows that it let something get away from it the first time, and it just decides not to let it happen again."

FISHING SPRINGS

On mountain lakes, there are often springs that bubble up from underneath the water, and the temperature of the spring water is warmer than the lake water during the winter months. The warmer water attracts huge schools of shad, and, of course, the baitfish draw the stripers.

Since most mountain lakes experience drastic drawdowns during the winter for flood control purposes, the springs are often boiling up in only four to eight feet of water by December. With the fish concentrated in such a small, shallow area and the water from the spring being clear, stripers get very wary and are easily spooked.

To overcome this problem, fish the springs at night when the majority of stripers are feeding. It is often best to fish a spring from the bank. Because most springs are situated in some type of slough or cove, and if you take a boat into such a confined area, it is easy to spook the stripers.

A variety of striper lures and live bait will produce when fished around a spring. Steve Baker's favorite lure is a swimming-minnow type plug which he slowly cranks across the surface.

FREE-LINE A GIANT RIVER HERRING FOR RIVER STRIPERS

When fishing specifically for a striper in the thirty- to forty-pound range, river expert Arthur Kelso of Loudon, Tennessee digs out his spinning rod and reel and catches a river herring on a small jig or even a trout fly. He doesn't want just any size river herring, however. The shad that he baits up with is fifteen to sixteen inches long and weighs over two pounds.

Kelso discovered the effectiveness of a big bait for a big striper while fishing the boils below a dam one day. He had fished all day without a strike when he caught a river herring that was over fourteen inches long while trying to catch smaller shad. Since he caught it, he decided to try it.

There were several other fishermen in the tailrace area. Kelso tried to hook the herring on and sneak it into the water without anyone seeing it, so that he wouldn't have to listen to their comments.

It didn't work. One of the anglers who knew Kelso hollered out, "Bear, (Kelso's nickname) when you get through with that shad, string it up. I want to take it home."

Kelso was embarrassed now that all the fishermen in the tailrace knew that he was fishing with a giant river herring. He shouldn't have been. Less than twenty minutes after baiting up, Kelso caught a thirty-five pound striper on the shad.

Since that experience, Kelso has used big river herring to boat some of his biggest stripers from the river. The places where he fishes river herring in excess of fourteen to fifteen inches long are the same places where he fishes smaller gizzard shad. (See Chapter 10.)

"The reason I use a big river herring is in the hopes of catching a really exceptional fish. I might not get more than one or two runs during several days of fishing a giant river herring, but one of those runs may weigh forty pounds or more," Kelso says.

To fish a fifteen- to sixteen-inch river herring, Kelso uses an unweighted line with a number 10/0 steel hook which is three inches long and has a one-half-inch hook bite. In fact, the hook is often used for shark fishing along the Gulf Coast.

Kelso runs the big hook through the herring's back just behind the dorsal fin. The hook doesn't impede a two-pound herring's movement at all. The hook just lies on its back as the giant herring swims around.

When using such a large size hook, Kelso says to check and make sure the eye of the hook is completely closed. If there is a gap, no matter how small, crimp it closed with a pair of pliers. "I've broken off some huge fish when the line would get jammed in the gap of an open hook eye," Arthur Kelso says.

IN SEARCH OF TROPHY STRIPERS

During Steve Baker's seventeen-year career as a professional striper guide, he has learned that the habits of a trophy striper are different from smaller, younger stripers which roam the same body of water. He compares the habits of a trophy striper with the habits of a trophy buck. Neither the striper nor the deer has reached its trophy size and avoided the den walls of thousands of sportsmen by being dumb. Both have become loners as age continues to make them wiser.

Steve Baker has dedicated his entire career to searching for that special breed of "trophy stripers." He has been fortunate enough to take several hundred fish in the trophy-size class.

When looking for that lone trophy fish, Baker doesn't always concentrate on structure located near deep water. He has caught numerous giant stripers from secondary points in the back of feeder creeks during the spring. The points are often far away from the main river channel. Baker believes that one reason why the big stripers are there is that they are seeking refuge from boat traffic and heavy fishing pressure.

Always try to remember that a trophy striper is wise to artificial lures and noisy boat traffic. When approaching a good area, Baker never disturbs the surface of the water where he is going to fish. He never washes any waves upon the point that he is approaching. Sometimes, Baker will stop a hundred yards from a point and move closer using only a trolling motor. Never slam the trolling motor down into the holding bracket. If you have ever thumped on the glass of an aquarium and watched the small fish run for their lives from the noise, what do you think a wise old striper does when it hears a commotion?

Underwater structure for a big striper will vary on

different lakes. Stripers often like old run-off ditches flowing into a lake which are thirty to forty feet deep. Big solitary stripers will hold on either side of the ditch or settle down toward the bottom of the ditch to wait on an easy meal.

When in shallower water, trophy fish will stay very close to the deep-water side of a hump or flat. This enables them to quickly escape any danger or disturbance.

Steve Baker has found that when live bait is the ticket for a big striper, the bait should, if at all possible, be caught from the lake you are fishing. Many anglers, especially out-of-town anglers, will transport live bait, either shad or herring, from their home lake or river.

At times, particularly in the hot summer months, shad can only be caught in great numbers below dams. Since an all-day trip usually requires four to six dozen shad, in order to keep a good lively shad on at all times, most anglers make a long drive to a dam in order to catch plenty of bait.

Again, a big striper is very wise and will notice small differences in bait size and shape. A gizzard shad that is caught from the clear water of a lake is usually fatter and has a lighter color than that of a river shad. As unimportant as that may seem, it will make a difference to a trophy striper.

In the spring, stripers are supposed to be in the headwaters or the large feeder creeks. This is true in part, but all stripers don't migrate at the same time. While most anglers will be waiting in line to get a cast at his favorite point up the river, Baker will work the almost unfished areas on the big water or in smaller, not so popular, feeder creeks. The summer and fall patterns work in the same manner. If a lake has a population of big fish, you can always find a few big fish somewhere in the areas of the lake that aren't receiving the greatest amount of pressure.

The size of a trophy striper varies from lake to lake. In some lakes, a twenty-pounder is a once-in-a-lifetime fish. Whereas on other lakes, thirty-pound fish are caught quite frequently. If you have a place designated on your den wall for a "trophy striper" from your lake, the tricks and methods Steve Baker has learned from years of hard work and practice will shorten the time that it takes to put your first trophy fish in the landing net.

TACTICS FOR LOW WATER LEVELS

Fishing a lake during low water levels in the winter can be one of the most productive periods of the year. Mathematically, the draw-down takes away hundreds of acres of water and limits the areas where stripers can be. On some lakes the entire acreage can be reduced by over one-third.

When fishing under low-water conditions, remember that the water temperatures will usually be in the high forties or low fifties. This temperature range allows stripers to move up from their deep-water summertime hide-outs. Steve Baker has seen schools of big stripers hold in a small cove or creek with less than twenty-five feet of water in its deepest point.

During the low-water period, most lakes will become slightly stained from winter rains and the violent winds that accompany cold fronts. Slightly stained water can break up bright sunlight and cause stripers to feed in shallow water even during the middle of the day.

As with any other period of the year, locating baitfish is the first step when searching for stripers. The same water temperature and water clarity conditions that draw stripers into shallow water also move baitfish closer to the surface.

An important fact to remember during the winter months is that stripers often feed on very small baitfish. When stripers are feeding on small shad, Baker prefers a bait he designed himself called the Poppen Spoon. The rig consists of a styrofoam cork with a concave mouth that creates a disturbance on the surface when jerked. Attached to the cork is a three-foot leader to which Baker ties a small Accetta spoon which resembles the small shad that the stripers are hitting.

One January, the water level on Norris was very low and frigid temperatures had lowered the water temperature to an unusually low forty-four degrees. Small threadfin shad were dying and washing up on the bank. The area where Baker docks his boats is a spring-fed creek which is considerably warmer in the winter than the open lake. Millions of tiny threadfins moved into the small creek to escape the cold water.

As you would expect, it didn't take long for the stripers to home in on an easy meal. The stripers seemed to ignore the shallow water and sunlight in both early morning and late afternoon to feed on the small shad. In a one week period, Baker and his wife, Pam, caught and released fifty-two stripers between thirteen and twenty-nine pounds while fishing from their dock. Most of the fish were caught on small bucktails which imitated the size of the threadfins.

When searching an unfamiliar lake for linesides during low-water levels, always be on the lookout for surface schooling. But don't let the surface action fool you, almost always when the fish are surfacing, the bulk of the heavier fish will be underneath the surface feeders. Always pay close attention to your chart recorder as you approach the activity. Many times, the smaller fish will be on top with hundreds of bigger fish underneath at twenty-five or thirty feet. Steve Baker has seen schools of big stripers twenty feet thick underneath the surface activity.

He uses the specially designed Tennessee Bait Weights to get a shad down to the suspended stripers. The weight rigged with a seven-foot leader gives a shad a natural movement that often draws an instant strike. A free line or balloon rig also works well on the suspended stripers.

A free line and a balloon rig need to run at least fifty yards behind the boat. Steve Baker has found that a big shad on a free line or balloon will draw strikes from the bigger fish even when they are feeding on smaller minnows.

During the winter draw-down is the only time of the year that the structure near the banks seems to make any difference. On Baker's home lake in Tennessee, the shallow sloping banks that are made up of shelf rock and stumps seem to attract stripers in the daylight hours. The gravel and sandy points seem to hold fish at night.

If he can catch the wind blowing just right, he likes to drift almost up against the rocky, stump-filled banks with a free line during the day. The wave action will break up the light penetration and stain the water just enough for the fish to move up into five or six feet of water. There's nothing more exciting than a thirty pounder exploding on a bait in shallow water.

Changing weather patterns don't seem to affect the feeding habits of a striper as much during the winter drawdown. Bluebird skies after a passing front will usually push stripers down a little deeper, but won't turn them off completely as often happens in the spring. Down rods with live bait are usually more productive than a shallow-running free line until the bright skies diminish.

Night-time plugging can be very good during low water levels as stripers move up to feed on shallow sand and gravel points. A Baby Mac seems to be a top producer when cast right near the bank and retrieved with a steady swimming action. Be ready for the strike to occur just as you begin your retrieve.

During mild weather, a topwater lure worked across shallow points can be deadly. With the low water levels, gravel points with good definition are easily visible at night.

Fishing a lake during the winter draw-down can definitely be one of the best times of the year to catch stripers regardless of whether you live on a shallow lake that fluctuates only a few feet or on a deep mountain lake that drops fifty to seventy feet. Taking away as much as one-third of a striper's backyard will cut your searching down immensely.